Information Literacy Beyond Library 2.0

edited by **Peter Godwin**
and **Jo Parker**

facet publishing

© This compilation: Peter Godwin and Jo Parker 2012
The chapters: the contributors 2012

Published by Facet Publishing,
7 Ridgmount Street, London WC1E 7AE
www.facetpublishing.co.uk

Facet Publishing is wholly owned by CILIP: the Chartered Institute
of Library and Information Professionals.

British Library Cataloguing in Publication Data
A catalogue record for this book is available from the British Library.

ISBN 978-1-85604-762-3

First published 2012

Mixed Sources
Product group from well-managed
forests and other controlled sources
www.fsc.org Cert no. SA-COC-1565
© 1996 Forest Stewardship Council

Text printed on FSC accredited material.

Typeset from editors' files by Facet Publishing in 10/14 pt University
Old Style and Zurich Expanded by Facet Publishing.
Printed and made in Great Britain by MPG Books Group, UK.

Contents

Contributors

Susie Andretta

Dr Susie Andretta is editor of the *Journal of Information Literacy* and a Senior Lecturer at the School of Information Management, London Metropolitan University. In 2005 she published *Information Literacy: a practitioner's guide* which promoted this practice as a foundation of independent and lifelong learning. In 2007 she edited the book *Change and challenge: information literacy for the 21st century* which covered the implementation of information literacy education from a range of UK-based and international perspectives. At this time, she also developed Facilitating Information Literacy Education (FILE), a CPD course commissioned by the London Health Libraries as part of their Learner Support Programme. Other publications include two chapters presenting information literacy provision that enhances the learning experience of information professionals as researchers and as information literacy facilitators (in Basili, C. (ed.), *Information Literacy as the Crossroad of Education and Information Policies in Europe*, CNR, 2008), and assessing the impact of FILE on the practice of the health librarians who completed this course (in Brine, A. (ed.), *Handbook of Library Training Practice and Development,* Volume 3, Ashgate, 2009). Her latest book, *Ways of Experiencing Information Literacy: making the case for a relational approach* (Chandos, 2012), proposes that information literacy is defined in terms of dynamic relationships between learner and information that operate in learner-constructed multiple contexts. Her study of transliteracy as the next stage of the literacy timeline is based on the view that transliteracy is the functional literacy required to operate within a Web 2.0 environment, and, in this respect, it succeeds information literacy, defined as the literacy required to function in a Web 1.0 information world.

Katie Birkwood

Katie Birkwood is a special collections librarian currently working on the online and physical exhibitions at Cambridge University Library. She has a BA in Music from Jesus College, Cambridge, and an MA in Library and Information Studies from University College London. Her first professional post was as Hoyle Project Associate at St John's College, Cambridge, where she catalogued a collection of personal papers and helped to develop the Library's outreach work. Her professional interests include historical bibliography, library history, exhibitions and outreach, and professional development for information professionals. She is part of the team that developed the TeachMeet event format for use by librarians, and is also part of the group that organized the 23 Things for Professional Development course. She blogs at http://maedchenimmond. blogspot.com and is also found playing the cello and knitting!

Karen Blakeman

Karen Blakeman is a freelance trainer, consultant and author. She originally trained as a microbiologist, receiving her degree from the University of Birmingham, and worked at the Colindale Central Public Health Laboratory for two years before joining Wellcome as an information scientist. Karen spent ten years in the pharmaceutical and health care industry before moving to the international management consultancy group Strategic Planning Associates, where she researched and provided information on the pharmaceutical, energy and telecoms sectors. In1989 she set up her company RBA Information Services and provides training and consultancy on finding and managing electronic information. Her business expanded in 1992 to embrace the internet, and now includes help and advice on using social and collaborative web tools. Past and current clients include public and corporate libraries, information providers, investment and financial services companies, organizations in the food and beverage industry, pharmaceutical companies and UK government departments.

Karen edits and publishes an electronic newsletter called *Tales from the Terminal Room* and the 7th edition of *Search Strategies for the Internet* is in production. Her blog can be found at http://www.rba.co.uk/wordpress/.

She is an Honorary Fellow of CILIP: the Chartered Institute of Library and Information Professionals, and a member of the Association of Independent Information Professionals (AIIP). In 2002 she received the Information World Review Information Professional of the Year award.

Susan Boyle

Susan Boyle is a Liaison Librarian for Nursing, Midwifery and Health Systems in the Health Sciences Library at University College Dublin, Ireland. Prior to working in librarianship, she qualified in advertising and has worked on a variety of brand campaigns in advertising and market research agencies. Her interest in information, technology, education and research led her to the library profession and she graduated with an Honours Masters in Library and Information Studies (MLIS). Susan has several years' experience as a liaison librarian. She is heavily involved in research consultation, library skills programmes and e-learning at UCD and has developed a particular interest in the design of treatment games to increase student engagement with information literacy. As an active member of the national Health Sciences Library Group (HSLG) committee, Susan has worked on various initiatives to support and advance the Irish health library sector. Over the past few years, she has presented and won awards at a variety of library conferences, published articles in various library journals and is also a peer reviewer for the *Journal of Information Literacy*. Susan enjoys tailoring trends to enhance library practice and translating her advertising skills to promote and convey library concepts. She has also developed keen research interests in the areas of creativity and innovation.

Phil Bradley

Phil Bradley is a qualified librarian who has acted as an internet consultant since the mid-1990s. He spends his time teaching other librarians about various aspects of the internet – most specifically .search and social media. He has written various books about the internet and is a well known and respected speaker at conferences and exhibitions. He contributes to various professional journals on a regular basis, notably CILIP's *Update* magazine with his Internet Q&A column, and he is also kept very busy writing two blogs on internet search and social media. For 2012 he will be CILIP President.

Christine Bruce

Christine Bruce is Professor in the Information Studies Group, within the Faculty of Science and Technology, Queensland University of Technology (QUT). She publishes and researches extensively on information literacy and higher education teaching and learning, including doctoral study and supervision. Christine is best known for her development of the phenomenographic approach to information literacy and information literacy education, based on the *Seven Faces of Information Literacy* (Auslib Press, 1997). Her most recent extension of that concept is published in *Informed Learning* (ACRL, ALA, 2008). Christine conducts seminars and workshops internationally and is regularly sought as a conference keynote speaker. Her thinking is informed by her research and by various professional roles over twenty-five years, including those of user education librarian, LIS educator, academic developer, and assistant dean, teaching and learning. In 2008 Christine was appointed a Fellow of the Australian Learning and Teaching Council. In 2010 she received a State Library Board of Queensland Award for contribution to information literacy, information literacy education and research.

Emma Coonan

Emma Coonan is Research Skills and Development Librarian, Cambridge University Library, and she directs and teaches on Cambridge University Library's Research Skills Programme, which supports and expands the information skills of students, researchers, and academics across the University of Cambridge. She holds a PhD in literary theory as well as a Masters in information and library management from Northumbria University. Her area of greatest professional interest is user behaviour, needs and expectations. She enjoys team-teaching and collaborative working, preferably over coffee!

Dean Giustini

Dean Giustini has an MLS and MEd, and is a biomedical librarian at the University of British Columbia (UBC) in Vancouver, Canada. In addition to his work within the Medical School Library, he teaches courses on health information, media literacy and social media at UBC's School of Library, Archival and Information Studies and School for Population and Public Health. He blogs at The Search Principle blog and coordinates volunteers for his wiki, HLWIKI Canada, which recently went over 750 pages of content and three million page views. He is a member of the Canadian Virtual Health Library catalogue team and sits as an editor on the *Canadian Journal of Pharmacy*.

Peter Godwin

Peter Godwin is currently working at the University of Bedfordshire as an Academic Liaison Librarian for the Business School in Luton, UK. Formerly he was Academic Services Manager at London South Bank University, in charge of subject support to all faculties. In the 1970s and 1980s he was Music and Media Librarian at Middlesex Polytechnic, and his interest in non-book materials and video led him to be Hon. Treasurer of British Film and Video Council for over ten years. His interest in information literacy has focused on support to academic staff in universities and the impact of Web 2.0 on information literacy in all information sectors. He has presented widely on Web 2.0 and how this affects the content and delivery of information literacy. In 2008 he co-edited the pioneering book *Information Literacy Meets Library 2.0* for Facet Publishing, which is still supplemented by a blog of the same name. He draws on many years' experience in academic library management and has presented at conferences in Europe, Asia, Canada and the USA. He has recently been incarcerated editing this sequel book *Information Literacy Beyond Library 2.0* and hopes to return to normal life shortly!

Hilary Hughes

Dr Hilary Hughes is Senior Lecturer and Course Coordinator for the Master of Education (Teacher-Librarianship) in the Faculty of Education, and co-leader of the Work and Play programme of the Children and Youth Research Centre at Queensland University of Technology (QUT). Her research interests cover: information literacy and informed learning; and the experiences and needs of learners in culturally diverse and online contexts. In 2010, she was sub-team leader for Reconceptualising and Repositioning LIS Education for the 21st Century (2010), a multi-institutional project funded by the Australian Learning and Teaching Council.

In teaching and research, Hilary draws on experience as reference librarian and information literacy educator at Central Queensland University Brisbane International Campus, QUT, Education Queensland Corporate Library, Northpoint Institute of TAFE (Brisbane), Longlands College of Further Education (UK) and (then) Sunderland Polytechnic (UK). She developed particular interest in the information and learning needs of international students, which prompted doctoral research entitled *International Students Using Online Information Resources to Learn* (QUT, 2009).

In 2010 Hilary was Fulbright Scholar-in-Residence at University of Colorado Denver, where she collaborated with Dr Mary Somerville, Auraria Library Director, as well as with other educators and LIS professionals. The residency's aim was to advance the academic success of international and less privileged students through informed learning. Hilary has an MA in Librarianship from the

University of Sheffield and is an Associate of the Australian Library Association. Follow her Fulbright experiences blog at http://fbdenver.blogspot.com/.

Carmen Kazakoff-Lane

Carmen Kazakoff-Lane is an Associate Librarian at Brandon University in Canada. Her interests in Open Content, Web 2.0 technologies, instructional videos, and finding smarter ways of working, led her to co-found the Animated Tutorial Sharing Project http://ants.wetpaint.com/. She currently co-ordinates the project and spends a great deal of time talking about how libraries can use it to collaboratively build and syndicate point-of-need educational videos that can be used for online or mobile instruction. Carmen has spoken about the project at numerous conferences, where she also advocates the creation of open educational resources that can be reused, redistributed, revised or remixed. She also serves as Online Editor for *The Canadian Journal of Native Studies* (www.brandonu.ca/library/CJNS).

Isla Kuhn

Never having imagined working in the health and medical library world, Isla Kuhn surprised herself when she got a job in the Cairns Library, University of Oxford's medical library based at the John Radcliffe Hospital. She's never looked back. A move to University of Leicester allowed her to set up and run a library outreach service for primary care and mental healthcare NHS staff working across Leicestershire and Rutland. Taking up her post at University of Cambridge Medical Library in 2005 allowed Isla to return to the mixed worlds of higher education, research and direct patient care. There are plenty of opportunities to contribute to education, learning, research and clinical care across both the University and Addenbrooke's, and to collaborate with colleagues from HE and the NHS. Providing support to student doctors, postgraduate researchers and clinical staff ensures that every day is different.

Isla has an MSc in Information and Library Studies from the University of Strathclyde. Her professional interests include Web 2.0 applications in library, educational and clinical settings and developing the educational role of librarians. She is a founder member of the first librarian TeachMeet, which encourages sharing of expertise in an informal setting. Not re-inventing the wheel is also important to her – so learning from colleagues seems like a good start. Any spare time is filled with dog walking and cooking!

Helen Leech

Helen Leech has worked for five local authorities, and there's not a lot she hasn't done in public libraries, from running storytimes to managing a re-organization. At one point, she even catalogued bricks. But throughout her career her key interest has always been in new technologies and the way that traditional library services translate into the online environment. She's now working for Surrey Library Service, where she's in her dream job: managing Surrey's Virtual Content Team, who are looking at the way the library service can use new tools to build a different relationship with customers. Contact her at helen.leech@surreycc.gov.uk or follow her at www.twitter.com/helenleech.

Jemima McDonald

Jemima McDonald is a Team Leader in the Information Services Department at the University of Technology, Sydney Library. She has been leading the team that coordinates information literacy at the library for three years. Jemima is particularly interested in the experience of first year students at university and working on ways to support them. She has driven the increased use of screencasts in the library to deliver information literacy as widely as possible. She is also an artist.

Sophie McDonald

Sophie McDonald is an Information Services Librarian at the University of Technology, Sydney Library. She is a member of the team responsible for developing information literacy programmes, with a special interest in mobile technologies and using social media to engage with clients. She has recently been involved in trialling a game-based learning model of information literacy for first year students using QR codes and mobile apps. She is a blogger and an app addict, and loves to read vampire fiction on her iPad!

Judy O'Connell

Judy O'Connell is an e-learning Lecturer in Library and Information Management in the Faculty of Education, Charles Sturt University. Prior to taking up this position in 2011 she was Head of Library and Information Services at St Joseph's College, Hunters Hill, for three years, following her work as consultant for Libraries and Web 2.0 developments for 80 primary and secondary schools in the Western Region of Sydney. Judy's professional leadership experience spans primary, secondary and tertiary education, at school and system level, with a focus on pedagogy, curriculum, libraries and professional development in a technology-enriched learning environment. She is passionate about global participation and collaboration; her ongoing commitment to global projects, including being an Australian Board member of the New Media Consortium's *Horizon Report: K-12 edition*, and Board member of the international journal *School Libraries Worldwide*, ensures that she remains at the forefront of 21st century learning innovation in schools. Find Judy online at http://heyjude.wordpress.com.

Jo Parker

Jo Parker is Head of Information Literacy at the Open University Library. This involves working in expert partnership with Library Services' subject librarian teams, leading strategic and curriculum change initiatives, developing information literacy products and services for students and providing staff development. She is a 'jolly good fellow' – a Winston Churchill Memorial Trust Fellow, and a Fellow of the HEA, as well as holder of an OU Teaching Award. Top of her to-do list at the moment are investigating learning design models to support the integration of information and digital literacies; employability; graduate attributes – and trying to remember to tweet more regularly!

Jane Secker

Dr Jane Secker is the Copyright and Digital Literacy Advisor working in the Centre for Learning Technology at the London School of Economics and Political Science, where she advises staff on copyright issues and runs a range of workshops and training on using new technologies in research and teaching. She has worked on numerous projects, most recently managing the DELILA (Developing Educators Learning and Information Literacies for Accreditation) project which produced a set of digital and information literacy materials as open education resources. She also managed the LASSIE (Libraries and Social Software in Education) project funded by the University of London, which explored libraries and Web 2.0 initiatives. She has published widely on topics such as information literacy, copyright and e-learning.

Jane is Conference Officer for the CILIP Information Literacy Group, organizing LILAC, the annual UK information literacy conference. She is a Fellow of the Higher Education Academy and teaches on the PGCert at LSE with staff from the Teaching and Learning Centre. Jane recently spent three months at Wolfson College, Cambridge, as an Arcadia Fellow, to develop a New

Curriculum for Information Literacy. She recently published *Copyright and E-learning: a guide for practitioners* (Facet Publishing, 2010).

Jane has a blog where you can find out more about her recent work at http://elearning.lse.ac.uk/blogs/socialsoftware/. You can also follow her on Twitter @jsecker.

Stacey Taylor

Stacey Taylor works in a secondary independent college that teaches both the local curriculum (NSW Board of Studies) and International Baccalaureate programmes. She has worked in both school and public libraries for over 25 years and is passionate about service. Stacey has a Masters of Information specializing in knowledge management and has just completed her Graduate Diploma of Teaching and Learning. She is an active member of the college's ICT strategic group and uses 'guided inquiry' processes in collaboration with classroom teachers. She is strategically involved with the management of large research tasks within the college, including senior Higher School Certificate level research and the IB Diploma research tasks including the Extended Essay and the Middle Years Program Personal Project. She believes that the most important set of skills to develop in students are the 'critical literacies', to teach students to be critical consumers of information. She also provides leadership in the college on copyright and acknowledgement. She has recently received the John Hirst Memorial Award for exemplary teacher librarianship. Stacey is a reflective practitioner who regularly shares her ideas via her blog http://librariansarego.blogspot.com where she invites discussion on some of the current issues for librarians.

Niamh Tumelty

Niamh has a Diploma in Higher Education, and is currently Assistant Librarian at the English Faculty Library, University of Cambridge. This is predominantly a reader services role, and she assists in the development and delivery of the User Education Programme at the Faculty of English. She has a particular interest in the educational role of the librarian, having originally qualified as a secondary school teacher in Ireland. She is currently researching information literacy levels at the transition to university as part of the MSc Econ. Information and Library Studies at the University of Aberystwyth. She has also worked in the Contemporary Music Centre, Dublin, An Chomhairle Leabharlanna/The Library

Council (a public sector advisory body for libraries in Ireland) and Cambridge University Medical Library.

Niamh has been involved in the Cambridge TeachMeet planning team since the idea first arose, has helped to organize both of the Cambridge TeachMeets held to date and, together with Katie Birkwood, presented a paper about TeachMeet at the 2011 LILAC conference at The British Library. She is actively involved in both CILIP: the Chartered Institute of Library and Information Professionals and the International Association of Music Libraries. She has also been instrumental in the development of the 23 Things for Professional Development programme (http://cpd23.blogspot.com), which developed the idea of an online training course on social media to include 'things' which help its participants from 22 countries worldwide to reflect on other aspects of their continuing professional development.

Andrew Walsh

Andrew Walsh, an Academic Librarian and National Teaching Fellow, thrives on making information skills relevant to all at the University of Huddersfield. He has championed online and mobile-friendly learning materials, and has done innovative work around mobile learning in libraries, using students' own mobile devices to facilitate learning. Over the last couple of years he has challenged professional colleagues to think how we can use mobile devices to blur the boundaries between our physical and virtual libraries, using techniques such as QR (Quick Response) Codes.

Increasingly he is invited to give keynote addresses at conferences internationally and is in demand to talk on information literacy, active learning and mobile learning. An active researcher practitioner, Andrew has published widely in journals and has written several book chapters. He is currently writing his second book (on mobile friendly library services).

Always looking for new ways to innovate, Andrew is currently leading a project to bring ideas borrowed from the gaming industry into the heart of the library. This project, Lemon Tree, will turn everyday library activities into points and badges within an online, mobile-friendly, social game, encouraging the use of library resources.

Lane Wilkinson

Lane Wilkinson is a Reference and Instruction Librarian and UC Foundation Assistant Professor at the University of Tennessee at Chattanooga, USA. Prior to becoming a librarian in 2009, he spent four years teaching Philosophy courses at Wayne State University in Detroit. As an active blogger, Lane writes on a variety of topics at his blog 'Sense and Reference' (http://senseandreference. wordpress.com), including the philosophy of information, the philosophy of librarianship, epistemology, metaethics, library instruction, transliteracy, and more.

Kristen Yarmey

Kristen Yarmey is the Digital Services Librarian at the University of Scranton Weinberg Memorial Library in Scranton, Pennsylvania, USA. She splits her time between digitization, digital preservation and emerging technologies and focuses her research on areas of intersection between technology and education. She holds a Bachelor's degree in chemistry from the Pennsylvania State University and a Master's degree in library science (with a specialization in archives and records management) from the University of Maryland.

Acknowledgements

An enormous thank you to our contributors for their excellent writing and willingness to work with us, and the many colleagues who have either pointed us in the direction of interesting and exciting work (such as Sarah Hammond at the BL), or tolerated our talking about this book for the past many months!

Peter Godwin and Jo Parker

This book has had more painful birth pangs than its predecessor, and I cannot thank my co-editor enough for her patience and hard work. I must also thank Professor Helen Partridge for her time and encouragement, Judy O'Connell for her inspirational help and hospitality, Dr Geoff Walton for his sage advice and Professor Sue Thomas for her most helpful suggestions. Finally, this book would have been impossible without the toleration of Jo Myhill and all my long-suffering friends and colleagues at the University of Bedfordshire. It would have been *absolutely* impossible without the support of my dear wife, Paula.

Peter Godwin

I didn't have to think very hard about agreeing to work with Peter again, and despite various frustrations we have remained cheerful and resolute; even with the benefit of hindsight, I would have still said 'yes' because not only is it flattering to be asked, it's also a fantastic opportunity to work with so many inspiring people who have interesting things to say. We have ended up with something a little bit different to what we originally intended. Peter has taken on a lot of the writing this time, for which I thank him. Thanks also to my family and friends for their support and patience.

Jo Parker

Introduction

Peter Godwin

Information Literacy Meets Library 2.0 was something of a journey into the unknown. The Web 2.0 'characters', as I often referred to them in my talks, were new, and to some, exciting. It was a fun time to write a book and we didn't think there'd be a sequel: despite requests from Facet Publishing, we would not emulate the Hollywood blockbusters and spawn another offering. So what changed my mind? One evening, while I was ambling home from the bus stop, reflecting gently to the strains of Telemann (or was it Siouxsie and the Banshees?) via an iPod, the possibility of a book seized me. A few days later I visited Jo Parker, my fellow editor, at the Open University and very tentatively suggested a sequel. To my great surprise she agreed to come on board – and here we have it.

Web 2.0 has affected the delivery of information literacy (IL), and somehow seems to have also affected what it means to be information literate. There has been much IL research questioning its nature, and I suspect that most of this has not reached the majority of practitioners. Indeed, I suspect there is something of a disconnect between IL research and IL practitioners. They often produce the MEGO (my eyes glaze over) effect on me, and I suspect that I am not alone! This is on the one hand understandable, due to the complex language used in some research articles, but on the other hand regrettable, because important insights are being gained that all practitioners should know about. My selection of these is bound to be incomplete, and I apologize in advance for any MEGO effects caused by my own writing! In the first chapters of this book I shall set the scene with a detailed discussion of what has happened to information literacy and Web 2.0 in the past three years. What was Library 2.0? Was it over-hyped? How did it connect with the so-called web generation? Then we will look at how social media have become mainstream and where there have been successes and failures. We will then examine what effects Web 2.0 has had on information literacy.

Then, in Chapter 4, Phil Bradley and Karen Blakeman give us an overview of the technical developments 'out there' on the web that are impacting on all of us, and how they are changing the way in which we are all operating in the information environment.

In Chapter 5 Susie Andretta looks at how literacies have changed and how transliteracy could become a better description of where IL is heading in the early 21st century.

As learning enters the cyber landscape, how can educators take advantage of social media and mobile environments to foster IL in the curriculum? Hilary Hughes, in Chapter 6, describes the concept of 'informed learning' developed by Christine Bruce, and how this may be applied in higher education (HE).

Part 2, our case study section, looks at how practitioners are 'entering the void', employing social media, finding new ways of interacting with their clientele or just doing things a little bit differently.

Sophie McDonald and Jemima McDonald (University of Technology, Sydney) show how active learning can be employed in HE to make induction more entertaining (Chapter 7).

Susan Boyle (University College, Dublin) has used games with great success to make her IL delivery more engaging and entertaining (Chapter 8).

Kristen Yarmey (University of Scranton) tells how her survey of mobile device use has influenced the way she approaches IL development (Chapter 9).

Andrew Walsh (University of Huddersfield) describes his experiences of using mobiles to deliver IL (Chapter 10).

Stacey Taylor (Monte School, Sydney) describes the employment of referencing training in her school using 2.0 tools EasyBib and Zotero (Chapter 11).

Carmen Kazakoff-Lane (Brandon University) introduces us to the Animated Tutorial Sharing Project (ANTS): an open source collection of library tutorials that can be shared – a development that makes so much sense in the 2.0 world (Chapter 12).

Hilary Hughes (Queensland University of Technology) has provided a case study from their institution to show how informed learning operates in reality with a postgraduate group (Chapter 13).

Dean Giustini (University of British Columbia) explains the importance of social media in LIS courses and how this has operated at UBC (Chapter 14).

Lane Wilkinson (University of Chattanooga) explains how the concept of transliteracy can be employed to good effect in our delivery of IL in HE (Chapter 15).

Jane Secker (London School of Economics) and Emma Coonan (University Library, Cambridge) present their new HE IL curriculum (Chapter 16).

Niamh Tumelty (University of Cambridge) helped to put on the first TeachMeet for IL librarians in the UK and with Isla Kuhn and Katie Birkwood shows how this developed from a Cambridge version of the 23 Things programme (Chapter 17).

Part 3 looks at how the changes and developments described in the previous section will change us and our mission. In Chapter 18 Helen Leech (Surrey County Libraries) analyses the ways in which public libraries in the UK are employing Web 2.0 in their services and how these could be improved. Judy O'Connell (Charles Sturt University) demonstrates in Chapter 19 the pivotal importance of school librarians as guides in the void and how they can influence curriculum delivery, providing inspiration and support.

I will then consider shifting literacies, which are now crucial, in Chapter 20, together with an appreciation of how to accommodate them in our own particular context. The transition from custodian of artefacts towards guide to and creator of material will bring about a significant change of emphasis in the way we operate in our information literacy role. In Chapter 21, we look at a variety of recent developments, trends and issues that are likely to affect our IL practice in the era beyond Library 2.0. Finally in Chapter 22, freed from the shackles of academic writing, I will draw together all the threads of the book in a short summary.

PART 1

Recent developments in information literacy and Library 2.0

Chapter 1
Library 2.0: a retrospective

Peter Godwin

When *Information Literacy Meets Library 2.0* was written in 2008 it was still 'cool' to use the 2.0 epithet. We did not attempt detailed definitions and skirted over any distinctions between Web 2.0 and Library 2.0. Now that the general enthusiasm has died down and scepticism about its merits has surfaced, we need to examine what it was all about in the first place and how it has turned out in practice. We shall see that there has been widespread adoption of certain elements of the 2.0 bandwagon, particularly in awareness, if not in the practice of all librarians. The importance of 2.0 in connecting to the so-called Net Generation was overplayed. The CIBER reports (2008) have demonstrated that the 'geeks' were in the minority. Now that the bubble has burst, we can begin to appreciate that social media (aka Web 2.0 tools) are here to stay. They have now become mainstream.

What was Web 2.0 and Library 2.0 about?

In 2004 something fundamental happened to the world wide web. It became a place for collaboration, more personal and driven by us, the users. The web itself, not extra software that had to be downloaded, became our platform and made it possible for us to share our thoughts, photos and videos and build or take part in building websites easily. The availability of the easy-to-use web tools for creating blogs and wikis and engaging in social networking seemed especially appealing to the young. This led university staff too, including librarians, to realize that it could be advantageous to start using them, both for plugging into their users' wavelength and for their marketing and educational potential. Then Michael Casey in his blog *Library Crunch* came up with the term Library 2.0, seeing it as a user-centred environment that helped people to learn and to fulfil their information needs and that also encouraged them to both create and share content (Sodt and Summey, 2009): 'Library 2.0 will look different for each library, based in part on users' diverse needs' (Casey and Savastinuk, 2007, 37). Library 2.0 was about constant change brought about through evaluation to see whether we were meeting our expected outcomes. It was about user participation, feedback and reaching out to new and existing users (Casey and Savastinuk, 2007). Brian McManus (2009) uses Web 2.0 and Library 2.0 interchangeably, and this has usually been my own approach. It has been a matter of how the 2.0 services could be applied in a library context: first for librarians to communicate with one another, creating and sharing content, and then doing the same with and for our users, sharing with them, guiding them, creating communities with and for them. The 2.0 phenomenon was not really about tools. It was more a state of mind, a way of thinking. It was about participation and collaboration (Melville, 2009). Hicks and Graber (2010) emphasize the sociological and philosophical elements and link them with the way educational theory has now embraced a constructivist approach, and what this could mean for the way students learn.

The risks of 2.0

The ability to use the web tools, to communicate and to share, promised so much. However, the apparently free tools have often come at the price of the invasion of privacy. We are the product that Facebook sells to its advertisers. Google continues to build up extensive information about us via its applications and our searches. Nicholas Carr (2010) believes that, just as the book promoted deep learning, so the internet promotes quick-fire glancing at little snippets from lots of places. We are losing our ability to concentrate, contemplate and reflect – to think! The most successful web tools, for example, YouTube, have become big business and their priorities are to sell and make money: priorities that do not accord with either state education or public libraries. Brian Lamb and Jim Groom (2010) believe that higher education should take action to promote 'safe spaces' on the web that are open and free from obvious commercial interests.

The risks of using free web tools are well summarized by Kelly et al. (2009). These include sustainability, and the prospect of Delicious, the social bookmarking site, ceasing earlier this year illustrates this perfectly. There are human factors involved too, as initial enthusiasm to create blogs or wikis can wither away. There can be copyright concerns (Wyatt and Hahn, 2011) with Web 2.0 services, particularly if users are encouraged to participate in the library website, copying and pasting documents that are in copyright. Thankfully, Creative Commons licences have gone a long way to making content more freely accessible. Herring (2011) notes that in schools the use of Web 2.0 has been hindered by limited time for developing resources or providing in-service training for librarians. Access to 2.0 sites may also be blocked by the firewall of the institution.

Web 2.0 – a waste of space?

We must face the proposition: was it all worth it? Was the innovative part of Library 2.0 – i.e. where the user is listened to and is central – not just something that good libraries have always been doing? Is not the library landscape filled with redundant wikis, blogs with no recent posts and Facebook pages with no interaction? Libraries experienced difficulties in staffing these extra, new services, which were launched in addition to existing services. Web 2.0 was already being criticized in 2005, even before Library 2.0 really got moving. Roddy Macleod (2010) summed up the blog situation beautifully in a post entitled 'Some university library blogs suck, some could do better, and some are quite good'. Walt Crawford (2011) makes the crucial point, saying that 'one truly beneficial result of the whole Library 2.0 phenomenon is that some (by no means all) library groups and libraries recognize the virtue of small, rapidly-deployed, "failable" projects: ones done without a lot of planning and deployment, ones that can grow if they succeed, die if they fail and in many cases serve as learning experiences'. There was obvious over-enthusiasm at the peak of the Library 2.0 movement in 2007/8, with institutions feeling that they should have a blog or a Facebook site. Sometimes this meant that services were set up with little or no evidence that the users required them or would even use them. There was therefore a disconnect between these initiatives and the announced aim of connecting and being user focused. We used social media just to be 'current' rather than 'useful' and the 2.0 concepts were just unfocused buzz words (Lankes, 2011).

The writer of the *Librarytwopointzero* blog noted: 'In many ways, the Library 2.0 seems a fallacy of the past. A word we used to start a conversation about. A word we used to bind us and throw around ideas. It was something new at the time' (Anon, 2010). Perhaps this is where we are now: 'the principles, tools, ideas that were temporarily gathered together into Library 2.0 – many of which preceded that nomenclature – are doing just fine and will continue to be relevant at least in part' (Crawford, 2011).

Social media comes of age

Web 2.0 as a term has arguably now been replaced by social media. We are well beyond the early adopter stage and therefore there is now more attention being paid to determining the value of the services and return on investment (ROI). For example, Dickson and Holley (2010) try to assess the take-up of Web 2.0 in US academic libraries. They can accept the potential for outreach to students but are concerned about the need for quantitative and qualitative research to show the effectiveness of the tools, rather than anecdotal evidence. Social media and ROI, taken together, have limited measurable goals (Glazer, 2009). How can a business case be made? What is the return on investment? Is it 'return on engagement' or should it be 'return on influence'? Surely success is measured over time and the ROI will depend on the starting-point. What was the adoption of a specific tool intended to achieve, and how well is it performing? Is it sustainable? It might be possible to do SWOT analyses of Web 2.0 developments (Fernandez, 2009). Measuring success can be hard, because success is intangible. With a blog, traffic and the number of comments are important measurement criteria, but there are also qualitative measures, such as 'tone' of conversation (Fichter and Wisniewski, 2008).

What are the consequences of increasing social networking usage? Hargittai (2010) surveyed over a thousand 18- to 19-year-old first-year students in an urban public research university in early 2007. The conclusion was that neither the amount of use of social networking sites (SNS) nor the social practices carried out on them bore any systematic relationship to academic performance. Just as there may be distractions from social networking there may be academic benefits too.

Library 2.0 – good thing for librarians

As far back as 2006, Stephen Abram challenged the information professional to become 'Librarian 2.0'. How has this transition taken place? How can we measure it? We have to bear in mind the difficulties of defining Library 2.0. As Helen Partridge says, 'regardless of how library 2.0 is ultimately understood, it will require a new type of LIS professional' (Partridge, 2011, 256). Focus groups held with Australian librarians from a variety of sectors revealed that they agreed that their profession was getting more complex and that they were responsible for their own continuing professional development. They should be inquisitive, like to play and experiment, and be happy to operate outside their comfort zone (Partridge, 2011). Most importantly, Partridge (2011) also suggested, from the focus groups' findings, that Library 2.0 represented a watershed moment, leading to a changed attitude and way of thinking.

How could this change have come about? The ground-breaking Learning 2.0 23 Things initiative of Helene Blowers at Charlotte and Mecklenburg County, North Carolina, in 2006 has been succeeded by many similar initiatives, many based directly upon it. Many library schools have adopted it, and Bawden et al., (2007) charted the ways in which their curricula were changing in Australia, Ireland, Lithuania, Slovenia and the UK, both by including 2.0 as topic and by use of 2.0 tools in course delivery.

Librarians' interest in Web 2.0 has developed for a variety of reasons. Raising awareness on behalf of library patrons is only part of the picture, and I believe it is useful to set this in the wider context of more general adoption. In her 2010 keynote at Internet Librarian International, Hazel Hall called on librarians to 'get real' about social media (Hall, 2010). This meant using them to amplify traditional service delivery, news and current awareness; to improve interaction with users; for marketing and raising our profile; for collaborative project work, peer review, staff development, virtual reference and training/teaching. We must acknowledge that these categories can overlap: for example promotional and marketing initiatives may also get users to engage with our services and be useful building blocks to enable users to make best use of library services.

The mobile dimension

Since our last book in 2008, the greatest changes have been the advent of Twitter and the explosion of mobile technology. Twitter began in a most unprepossessing way in 2006, as a sort of SMS system for offering friends the chance to keep up with each other's whereabouts. The idea that 140 characters could be sufficient to communicate anything worthwhile seemed remote. Yet this limitation can be seen as a strength, the short bursts proving easier for our brains to cope with and manage. In May 2011 a Pew Research Center report found that 13% of online adults used Twitter - a significant increase from 8% in November 2010 (Pew Research Center, 2011). This will undoubtedly increase, as Apple considers integrating Twitter into their operating system for future iPhones (Carlson and Hamburger, 2011). Pew data showed that, in 2010, 65% of US households had broadband, and this was more common in white, better educated and affluent households (Purcell, 2011). This will speed up the adoption and facilitate the use of Web 2.0 applications. In 2011, 85% of US adults had a mobile phone; wireless

Figure 1.1
It's social and mobile! (Photograph:
University of Bedfordshire)

internet use is growing, with young adults leading the way. Of those who use the internet on their mobile, 55% do this daily, up from 36% in 2009. The use of SNS has rocketed from 8% in 2005 to 35% in 2008 and 61% in 2011. Overall, 37% of internet users have contributed news content, or made comments or sent out content of some description through SNS (Purcell, 2011). So what does all this mean? Social media or 2.0 is now 'hand in glove' with mobile devices, as they feed off each other. The web is going social and mobile (Figure 1.1)!

Worldwide, 81 million smartphones were sold in the third quarter of 2010 - nearly twice as many as in the same period of 2009 (Dowell, 2010); 7.5 million iPads were sold in the first 6 months following the device's release (Dowell, 2010). In the USA 85% of adults own mobile phones and 90% of all adults worldwide (including 62% aged 75 and over) live in a household with at least one operational mobile phone. In the USA nearly half of all adults own an iPad or other MP3 player, including 74% of adults aged 18-34 (Zickuhr, 2011). From January to March 2011, 24% of the mobile phones sold in Western Europe were smartphones, up from 15% for the same period in 2010. Sales of smartphones have now exceeded sales of PCs (Arthur, 2011). The sale of mobiles and tablets seems likely to buck the recession, as Apple made a record profit during the quarter ending June 2011, primarily due to massive sales of iPads and iPhones (British Broadcasting Corporation, 2011). A few institutions are giving new students iPads; for example, Illinois Institute of Technology gave 400 incoming freshmen an iPad; Abilene Christian University became renowned for a similar gesture with iPhones and iPods (Raths, 2010).

The use that students will make of mobile devices during their course of study will depend much on their subject area. Students of health, business or journalism may well prove to be the early adopters. We can see this in operation at the University of Leeds, where 520 medical students are being loaned iPhones containing dedicated apps allowing them to record notes in hospitals and test their knowledge of procedures, alongside copies of key textbooks, reference books and guidelines on administering drugs (University of Leeds, 2010).

Preliminary data from the responses of 100 students interviewed at Manchester Metropolitan University during January to March 2011 (JISC, 2011) showed that 79 of them used mobiles to access technologies used in learning in the university, 81 used them for access at home, 67 on the train/bus and 57 in the café/pub and 32 at work. Significantly, desktop usage exceeded mobile and laptop use for only one activity – accessing e-books and journals.

Web generation

At the time of our previous book, the notions of the digital native and the web or Net Generation being distinct were very much to the fore. I believe that these concepts were useful as a wake-up call of sorts. However, since then they have largely been debunked as too simplistic. Selwyn (2009) does much to defuse the debate about a huge gulf between generations. He sees the digital native as just another manifestation of the usual stereotype of young people being different from older generations. What we are now seeing is involvement with Web 2.0 by all generations, and that the distinctions are breaking down as we all become part of that web generation

Figure 1.2
A student of today in the British Library (Photograph: Paula Dilger)

(Fieldhouse and Nicholas, 2008). Jones et al. (2010) concluded that there was no clear distinction in the use of technology between so-called Net Generation and non-Net Generation users. Other more complex factors were involved, like nationality, gender and university affiliation. The 'geeks' were always in the minority, and we now view the student body as a complex collection of individuals from different backgrounds and cultures and with differing experience – rather as we did before Web 2.0 – but just different characters (Figure 1.2)! In 2011, I prefer to echo Wheeler (2011): 'There are no digital natives. There is no net generation. We are all in this together. That is all.'

Digital divide?

What is new is the collision of this sudden cornucopia of unreliable information, ubiquitous powerful cultural technologies and a generation for whom the Web is not an innovation, but a feature of the environment, like running water.

(Rheingold, 2011)

Is there equal access now to this 'running water'?

The *Higher Education in a Web 2.0 World* report (Melville, 2009) found that the digital divide had not been wholly wiped out, particularly with regard to individual ability, access to and engagement with technology, and what that technology could do. Use of Web 2.0 in learning and teaching in higher education was patchy and not systematic. A series of recommendations were made regarding learner skills, staff skills, and infrastructure. These were instrumental in helping to improve awareness of the competencies required among staff and students. The present economic climate is not going to help their implementation.

Do the young acquire the key participatory skills required for today's digital world by themselves, or by interacting with popular culture? Do they need guidance or help? There is still unequal access to information, and a need to foster understanding of how media affects an individual's perception of the world and how material on the web can be used ethically. We should see the 'divide' as being more about cultural and social issues, rather than about technological ones, and focus on the importance of social skills acquired through collaboration and networking. Transmedia navigation is one of these skills (Jenkins, 2009), and this is a theme to which we shall return later. If kids lack access to the internet at home, and meet with site blocking at public libraries and in schools, they are twice discriminated against in being able to use the web for social communication and common culture (Ito et al., 2009). Greenhow, Walker and Kim (2009) surveyed 852 students from lower-income families in 13 urban high schools. Although in ownership of hardware and access to the internet they had practically caught up with the higher-income students, their usage was likely to be lower because of other circumstances at home, such as sharing of a machine and running costs.

Social media in higher education

Head and Eisenberg (2010), in their Project Information Literacy (PIL) study, found that 'even though students may be heavy users of SNS such as Facebook,

Web 2.0 applications for course research have not yet found their way into students' research repertoire – yet. Recent research suggests that this trend is very likely to change within the next few years as students' demand for digital course work and time-shifted instruction inevitably increase.' Also 'few students had used Web 2.0 applications within the last six months for collaborating, sharing, and building knowledge for course work with others'. Yet they found that 70% of students frequently used social networks like Facebook to solve information issues in their daily lives. Therefore students have information solutions that academia ignores or even prohibits (Wikipedia is a key example here). This getting out of step with reality should be seen as a huge missed opportunity. To bridge this gap, Head and Eisenberg want a dialogue between administrators, academics and librarians. This dialogue should be extended outside the sector, to schools, because their research discovered that students develop a narrow kind of research process earlier in life, whilst at school. Here is an opportunity for school librarians and for the publishers (print, software, hardware producers) to be 'active partners in developing valued, college-level skills as well as content'. PIL interviewed Howard Rheingold about the lack of engagement with Web 2.0 (Rheingold, 2011). He thinks their 2011 PIL survey will show an increase in the figures for student use of social media, and sites like tumblr (www.tumblr.com/) could be a catalyst for this, because of the effortless sharing ability that they offer. At present he sees social media being used only in diverse and fragmentary ways. Indeed, if teachers are not using Twitter, wikis, or social bookmarking, why should we expect students to do so? The failure of social media in education has been because educational establishments were slow to change, lacked funds and were afraid to innovate.

The annual ECAR study (Smith and Caruso, 2010) is an important means of identifying how student behaviour is changing. From the 2010 study, we see that two-thirds of students surveyed now own a mobile device capable of accessing the internet, and about half of these say that they access the web daily, which is a substantial increase over the previous year's one third. Very high usage of SNS was evident, but only about 30% of students were using them in their courses. It appears that students are gradually including SNS and other web tools in their academic lives, but the rise of mobile computing and cloud-based applications can be seen much more clearly.

Web 2.0 in academic libraries

Knowledge of the extent of adoption of Web 2.0 in academic libraries is still quite limited. Kim and Abbas (2010) did a limited survey of US academic libraries in 2009, achieving a sample size of 230 libraries out of a possible 459. Library websites were trawled for evidence of Web 2.0 implementation; 73% showed evidence of ability to subscribe to library RSS feeds, with figures of 65% for blogs and 27% for podcasts. Various categories of users were surveyed from two sample Midwest US universities and it was concluded that their use of Web 2.0 tools did not match the tools that were most often offered. Although 73% of libraries had RSS feeds, only 10% of users in the two universities used them. This mismatch may not be significant, but it could suggest that libraries are offering services that users neither understand (yet) nor have a strong desire for. Tools that were initiated by users, like tagging and wikis, were also rated as low use. A survey in 2009 of 81 academic libraries in New York State showed that seven Web 2.0 tools had been employed to varying degrees by 34 libraries. There seemed to be more enthusiasm for them among librarians, than among users (Xu, Ouyang and Chu, 2009).

Tripathi (2009) did a survey of 277 university libraries in the UK, USA, Canada and Australia which revealed instant messaging in 53%, blogs in 43% and RSS use in 39%. A study of 120 academic and public libraries in North America, Asia and Europe (Chua and Goh, 2010) found that take-up of RSS and instant messaging was particularly popular. European and Asian libraries lagged behind the North American libraries in their adoption of 2.0 tools, particularly instant messaging and social networking. In 2007 a survey of take-up by Chinese libraries (30 university, 6 public, 3 national) showed early adoption, with especial interest in SMS (Cao, 2009). Park (2010), in a survey at Yonsei University, Seoul, South Korea, found that undergraduate students were the most receptive to the use of social networking and recommended that SNS be regularly upgraded and updated. Interestingly, he concluded by hoping that SNS would allow users to control their own relationship boundaries and groups: exactly what Google Plus has since brought in.

Just as web tools are appearing at a greater rate than any academic institution can cope with, I believe this is exactly the same for academic libraries.

Researchers and Web 2.0

Researchers as a group of library users are receiving a lot more attention in the UK at present. This is because in the past they have sometimes been sidelined and recent reports have shown that they are not using library resources to the full and need support.

Researchers do not appear to be heavily concerned with Web 2.0 applications. Stuart (2009) rated researchers as conservative and slow to take on board the potential benefits offered. For example, when the Nature publishing group offered a process of voluntary open peer-review, most writers opted out, and those who did try it received few comments. Drabble (2011) describes a survey of 2414 researchers from 215 countries that shows a big gap between awareness and actual use of social media; little difference of use by age group; but great prospects for identifying research opportunities and boosting dissemination. The survey found that librarians were undervalued, and the researchers surveyed wanted libraries to become more like Google. Earlier this year (2011) the Researchers of Tomorrow three-year joint British Library and JISC study, which is tracking the research behaviour of 'Generation Y' doctoral students, showed that take-up of social media was still disappointing (Carpenter, Tanner and Smith, 2011). This is a longitudinal study, and there is evidence this year that use of some social media and networking is on the increase. The reasons for low take-up include reluctance to accept training opportunities and preference for learning from supervisors, who may not display current best practice.

An earlier report from Research Information Network (2010) concluded that researchers will not take the time to learn about and experiment with new tools and services unless they can see the benefit that might flow (Research Information Network, 2010, 48) and 'Web 2.0 services are currently being used as supplements to established channels, rather than displacing them' (Research Information Network, 2010, 49). While a few researchers are making frequent and innovative use of Web 2.0 tools, most use them sporadically, or not at all'. The need for training and encouragement from librarians is clear. I can report that I ran a successful social media workshop for researchers in our Staff Conference at the University of Bedfordshire in July 2011 – a drop in a large ocean. I am sure that colleagues are attempting similar initiatives in other institutions.

Public libraries and Library 2.0

What has been the attitude of the public library to Library 2.0? Hammond (2010), in surveying the take-up of Library 2.0 by public libraries in the UK, started by looking at their use of blogs. In September 2009 she identified only

13 active public library blogs. Helen Leech's study (Chapter 18) is a pioneering account of what is going on, and what should be done in our UK public libraries to unleash the full potential of Web 2.0 in a time of national recession.

Anttiroiko and Savolainen (2011) attempt a qualitative summary of public library activity with Web 2.0 mainly in the USA, Canada, the UK, the Netherlands, Australia and the Nordic countries. Developments are seen as fairly positive and encouraging for the future of Library 2.0. There is evidence of short messaging, blogs and social networking, but the authors indicate 'only a weak signal of the direction of change' (Anttiroiko and Savolainen, 2011, 97), and 'it remains to be seen how Web 2.0 applications will diffuse and contribute to the redesign of library services and reorganization of public libraries all over the world' (Anttiroiko and Savolainen, 2011, 97).

In the United States, Lietzau and Helgren (2011) compare selected US public library websites for evidence of use of Web 2.0 technologies in 2007 and 2010. There has been a marked increase in adoption, particularly of social networking. Overall, Facebook adoption has increased from 2% to 18%. The most growth has been in larger libraries. However, there is evidence of experimentation by more libraries. Very few libraries were particularly aiming at mobile users, but this was expected to change. Surveys by Curtis Rogers (2010) of libraries in the USA provide some data. His third survey on the promotion and use of Web 2.0 elicited 664 responses: 78.6% were using social networking, 51.9% were using blogs, 40.2% photo sharing and 29.1% online video.

In Australia case studies from the Melbourne area (Casey-Cardinia Library Corporation, Eastern Regional Libraries and Frankston Library Service) show how Web 2.0 tools can be used to reach library users (Gosling, Harper and McLean, 2009).

In general, I believe that the role of public libraries in information literacy deserves more attention than it currently seems to be getting. It represents an area of great opportunity and I hope that the case studies and later chapters in this book will help this to be recognized and taken up.

From 2.0 to social media

We may no longer be speaking about 2.0 in the way we did four years ago, but the ground-breaking changes for everyone in use of the web as a platform for creation, sharing and innovation remain with us. Nowadays we speak of social media and this may reflect the fact that the 2.0 concept is coming to some kind of maturity. There is no longer an argument: social media (aka Web 2.0, Library

2.0) are now mainstream and will continue to evolve, challenging the way we, as librarians and as citizens, operate in the world to come.

References

Anon (2010) Is Library 2.0 Dead? *Librarytwopointzero* (blog) 25 February, http://librarytwopointzero.blogspot.com/2010/02/is-library-20-dead.html.

Anttiroiko, A. and Savolainen, R. (2011) Towards Library 2.0: the adoption of Web 2.0 technologies in public libraries, *Libri*, **61** (2), 87–99.

Arthur, C. (2011) How the Smartphone is Killing the PC, *Guardian* (5 June), www.guardian.co.uk/technology/2011/jun/05/smartphones-killing-pc.

Bawden, D. et al. (2007) Towards Curriculum 2.0: library/information education for a Web 2.0 world, *Library and Information Research*, **31** (99), 14–25.

British Broadcasting Corporation (2011) Apple Makes Record Profit as iPhone and iPad Sales Leap, *BBC Business News* (19 July), www.bbc.co.uk/news/business-14211938.

Cao, D. (2009) Chinese Library 2.0: status and development, *Chinese Librarianship*, (27), 4.

Carlson, N. and Hamburger, E. (2011) Apple is Building Twitter into your iPhone and it's a Game-changer, *Business Insider* (2 June), www.businessinsider.com/apple-is-building-twitter-into-your-iphone-and-its-a-game-changer-2011-6.

Carpenter, J., Tanner, S. and Smith, N. (2011) *Researchers of Tomorrow: a three year (BL/JISC) study tracking the research behaviour of 'Generation Y' doctoral students, Second Annual Report, 2010–2011*, http://explorationforchange.net/index.php/rot-home/59-researchers-of-tomorrow-2nd-year-report.html.

Carr, N. (2010) *The Shallows: what the internet is doing to our brains*, New York: W. W. Norton & Co.

Casey, M. E. and Savastinuk, L. C. (2007) *Library 2.0: a guide to participatory library service*, Information Today Inc.

Chua, A. Y. K. and Goh, D. H. (2010) A Study of Web 2.0 Applications in Library Websites, *Library and Information Science Research*, **32** (3), 203–11.

CIBER (2008) *Information Behaviour of the Researcher of the Future*, CIBER briefing paper, www.jisc.ac.uk/media/documents/programmes/reppres/gg_final_keynote_11012008.pdf.

Crawford, W. (2011) *Library 2.0: a cites and insights reader*, Cites & Insights Books.

Dickson, A. and Holley, R. P. (2010) *Social Networking in Academic Libraries: the possibilities and the concerns*, Wayne School of Library and Information Science Faculty Research Publications, Paper 33, http://digitalcommons.wayne.edu/slisfrp/33.

Dowell, A. (2010) The Rise of Apps, iPad and Android, *Wall Street Journal Technology* (27 December), http://online.wsj.com/article/ SB10001424052748704774604576035611315663944.html.

Drabble, A. (2011) So What Is the Real Impact of Web 2.0 on Researcher Workflow? Presentation at ALISS Conference, 20 July, www.slideshare.net/heatherdawson/coventry2011drabble.

Fernandez, J. (2009) A SWOT Analysis for Social Media in Libraries, *Online*, **33** (5), 35-7.

Fichter, D. and Wisniewski, J. (2008) Social Media Metrics: making the case for making the effort, *Online*, **32** (6), 54-7.

Fieldhouse, M. and Nicholas, D. (2008) Digital Literacy as Information Savvy: the road to information literacy. In Lankshear, C. K. M. (ed.), *Digital Literacies: concepts, policies and practices*, International Academic Publishers.

Glazer, H. (2009) Clever Outreach or Costly Diversion? An academic library evaluates its Facebook experience, *College and Research Libraries News*, **70** (1), 11-19.

Gosling, M., Harper, G. and McLean, M. (2009) Public Library 2.0: some Australian experiences, *Electronic Library*, **27** (5), 846-55.

Greenhow, C., Walker, J. D. and Kim, S. (2009) Millennial Learners and Net-savvy Teens? Examining internet use among low-income students, *Journal of Computing in Teacher Education*, **26** (2), 63-8.

Hall, H. (2010) *Getting Real about Social Media. Keynote presentation at Internet Librarian International Conference*, October, www.csi.napier.ac.uk/c/news/newsid/13366609.

Hammond, S. (2010) Public Library 2.0: culture change? *Ariadne: A Web and Print Magazine of Internet Issues for Librarians and Information Specialists*, **30** (64), 16, www.ariadne.ac.uk/issue64/hammond/.

Hargittai, E. (2010) Digital Na(t)ives? Variation in internet skills and uses among members of the 'net generation', *Sociological Inquiry*, **80** (1), 92-113.

Head, A. J. and Eisenberg, M. B. (2010) *Truth be Told: how college students evaluate and use information in the digital age. Project Information Literacy Progress Report*, http://projectinfolit.org/pdfs/PIL_Fall2010_Survey_FullReport1.pdf.

Herring, J. E. (2011) *Improving Students' Web Use and Information Literacy*, Facet Publishing.

Hicks, A. and Graber, A. (2010) Shifting Paradigms: teaching, learning and Web 2.0, *Reference Services Review*, **38** (4), 621-33.

Ito, M. et al. (2009) *Living and Learning with New Media: summary of findings from the Digital Youth Project*, Cambridge, MA: MIT Press.

Jenkins, H. (2009) *Confronting the Challenges of Participatory Culture: media education for the 21st century*, MIT Press.

JISC (2011) Responses from 100 Device-led Student Interviews, *JISC W2C Project Blog* (11 June), http://lrt.mmu.ac.uk/w2c/2011/06/11/responses-from-100-device-led-student-interviews/.

Jones, C. et al. (2010) Net Generation or Digital Natives: is there a distinct net generation entering university? *Computers and Education,* **54** (3), 722-32.

Kelly, B. et al. (2009) Library 2.0: balancing the risks and benefits to maximize the dividends, *Program: Electronic Library and Information Systems,* **43** (3), 311-27.

Kim, Y. M. and Abbas, J. (2010) Adoption of Library 2.0 Functionalities by Academic Libraries and Users: a knowledge management perspective, *Journal of Academic Librarianship,* **36** (3), 211-18.

Lamb, B. and Groom, J. (2010) Never Mind the Edupunks: or, the great Web 2.0 swindle, *Educause Review,* **45** (4), 50-8.

Lankes, R. D. (2011) *The Atlas of New Librarianship,* Cambridge, MA: MIT Press.

Lietzau, Z. and Helgren, J. E. (2011) U.S. Public Libraries and Web 2.0: what's really happening? *Computers in Libraries,* **29** (9), 6-10.

Macleod, R. (2010) Some University Library Blogs Suck, Some Could Do Better, and Some Are Quite Good, *Roddy Mcleod's blog* (9 November), http://roddymacleod.wordpress.com/2010/11/09/some-university-library-blogs-suck-some-could-do-better-and-some-are-quite-good/.

McManus, B. (2009) The Implications of Web 2.0 for Academic Libraries, *Electronic Journal of Academic and Special Librarianship,* **10** (3), www.openj-gate.com/browse/ArticleList.aspx?issue_id=1246473&Journal_id=81151.

Melville, D. (2009) *Higher Education in a Web 2.0 World,* www.jisc.ac.uk/publications/generalpublications/2009/heweb2.aspx.

Park, J. (2010) Differences among University Students and Faculties in Social Networking Site Perception and Use: implications for academic library services, *Electronic Library,* **28** (3), 417-31.

Partridge, H. (2011) Librarian 2.0: it's all in the attitude, paper presented at ACRL 2011, Philadelphia, 30 March-2 April, http://www.ala.org/acrl/sites/ala.org.acrl/files/content/conferences/confsandpreconfs/national/2011/papers/librarian2.0.pdf.

Pew Research Center (2011) *Twitter Update 2011,* Pew Internet and American Life Project, 26 April-22 May, www.pewinternet.org/Reports/2011/Twitter-Update-2011/Main-Report.aspx.

Purcell, K. (2011) Information 2.0 and beyond: where are we, where are we going?, presentation given at APLIC Annual Conference, Washington, DC, March, www.pewinternet.org/Presentations/2011/Mar/APLIC.aspx.

Raths, D. (2010) Mobile Learning on Campus: balancing on the cutting edge, *Campus Technology*, http://campustechnology.com/articles/2010/11/01/balancing-on-the-cutting-edge.aspx.

Research Information Network (2010) *If You Build It Will They Come? How researchers perceive and use Web 2.0*, Research Information Network.

Rheingold, H. (2011) Crap Detection 101: required coursework, *Project Information Literacy, 'Smart Talks'*, no. 5, 3 January, http://projectinfolit.org/st/rheingold.asp.

Rogers, C. R. (2010) Social Media, Libraries, and Web 2.0: how American libraries are using new tools for public relations and to attract new users – third survey, November 2010, www.slideshare.net/crr29061/social-media-libraries-and-web-20-how-american-libraries-are-using-new-tools-for-public-relations-and-to-attract-new-users-third-survey-november-2010.

Selwyn, N. (2009) The Digital Native – Myth and Reality, *Aslib Proceedings*, **61** (4), 364–79.

Smith, S. D. and Caruso, J. B. (2010) *ECAR Study of Undergraduate Students and Information Technology, 2010*, Educause Center for Applied Research, www.educause.edu/Resources/ECARStudyofUndergraduateStuden/217333.

Sodt, J. M. and Summey, T. P. (2009) Beyond the Library's Walls: using Library 2.0 tools to reach out to all users, *Journal of Library Administration*, **49** (1), 97–109.

Stuart, D. (2009) Web 2.0 Fails to Excite Today's Researchers, *Research Information*, (44), 16–17.

Tripathi, M. (2009) Use of Web 2.0 Tools by Academic Libraries, *IATUL Proceedings*, www.iatul.org/conferences/pastconferences.

University of Leeds (2010) Generation Y Student Doctors Swap Textbooks for iPhones, www.leeds.ac.uk/news/article/895/generation_y_student_doctors_swap_textbooks_for_iphones.

Wheeler, S. (2011) The Natives Are Revolting, *Learning with 'e's* (blog) (2 May).

Wyatt, A. M. and Hahn, S. E. (2011) Copyright Concerns Triggered by Web 2.0 Uses, *Reference Services Review*, **39** (2), 303–17.

Xu, C., Ouyang, F. and Chu, H. (2009) The Academic Library Meets Web 2.0: applications and implications, *Journal of Academic Librarianship*, **35** (4), 324–31.

Zickuhr, K. (2011) *Generations and Their Gadgets*, Pew Report, www.pewinternet.org/Reports/2011/Generations-and-gadgets/Overview/Findings.aspx.

Chapter 2

Information literacy and Library 2.0: an update

Peter Godwin

We could easily have coined the phrase 'Information Literacy 2.0' when we wrote our first book. There was very little usage of this term at that time, but we have no regrets. To use such a label then would have threatened hours of creating a definition, satisfying no one! Since then, Špiranec and Zorica (2010) have interpreted Information Literacy 2.0 as a subset of information literacy (IL), and we shall return to this later. It was an exciting time, and I believe it was useful then to concentrate more on how the tools could be used to deliver IL. We could, however, have spent more time considering the effects it would have on what it meant to be information literate. That is the aim of this chapter!

What is IL?

In the past the seemingly endless debates about what information literacy is and whether it is a good label have been a huge bore. It is so easy to say that we must define something before we can do anything about it. Most practising librarians who are involved with educating their users just get on with it and don't agonize over the niceties. It concerns me that much of the research in IL never really permeates down to practitioners, not least because of the portentous language used in the name of scholarship to make it appear appropriately impressive. How many paradigm shifts have you read about? Should I be concerned about the ontological and epistemological positions of my praxis?! Julien and Williamson (2010) are similarly concerned about the disconnect between researchers and practitioners, but for rather different reasons. They are concerned that researchers criticize the IL standards approach but, with some exceptions, are not replacing it with anything based on sufficient observed behaviour.

When necessary, we have to provide IL documentation for institutional learning and teaching plans or reviews, and these tend to refer to generally recognized frameworks like the Big Six or SCONUL Seven Pillars. This can be extremely useful to aid discussion and understanding among colleagues from outside the library. The danger is that they become the blueprint for our IL initiatives day by day. Such frameworks too easily become a series of tick-boxes for skills development. Markless (2009) questioned whether we should 'continue to present students with generic IL frameworks, models and processes': IL has always been more complex than this.

IL has evolved from 'user education' into something of a totem for the modern librarian. It is usually academic librarians who have been most concerned about IL, and it is in this sphere that the most developed models of what it consists of and how to deal with it have been developed. This has led IL to be portrayed as short-sighted and too higher-education oriented (Hoyer, 2011). Most of our students will not continue in academia and will instead go into the public, private or non-profit job markets. IL is usually encountered only in library-related journals. However, librarians in all sectors have begun to be involved with it. Somehow it has become our territory (whatever it is), and to some it must seem like a justification for our existence. In reality, IL has developed as a response to the needs of the modern individual, from school through college or university and across lifelong learning (Lloyd and Talja, 2010), and librarians have an important part to play in this. Yet there is a residual view that it is about using library catalogues and databases in higher education (HE) (Lloyd and Talja, 2010). The ones who get most excited about IL are HE librarians. *Mea culpa!* IL is much bigger than just the library, but who is better qualified than the librarian to act as guide to navigating the web?

Information literacy: going beyond skills

The root of the problem is that we have always been unlucky with the term IL because it is very hard to define either 'information' or 'literacy' (Lloyd, 2010; Bawden, 2001). No wonder that, when used together outside libraries, they often elicit puzzled looks. Having been critical of long debates about the nature of IL, I must avoid giving a lengthy history of how we got to the term! The ALA definition in 1989 (American Library Association Presidential Committee on Information Literacy, 1989) had great influence, and has formed the basis of most other formulations (Bawden, 2008). The SCONUL definition carried it further and has been much used in planning IL programmes. However, as we have seen, these frameworks have encountered a lot of criticism in recent years and have become regarded as too skills based and restrictive. Whitworth (2006) goes further, and from a critical social theory perspective demonstrates that the ACRL (Association of College and Research Libraries) framework encourages a prescriptive view of the information landscape that is harmful to autonomous learning and to students developing their own information landscape.

IL is too often about libraries and resources, searching, and technical tips, and the frameworks can encourage this. We should not be trying to make our students into librarians! Stanley Wilder said this in a particularly famous article in 2005 (Wilder, 2005). He was especially critical of IL and recommended that librarians should concentrate on building up students' understanding of their chosen discipline: an approach that will resonate with much I shall say later. Standard frameworks like the 1999 SCONUL Seven Pillars tended to see the development of the skills in a set order. I can remember teaching students like that myself. It was an order that I imposed because it provided a structure and it helped me. However, this is not the way that students actually research, and increasingly I have been moving away from that approach. Markless (2009) emphasizes this by saying that students may find this kind of chain of information useful for facts, but 'it is of little use when trying to influence behaviour and judgement' (Markless, 2009, 27). And that is exactly what many of us are trying to do with our students now, whatever their background.

Standard perceptions of IL have been under criticism for a number of years now (Markless, 2009; Markless and Streatfield, 2007). From a number of writers and influential thinkers far more learned than myself, we encounter the idea that knowledge is constructed individually and socially. Ever since Christine Bruce's phenomenological approach in her *Seven Faces of Information Literacy* (Bruce, 1997), things have never really been the same (Julien and Williamson, 2010). IL has become more complicated. Frameworks were only part of the story. Yet how far has the phenomenological approach to IL reached the practitioners? This is part of the serious disconnect between IL researchers and practitioners (Julien and Williamson, 2010.) In a small way, this book is aiming to make more accessible such crucial insights.

Information literacy as a social practice

We need to get back to basics: what are the types of literacy? There are three types, according to Lupton and Bruce (2010). They are:

1   Generic skill sets to be learned by the individual
2   Situated in a particular social context
3   Transforming persons and groups to challenge the status quo.

If we map IL against these criteria, we see that the standard IL frameworks fall mainly into the first category. In the past there has been a lot of emphasis on generic skill sets and some partial acceptance of the (second) social context approach. The third, transformative approach, has outcomes for the individual and for society, and is the hardest to achieve. It is a most illuminating analysis. On the one hand we have IL as generic, then as part of a social practice and finally as challenge and question. The tension between the three is best reconciled by seeing them as inclusive, but as a hierarchy. So far I have only considered the first approach.

We will now consider the social practice aspect, because this is, in my view, the most crucial and helpful for practitioners. Lloyd (2010) has written that 'IL is a social practice that facilitates knowing about the information landscapes within which a person is situated'. This would not have meant much to me until recently. Illumination came from the work of Lankshear and Knobel (2007). They have defined literacies as 'socially recognized ways of generating, communicating and negotiating meaningful content through the medium of encoded texts within *contexts* of participation in Discourses'. Don't be put off by this! I emphasize the word 'contexts'. The social, cultural, political, economic and historical practices in a country or organization provide the context for literacy development. From the work of Gee (1996, cited in Lankshear and Knobel, 2007) we can see our literacy being determined by, first, how we learn to do things and be ourselves and, second, our participation in outside groups.

IL can no longer be seen as individual skill development and a workforce requirement without considering the particular context in which each individual operates. They will differ. This socio-cultural approach starts from the assumption that all human practices are social and that the way we do things comes from a body of practitioners. These communities of practice have common concerns and use similar language. Think of schools, universities, small companies, tax offices, hospitals, church communities. If we think about IL in relation to *all* of these, how do the standard IL frameworks apply? In the past I might have tried to defend the SCONUL framework and implied that some parts were more important than others. The truth is that such frameworks do not really apply. IL will alter according to the context.

Frameworks try to apply to everyone, but apply to no one because they ignore context. What are the cultural and social practices in the discipline? This could be based on a departmental way of operating, the standards set by professional boards, and assessment criteria. These will vary across disciplines and affect the way students may approach problems. Furthermore, it follows that IL cannot be taught well out of context, in standalone general units at the start of an undergraduate course (Woolwine, 2010). Most of our students will not continue in academia and will instead go into the public, private or non-profit job markets. There they will need a different focus in order to evaluate and fulfil their information needs, because IL depends on context. Workplace IL is different, and social interactions and relationships will be paramount (Hoyer, 2011). Lloyd undertook important research into how emergency services developed their IL (Lloyd-Zantiotis, 2004). 'As ... practitioners we need to understand how IL practices occur in other contexts so that our own pedagogical practice prepares our users for the transition from our landscape to another' (Lloyd, 2010, 138). Information landscapes develop over time via collaboration, and carry on through membership and have their own language and narrative. Maybe we should begin to think of information literacies in the plural, rather than a single manifestation?

Information literacy and 2.0

A key part of the 2.0 approach was to know our users (Booth, 2009). I suspect that in the past we gave them what we thought was good for them and what we thought they needed. I can see from the above social practice approach that this was not such a good idea. Markless (2009) refers to the importance of knowing something about the students' intentions in learning. Are they concerned about understanding and seeking meaning, or are they just concerned about assessment and getting the best marks? It is all very well for us to have high-blown theories about lifelong learning and equipping them for life, but is that what they need? Is there a mismatch here? We need to equip them for both, and Web 2.0 can assist in this. It uses territory that they already know or that, in some subject areas, is essential to know about, and can help them to gain knowledge, build understanding, do better assignments and become adaptive players in the world later on. Teachers and librarians in schools should support this social constructivist approach, which gets students to construct their own knowledge by building upon what they already know (Herring, 2011). Just because you point to lifelong learning advantages, this approach may not appeal to all individuals (Shenton and Fitzgibbons, 2010) at school level. Motivation in schools can come from allowing pupils to research their own interests. The essence is, as the CILIP School Libraries Group said in 2007, that schools in the 21st century should aim to 'light sparks rather than fill vessels' (Shenton and Fitzgibbons, 2010). This is all very 2.0.

Furthermore, there is often a disconnect between what librarians think it is important to teach first-year undergraduates and what academics think. In a representative survey of librarians, academics and students at California State University, the librarians' priority for teaching was to distinguish between scholarly and non-scholarly material, while the academics' first priority was how to quote and paraphrase information in assignments. Also librarians and students had differing perceptions concerning the skills students found the most difficult. The librarians thought search strategy and the right tool, whereas the students said choosing/narrowing down a topic (Cunningham, Carr and Brasley, 2011).

Has Web 2.0 fundamentally changed how we approach IL? This is a topic we shall return to in Chapter 20. Markless (2009) admitted in her IL framework for the University of Hertfordshire that some changes had to be made as a result of Web 2.0. Although the new social media did not change the basic processes of learning, they did have implications for IL. The satisfaction of information needs may now come more frequently from peer web pages, social bookmarking and interest groups than from the systematic searching suggested by librarians, because students interact differently in their use of online material (CIBER, 2008). Web 2.0 sources are likely to encourage a more chaotic way of information gathering, in contrast to the fixed certainties of the IL frameworks. Oblinger and Oblinger (2005) foresaw a generation of digitally literate students who could expect to operate in a social manner, in teams, and who would expect interactivity in environments that are far less text heavy. The mobile element will reinforce the trend toward information searching that is uncontrolled and 'on the fly'. There is no going back: we are all part of a 2.0 world, uncertain, chaotic; and it is now time to look at what this has meant for the way we have been delivering IL of late.

References

American Library Association Presidential Committee on Information Literacy (1989) *Final Report,* American Library Association.

Bawden, D. (2001) Information and Digital Literacies: a review of concepts, *Journal of*

Documentation, **57** (2), 218-59.

Bawden, D. (2008) Origins and Concepts of Digital Literacy. In Lankshear, C. K. M. (ed.), *Digital Literacies: concepts, policies and practices*, New York: Peter Lang.

Booth, C. (2009) *Informing Innovation: tracking student interest in emerging library technologies at Ohio University*, Chicago: ACRL.

Bruce, C. (1997) *Seven Faces of Information Literacy*, Adelaide: Auslib Press.

CIBER reports (2008) *Information Behaviour of the Researcher of the Future*, CIBER briefing paper.

Cunningham S., Carr, A. and Brasley, S. S. (2011) Uncovering the IL Disconnect: examining expectations among librarians, faculty and students, *Proceedings of the 2011 ACRL Conference*, 466-70.

Herring, J. E. (2011) *Improving Students' Web Use and Information Literacy*, Facet Publishing.

Hoyer, J. (2011) Information Is Social: information literacy in context, *Reference Services Review*, **39** (1), 10-23.

Julien, H. and Williamson, K. (2010) Discourse and Practice in Information Literacy and Information Seeking: gaps and opportunities, *Information Research*, **16** (1), Paper 458.

Lankshear, C. and Knobel, M. (eds) (2007) *A New Literacies Sampler*, New York: Peter Lang.

Lloyd, A. (2010) *Information Literacy Landscapes: information literacy in education, workplace and everyday contexts*, Chandos Publishing.

Lloyd, A. and Talja, S. (eds) (2010) *Practising Information Literacy: bringing theories of learning, practice and information literacy together*, Wagga Wagga, New South Wales: Centre for Information Studies, Charles Sturt University.

Lloyd-Zantiotis, A. (2004) Working Information: a grounded theory of information literacy in the workplace, Armidale, Australia: University of New England (unpublished).

Lupton, M. and Bruce, C. (eds) (2010) *Windows on Information Literacy Worlds: generic, situated and transformative perspectives*, Wagga Wagga, New South Wales: Centre for Information Studies, Charles Sturt University.

Markless, S. (2009) A New Conception of Information Literacy for the Digital Learning Environment in Higher Education, *Nordic Journal of Information Literacy in Higher Education*, **1** (1), 25-40.

Markless, S. and Streatfield, D. (2007) Three Decades of Information Literacy: redefining the parameters. In Andretta, S. (ed.), *Change and Challenge: information literacy for the 21st century*, Adelaide: Auslib Press.

Oblinger, D. G. and Oblinger, J. L. (2005) *Educating the Net Generation*, Educause E-Book.

Shenton, A. K. and Fitzgibbons, M. (2010) Making Information Literacy Relevant, *Library Review*, **59** (3), 165–74.

Špiranec, S. and Zorica, M. B. (2010) Information Literacy 2.0: hype or discourse refinement? *Journal of Documentation*, **66** (1), 140–53.

Whitworth, A. (2006) Communicative Competence in the Information Age: towards a critical theory of information literacy education, *Italics*, **5** (1).

Wilder, S. (2005) Information Literacy Makes All the Wrong Assumptions, *Chronicle Review*, **51** (18), B13,
http://faculty.philau.edu/kayk/kkay/articles/searching/Information%20Literacy%20Makes%20All%20the%20Wrong%20Assumptions.pdf.

Woolwine, D. E. (2010) Generic versus Discipline-specific Skills. In Lloyd, A. and Talja, S. (eds), *Practising Information Literacy: bringing theories of learning, practice and information literacy together*, Wagga Wagga, New South Wales: Centre for Information Studies, Charles Sturt University.

Chapter 3

The story so far: progress in Web 2.0 and information literacy

Peter Godwin

I have delivered many presentations suggesting that the IL and Web 2.0 connection might be overplayed (Godwin, 2009a). How much evidence is there that libraries and librarians are really viewing the information landscape as different, requiring Web 2.0 to be included and used to teach IL? How much impact is it having on student learning?

Luo (2010) conducted a survey of IL instruction librarians who were members of the Information Literacy Instruction Discussion List sponsored by the Association of College and Research Libraries. Fifty valid responses were received, which were then followed up by eight interviews which revealed some great ideas of how librarians have employed blogs, wikis, social bookmarking sites, YouTube and Flickr. Luo separates his respondents into those who use Web 2.0 for their own purposes, those who use them for facilitating delivery of IL to students and those who use the facilities of certain Web 2.0 tools to enhance the teaching of specific aspects of IL. An example of the latter was where the respondent had used Flickr to get the students to collect some digital images and apply attribution, in order to explain Creative Commons, and then doing a similar exercise with Wikipedia. Luo concludes that 'it is indisputable that Web 2.0 is becoming more and more prevalent and its value to facilitating IL instruction is recognized' (Luo, 2010, 39), but more research is needed, particularly around assessing how the students react to it and how it affects learning outcomes. There is still a feeling that students regard social media as their own province and resent their use for academic purposes.

It is possible to get some clues regarding take-up from Tripathi (2009), who surveyed university libraries: 82 in the UK, 151 in the USA, 37 in Canada and 7 in Australia. Of the 45% that had blogs, 20.53% used them for search tips and

8.53% for IL. Most of the 11% that used podcasts and the 6% that used vodcasts did so for some IL purpose. Tripathi also notes that the 300 University Grants Commission-recognized universities in India had yet to start using Web 2.0 tools. In the Philippines, Lapuz (2009) enthusiastically and successfully championed their use in library schools, but found school teacher-librarians much less receptive.

Bobish (2010) reports a survey of 122 Association of Research Libraries instructional websites between February and April 2008. Instant messaging was used by 72%, some kind of media (video, flash, screen capture, podcasts) by 48%, but blogs by only 8% and social bookmarking by 5%. He also compares these results with keyword mentions on the EBSCO Library, Information Science and Technology Abstracts database. This interesting idea showed that social networking, gaming and Second Life were written about because they sounded 'sexy' – yet in reality were hardly used. Blogs were the most heavily documented medium, but one of the least mentioned in the website survey. More up-to-date research is needed to see whether these imbalances between interest and application still exist and to get a truer picture of the uptake of Web 2.0. Bobish concludes that librarians are willing to experiment but reluctant to let their users participate directly in the creation of materials, e.g. wikis.

I believe we are a long way from fulfilling all the potential of Web 2.0 tools for IL teaching, but there are plenty of success stories. Some of these have been showcased on our blog *Information Literacy Meets Library 2.0* (http://infolitlib20.blogspot.com/). It was also good to read Carolyn Carpan's article where she says that our first book 'signals a shift in how libraries are thinking about using Web 2.0 tools' (Carpan, 2010, 107), and to read how she introduced her classes to Delicious and PBWiki. In presentations I have given (Godwin, 2009b) I have suggested ways in which the various tools could help to deliver elements of the SCONUL Seven Pillars. Špiranec and Zorica (2010) spoke of the need for us to employ the tools in our teaching not as isolated tools, but fully within our IL teaching programmes. Williams (2010) stresses the need for students to be able to do more than find information and emphasizes the validation process, that is, making sense and creating new meaning from what has been found. She demonstrates this in her article, identifying Web 2.0 tools such as blogs, podcasts, screencasts, games and Second Life as able to play a significant part in the process.

Bobish (2011) has provided a comprehensive list of how Web 2.0 tools could be employed against each of the ACRL (Association of College and Research

Libraries) Learning Outcomes. He states: 'Web tools, if used thoughtfully in information literacy instruction, are not simply the latest flashy trend, but can have a solid pedagogical basis that enhances student learning while at the same time making connections with technologies that are already being used for research purposes and in daily life outside the classroom.' His list is brilliant and shows how far we have to go to use these tools to their full potential.

Let us now take a look at the 2.0 success stories.

Podcasts

Ever looked at the number of train commuters in their own sound world, wearing headphones? (How did I survive most of my 19 years' commuting without them?!) Sound is a huge opportunity for learning and Brabazon (2010) recommends the use of podcasts because they utilize the undervalued ability to listen. We plug into our own world of listening. Podcasts are quick and easy to produce and are a useful means of presenting learning materials, a space for interaction between learner and information environment, a way of communicating between teacher and learner – and vice-versa – and between teachers. Sarah Ison, creative media librarian at the University of Brighton, created a welcome message for new students as part of their orientation, and this was a powerful way of first meeting them aurally, before meeting them in person. Sutton-Brady et al. (2009) provide a convincing account of how podcasting was used at the University of Sydney to enhance their communication with a large and diverse student group. Podcasts should be short and provide support for student assessments.

Images

The ability to illustrate an argument, brighten up a presentation by using images legally on the web via Web 2.0 repositories such as Flickr, is one of the most obvious success stories. We can use them and we can recommend that our students use them. The challenge is to understand which services are 'free' of charge to use and also free of any copyright restrictions (an IL skill in and of itself). Flickr has a Creative Commons filter, but there are many other ways to deal with this and find out about freely usable images. O'Connell (2011) gives a great list of these, and also draws attention to ImageCodr.org, a service that helps you to decipher how you can use a particular Flickr image and how to cite it.

Visualization tools

We are drowning in data. One of the great success stories of the past few years lies in the development of web tools that allow the visualization of this data. They can pull together vast amounts of data into a graphical form and are now known as 'infographics'. Twitter is one service that has created this mound of data, and it needed some way of representing its trends visually. Twitter's API is public, so it can be 'mashed' – manipulated by anyone with the necessary skills into something new that illustrates data visually (Booth, 2010). Twitter has spawned sites like Twitterverse. Think of Wordle, which is widely used to create word clouds showing the prevalence of the words used in a text: it is really useful in schools and beyond to emphasize ideas in a speech, for example (Watt, 2011). Infographics make information more accessible, comprehensible and engaging. They are now becoming much more common for publicity campaigns, e.g. National Library Week 2011 in the USA.[1] The ability to interpret them, sort and search visually and create them will be a future trend. Watt (2011) recommends infographics to help develop critical literacy in students, which could involve framing a good research question, finding reliable data, gathering images under Creative Commons Licence and designing the infographic itself. Great advice for this is available on Kathy Schrock's website.[2]

Video and screencasts

To me, online video and screencasts that can be produced and shared on the web represent the most exciting part of the 2.0 revolution. Jeffery Loo (2010) from the University of California, Berkeley, made online instructional videos about PubChem using free open source software (GIMP, Audacity, Windows Live MovieMaker, YouTube). Hartnett and Thompson (2010) at the University of Texas A&M used Jing, Camtasia and Captivate to create screencasts, and these screencasts have been particularly helpful for communicating with and assisting their overseas students in Qatar.

Sparks (2010), from Arizona State University, wrote enthusiastically about how to do quick, simple screencasts to answer reference queries, for class instruction (an example used five separate screencasts) and for embedding sessions into LibGuides. In particular she used screenr, an easy-to-use free software package on the web that authenticates via Twitter. (I have used this myself with great success.)

Oehrli et al. (2011) set out to find out whether screencasts really work. They selected fifteen undergraduate students from different years, aged between 18 and 22, at the University of Michigan Undergraduate Library. From their findings they suggested that screencasts should be two minutes or less in length. It is better to show two screencasts of two minutes than one of four minutes because a single concept can be focused upon in a shorter time span. Creating a context for the learning point can be a challenge. They suggest that the length of time spent on preparation varies according to the purpose and intended audience. They conclude that screencasts do indeed facilitate student learning.

Sekyere (2010) notes how reference services often embrace e-mail and chat/instant messaging (IM), but these can be problematic when dealing with more complex queries. Some libraries are meeting this challenge by creating short on-the-fly videos and screenshots. Jing is particularly recommended because the librarian can record a search within Jing whilst sharing it with the user on the fly during the conversation, and can then upload it into a screencast, using a URL that can be sent to the user.

The Animated Tutorial Sharing Project (ANTS) has given libraries a significant way of building up a collection of tutorials that can be shared and used by any library via LibGuides, course management systems, blogs or Facebook sites, as required. Carmen Kazakoff-Lane (from Brandon University, Manitoba) describes this in a case study in Chapter 12.

Presentation software

Freely available software on the web helps us to improve presentations and avoid 'death by PowerPoint'! For example, Prezi is a useful alternative, and with judicious use of the zoom feature can be powerful (Herring, 2011). SlideShare has proved to be an invaluable resource for librarians to share their cutting-edge presentations, just as YouTube continues to provide a great treasure trove of material for learning and 'edutainment'.

Offsite reference

How has the provision of offsite reference progressed? This can involve e-mail, FAQs on your website, IM, chat and SMS text messages. Virtual reference (aka chat) has become mainstream in the US and Australia (Geeson, 2011) but has been slower to evolve in the UK. For example, Southeastern Louisiana University Library started with SMS, using Altarama in 2005, and already offered phone, e-mail and online chat reference. Over the five years to 2010, e-mail traffic has decreased, chat reference has stayed the same, but SMS has increased dramatically (Stair, 2011).

SMS text messaging has become a quick win for most libraries. Seen as an addition to the standard face-to-face reference library function, such services have grown alongside the general popularity of texting. Text messages can supplement induction or be part of a treasure hunt in the library (Walsh, 2010a). With their SMS service at New York University Library, Pearce, Collard and Whatley (2010) found a higher-than-expected variation in the length of transactions. However, on average, reference queries took 4.85 hours and their findings supported the idea that users do not expect a purely synchronous service, and there was evidence of a correlation between the speed and thoroughness of answers and higher user satisfaction.

Wikis

The use of a wiki to deliver a course project for honours freshmen in their Introduction to Education course at the University of Rhode Island is documented in Niedbala and Fogleman (2010). They show how a wiki was used as a shared workspace to combine library instruction, online research and peer evaluation. During the process it was interesting to note that students became dramatically more comfortable with using RSS feeds, Google Reader, social bookmarking, Diigo and the online citation manager Zotero.

Warlick (2004) believes we should stop teaching students to assume that things are authoritative and start by asking them to prove authority. I have pursued a similar approach in my teaching, announcing to students that I am turning them all into detectives and that they ought always to be suspicious of what they read, hear or see. Wikipedia is a great asset for this approach. Head and Eisenberg (2010) researched Wikipedia usage as part of Project Information Literacy (PIL) during 2008 and 2009. The focus groups and survey concluded what most of us already felt: that students wanting background information go to Wikipedia early in their research as a quick and easy solution. Research for their course may begin there, but it seldom ends there. Students use it understanding its limitations, but do so because it is a quick fix that has some credibility. A small-scale test was undertaken at the University of Illinois to see how the Wikipedia app for the iPhone might be used and how it might affect the research process (Hahn, 2010). The students tended to use it more for recreational use and for short, factual topics. Despite this they did report that they used some of the information found as part of their research. All were satisfied with the information they found.

Portals

Information portals are proving to be a great way to create an easy-to-update dynamic resource for student groups on a particular topic. These portals are easily constructed collections of RSS feeds from sites such as PageFlakes, iGoogle and NetVibes. Kolah and Fosmire (2010) give an excellent account of their experiences with two cohorts of students: graduate physics students at Rice University and general science undergraduates at Purdue University. In both cases the students' appreciation of what RSS feeds can accomplish was marked. One student remarked: 'in my opinion, this will be one of the most useful assignments we have had this semester, I am very likely to use this in other classes, and just in general to help collect and organize information'. This is a superb example of what we are trying to do: provide techniques that students will reuse and that may eventually become part of their normal everyday practices.

Social networking

Mitchell and Smith (2009) describe their use of social media at Wake Forest University, North Carolina, for an elective one-credit course on IL. Facebook was used as a substitute for Blackboard, along with Wiki Project (using MediaWiki) Walton and Hepworth (2011) describe how Web 2.0 social networking was used in a year one Sport and Exercise module at Staffordshire University. This showed conclusively that use of the Blackboard message board helped students' critical thinking.

Social bookmarking

Social bookmarking via Diigo, Delicious, Connotea, LibMarks and the H20Playlist from Berkman Center for Internet and Society at Harvard Law School all offer the possibility of saving bookmarks which then can be accessed from anywhere, and can promote interaction between users. This may be more about helping students to organize themselves and fostering serendipitous discovery, rather than encouraging lots of sharing of resources. Alas, in my experience, group work in general can bring its own problems, with unequal participation leading to unwillingness to share resources.

Delicious has been one of my favourite Web 2.0 tools. However, the very recent change of ownership (at the time of writing) may be discouraging its use. This should not stop librarians from using such services for their own purposes or in instruction. Fortunately, migration from one service to another can often be accomplished easily, e.g. Delicious to Diigo.

Social tagging could make library catalogues collaborative and interactive (Redden, 2010). LibraryThing for Libraries can enhance library catalogues with tag browsing and book recommendations, ratings and reviews, and LibMarks can be integrated into catalogues with LibGuides. Tagging, if taught imaginatively using the examples of blogs and social bookmarking, could be the link that makes users understand the value of summarizing their topic, by using labels and comparing them with the controlled vocabulary used in subject terms in databases.

LibGuides

Yelinek et al. (2010) explain how they were able to use LibGuides at Bloomsburg University of Pennsylvania for their revised IL tutorial. It is an interesting tale of permitted reuse of material from another university (Go for Gold from James Madison University), which subject librarians updated collaboratively, creating their own branded tutorial. Curtis-Brown (2011) explains how LibGuides was chosen at Middlesex University to get over the inability of previous web pages to integrate Web 2.0 easily. This has helped staff to create larger numbers of guides aimed at more areas and to integrate podcasts and Delicious RSS feeds.

Blogs

Blogs have become popular for providing IL support. Chan and Cmor (2009) describe how a course blog was developed at Hong Kong Baptist University to provide support for a first-year politics course with a cohort of 94 students. In addition to sessions with the librarian, the students were encouraged to undertake a small project on the blog each week. The authors stress the importance of the backing of the academic tutor and his insistence on a minimum participation requirement. In the public library world, the ability to use blogs to form user communities is highlighted by Pieper (2010), where the Gold Coast City Library blog, *Book Coasters*, promotes reading and informal learning in an informal way, providing book recommendations, reviews and short discussions on current themes. Walton and Hepworth (2011) have demonstrated that online social-networked learning (in this case forums on Blackboard), when problem based and used with groups, has beneficial effects on their learning that also foster the development of higher-order skills so that they can synthesize their new knowledge and become producers as well as consumers of knowledge.

The mobile dimension

Users' views on what mobile services they would like to see were investigated at the University of Huddersfield (Walsh, 2010a). Attitudes to services were dependent on students' being clear about their usefulness. SMS was very positively received, e.g. for overdue reminders. There was no desire to experiment with new services outside the library, partially because of concerns about the cost of internet access (Walsh, 2010a). The ability to search from a mobile device came second in the rating by the student groups, despite possible fears about internet connection costs. There were mixed feelings about SMS support; tips by text message received some support, but vodcasts, podcasts and Quick Response (QR) codes featured low in the students' recommendations.

Smartphones provide opportunities for constructive learning in general, some of which are being followed up in libraries. These include video streaming, geotagging, microblogging, text notifications, direct image and video blogging, QR codes, student podcasts and social networking (Cochrane and Bateman, 2010).

QR codes are being displayed on walls, on machines and in publications, anywhere that a mobile can read them for the information that can then be linked to on the web. Pulliam and Landry (2011), from Providence College, Rhode Island, warn that QR scanning is not automatically available on mobiles. They warn against overuse of QR codes because they can lose their impact if they cover every surface of the library. The University of Huddersfield experimented with a range of uses, from linking to a Text a Librarian service, to instructional videos and electronic resources. In general, use was low and disappointing at the time (Walsh, 2010b) (see Chapter 10). Brigham Young University carefully introduced an audio tour connected by QR codes. Its reflections show that users were not really ready for use of QR codes. The locations of QR codes need to be clear, and they maybe work better if a game like SCVNGR is also employed (Whitchurch, 2011).

iPads are great for designing our own media consumption. Flipboard (http://flipboard.com) is an example of this, as it can aggregate Facebook and Twitter and display content in an attractive way. iPads used as e-readers allow bookmark searching, and tagging and sharing of content: compare the potential of this as opposed to the paper textbook! In my opinion, the iPad is the start of something big, and others will follow. The applications that live in these spaces shared by education and entertainment could be a powerful way of encouraging student learning (Educause, 2011). Berkeley College students use iPads to keep journals of their life as students (Cortes, 2011), and the device is a great roaming reference tool (King, 2010). I have found my iPad to be an invaluable aid when providing help to individual students, either within the library or elsewhere on campus, because of its flexibility in providing point-of-use help and the ability to move so swiftly between the many windows that I may have open. The iPad has given us a great device to use with our public that is limited only by cost, security and our imaginations: for access to e-books, lending to customers, easy access to dedicated research collections and rare materials, for individual use of training material, and so on (Online College, 2011).

Daring Librarian (Gwyneth A. Jones at Murray Hill Middle School) has created a great scavenger hunt for library orientation aimed at her ESOL (English for speakers of other languages) class (see Figure 3.1), which has used images from Flickr and QR codes (Jones, 2011).

Library tours for iPod can also be created. University of California, Merced, developed an iPod Touch tour, with 15 iPod Touches available for use in leading students around the building and highlighting services and resources (Mikkelsen and Davidson, 2011). Tours usually took about 30 minutes. California Polytechnic State University has created a GPS guided tour (CalPoly, 2011) that can also be downloaded as an app from iTunes.

Conclusion

We have clearly gone well beyond the early adopter and 'do it because it's fashionable' stages in the use of Web 2.0 tools in our IL interventions. The ever-increasing number of possibilities should not deter us. The value of the tools will vary according to the context in which they are being used, and we will no doubt all experience failures. There is some evidence of the impact on student learning, but, as with IL in general, this is hard to prove conclusively. However, this is not stopping experimentation, as we shall see from the case studies in later chapters. I believe that the use of Web 2.0 tools should form a crucial part of any 21st-century IL professional's time.

Notes

1   See www.archives.com/blog/industry-news/national-library-week-2011.html.
2   https://sites.google.com/a/kathyschrock.net/infographics/links.

Figure 3.1 A poster explaining and promoting QR codes by Gwyneth A. Jones (Daring Librarian) reproduced under CC BY-SA 2.0 licence (www.flickr.com/photos/info_grrl/5281436894/in/set-72157625298744518/)

References

Bobish, G. (2010) Instruction 2.0, *Communications in Information Literacy*, **4** (1), 93-111.

Bobish, G. (2011) Participation and Pedagogy: connecting the social web to ACRL learning outcomes, *Journal of Academic Librarianship*, **37** (1), 54-63.

Booth, C. (2010) Stacking the Tech: Twitter and the visual dataverse, *Library Journal* (1 July), www.libraryjournal.com/article/ CA6713635.html?nid=2673&source=title&rid=1105906703.

Brabazon, T. (2010) The End of 'Shhhhh' in the Library, *Times Higher Education* (20 October), www.timeshighereducation.co.uk/story.asp?storycode=413927.

CalPoly (2011) Self-guided Tours, (July 14), http://admissions.calpoly.edu/visit/selfguided.html.

Carpan, C. (2010) Introducing Information Literacy 2.0, *College and Undergraduate Libraries*, **17** (1), 106-13.

Chan, C. and Cmor, D. (2009) Blogging toward Information Literacy: engaging students and facilitating peer learning, *Reference Services Review*, **37** (4), 395-407.

Cochrane, T. and Bateman, R. (2010) Smartphones Give You Wings: pedagogical affordances of mobile Web 2.0, *Australasian Journal of Educational Technology*, **26** (1), 1-14.

Cortes, D. A. (2011) Berkeley College Embraces the iPad, *President of Berkeley College* (blog), http://presidentofberkeleycollege.blogspot.com/2011/03/berkeley-college-embraces-ipad.html.

Curtis-Brown, L. (2011) LibGuides: the implementation of new library subject guides at Middlesex University, *ALISS Quarterly*, **6** (2), 8-12.

Educause (2011) Seven Things You Should Know about iPad Apps for Learning, (18 August), www.educause.edu/Resources/7ThingsYouShouldKnowAboutiPadA/223289.

Geeson, R. (2011) Virtual Advice Services. In Dale, P., Beard, J. and Holland, M. (eds), *University Libraries and Digital Learning Environments*, Ashgate, 87-103.

Godwin, P. (2009a) Information Literacy and Web 2.0: is it just hype? *Program: Electronic Library and Information Systems*, **43** (3), 264-74.

Godwin, P. (2009b) Shots in the Dark: information literacy in the 21st century, CONUL Annual Information Literacy seminar in Dublin, 28 May, www.slideshare.net/godwinp/shots-in-the-dark-information-literacy-in-the-21st-century.

Hahn, J. (2010) Information Seeking with Wikipedia on the iPod Touch, *Reference Services Review*, **38** (2), 284-98.

Hartnett, E. and Thompson, C. (2010) From Tedious to Timely: screencasting to troubleshoot electronic resource issues, *Journal of Electronic Resources in Librarianship*, **22** (3-4), 102-12.

Head, A. J. and Eisenberg, M. B. (2010) How Today's College Students Use Wikipedia for Course-related Research, *First Monday*, **15** (3).

Herring, J. E. (2011) *Improving Students' Web Use and Information Literacy*, Facet Publishing.

Jones, G. A. (2011) QR Code Quest: a library scavenger hunt, *The Daring Librarian* (blog) (23 July), www.thedaringlibrarian.com/2011/03/qr-code-quest-library-scavenger-hunt.html.

King, D. L. (2010) iPad - a Game Changer? *David Lee King blog* (31 May), www.davidleeking.com/2010/01/28/ipad-a-game-changer/.

Kolah, D. and Fosmire, M. (2010) Information Portals: a new tool for teaching information literacy skills, *Issues in Science and Technology Librarianship*, Winter, www.istl.org/10-winter/refereed1.HTML.

Lapuz, E. B. (2009) *Teaching Web 2.0 Applications in the Planning and Development of Information Literacy Programs: reaching out to librarians and information professionals*, IATUL Conference, www.iatul.org/doclibrary/public/Conf_Proceedings/2009/Lapuz-text.pdf.

Loo, J. (2010) *Library Instruction through Online Video and Social Media*, www.lib.berkeley.edu/CHEM/instruction/video/index.htm.

Luo, L. (2010) Web 2.0 Integration in Information Literacy Instruction: an overview, *Journal of Academic Librarianship*, **36** (1), 32-40.

Mikkelsen, S. and Davidson, S. (2011) Inside the iPod, outside the Classroom, *Reference Services Review*, **39** (1), 66-80.

Mitchell, E. T. and Smith, S. S. (2009) Bringing Information Literacy into the Social Sphere: a case study using social software to teach information literacy at WFU, *Journal of Web Librarianship*, **3** (3), 183-97.

Niedbala, M. A. and Fogleman, J. (2010) Taking Library 2.0 to the Next Level: using a course wiki for teaching information literacy to honors students, *Journal of Library Administration*, **50** (7), 867-82.

O'Connell, J. (2011) Find Free Images Online, *HeyJude* (blog), http://heyjude.wordpress.com/find-free-images-online/.

Oehrli, J. A. et al. (2011) Do Screencasts Really Work? Assessing student learning through instructional screencasts, *ACRL 2011 Annual Conference Proceedings*, 127-43.

Online College (2011) Twenty Coolest iPad Ideas for Your Library, *Online College* (blog), www.onlinecollege.org/2011/09/05/20-coolest-ipad-ideas-for-your-library/.

Pearce, A., Collard, S. and Whatley, K. (2010) SMS Reference: myths, markers, and modalities, *Reference Services Review*, **38** (2), 250-63.

Pieper, L. (2010) Information Literacy in Public Libraries: a covert operation, ALIA Access, 1-3 September, Brisbane.

Pulliam, B. and Landry, C. (2011) Tag, You're It! Using QR codes to promote library services, *Reference Librarian*, **52** (1-2), 65-74.

Redden, C. (2010) Social Bookmarking in Academic Libraries: trends and applications, *Journal of Academic Librarianship*, **36** (3), 219-27.

Sekyere, K. (2010) Less Words, more Action: using on-the-fly videos and screenshots in your library's IM/chat and email reference transactions, *Community and Junior College Libraries*, **16** (3), 157-61.

Sparks, O. B. (2010) Five Minute Screencasts - the Super Tool for Science and Engineering Librarians, *Issues in Science and Technology Librarianship*, (Winter), www.istl.org/10-winter/tips.html.

Špiranec, S. and Zorica, M. B. (2010) Information Literacy 2.0: hype or discourse refinement? *Journal of Documentation*, **66** (1), 140-53.

Stair, B. (2011) Reference Service: five years later, *Reference Librarian*, **52**(1-2), 9-19.

Sutton-Brady, C. et al. (2009) The Value of Using Short-format Podcasts to Enhance Learning and Teaching, *ALT-J Research in Learning Technology*, **17** (3), 219-32.

Tripathi, M. (2009) Use of Web2.0 tools by academic libraries, *IATUL Proceedings*, www.iatul.org/doclibrary/public/Conf_Proceedings/2009/Tripathi-text.pdf.

Walsh, A. (2010a) Mobile Phone Services and UK Higher Education Students, What Do They Want from the Library? *Library and Information Research*, **34** (106), 22-36.

Walsh, A. (2010b) QR Codes – Using Mobile Phones to Deliver Library Instruction and Help at the Point of Need, *Journal of Information Literacy*, **4** (1), 55-63.

Walton, G. and Hepworth, M. (2011) A Longitudinal Study of Changes in Learners' Cognitive States during and following an Information Literacy Teaching Intervention, *Journal of Documentation*, **67** (3), 449-79.

Warlick, D. (2004) *Redefining Literacy for the 21st Century*, Columbus, OH: Linworth.

Watt, D. (2011) Becoming the Embedded School Librarian Begins with Understanding Our Place in the New Zealand Curriculum, *Half Pint of Wisdom* (blog), http://halfpintofwisdom.wordpress.com/2011/07/22/becoming-the-embedded-school-librarian-begins-with-understanding-our-place-in-the-new-zealand-curriculum/.

Whitchurch, M. (2011) QR Codes and the Library: the library audio tour, *ACRL 2011 Annual Conference Proceedings*, 363-68.

Williams, S. (2010) New Tools for Online Information Literacy Instruction, *Reference Librarian*, **51** (2), 148-62.

Yelinek, K. et al. (2010) Using LibGuides for an information literacy tutorial, *College and Research Libraries News*, **71** (7), 352-5.

Chapter 4

The changing web: sites to social

Phil Bradley and Karen Blakeman

Introduction

We would all agree that the internet is in a constant state of change. There are, however, many different types of change that we can observe. For example, there is the very crude measurement of the number of hours of YouTube video posted every minute, the number of tweets per second and the number of blogs that are created. These figures are generally quite mind boggling, but because they are available in easy, bite-sized chunks they are easy to digest and understand.

What are rather less easy to understand, however, or indeed to know, are some of the longer-term changes in trends that influence the growth and change of the internet. We could, for example, consider the way in which the internet has become more of a medium for the creator than for the consumer; or the extent to which newspaper publishing has moved onto the net at the expense of the more traditional printed format; or the way in which various groups or indeed societies are able to change both politically and socially. What is of particular interest to the information professional, however, is the slow but sure way in which the whole process of internet search is moving away from the institutional and towards the individual. This is of course part and parcel of the increasing importance of the information creator and needs to be considered within that context.

Issues of personalization

Search engines have always had as their Holy Grail the ability to tailor their results directly to the individual's needs. Once they are able to do that they can also much more closely tailor the adverts that they present to individual users, and thus make more money for themselves. Until now it has been almost impossible to achieve this except in the very broadest sense. Search engines have had to rely on what sites people click on and the links to those sites. With the rising volume of individual data flooding onto the net, however, search engines can now start to become much more precise in the way in which they tailor their information. Let's assume a really basic example. Suppose that you are interested in finding out about librarians. In the past you would run your search and the search engine would return results based primarily on web pages and the way in which those web pages were ranked or valued by others using the internet. However, a search engine now can interrogate a resource such as Twitter. It can see who is tweeting on the subject of librarians, it can check the biographies of tweeters to see if any of them are librarians and it can also use new algorithms to check who those individuals are, how often they are re-tweeted and how many people are following them. That provides the search engine with a group of individuals who have an interest in the subject area. It is then possible to follow several other lines of enquiry by looking at the pages they bookmark, the size of their network in their favourite bookmarking resource, whether they have published anything in a presentation format, the pages of information that they have written, their websites and how often those websites have been looked at by other internet users. It is thus possible for the search engine to display data based on social networks generated by influential users in a specific subject area.

The search engine can also begin to make a leap from that data to information about you and can start to correlate it. For example, are any of the people in your own social networks related in any way to the influential individuals that were previously identified? If so, the work referenced by those particular influential people can be ranked much more highly for your own results. Have any of the friends or colleagues in your social network indicated a particular liking or preference for any of the material that the search engine has returned? If so, that material can once again be pushed further up the set of results. Consequently your own social network becomes a valuable criterion for assessing the importance of the data that the search engine has found, and the data is tailored specifically towards you. The search engine can then utilize more algorithms based on its knowledge of your own preferences and can narrow and rerank the results based on such criteria as your preferred reading level, the medium in which you prefer to receive your information, the language used, the geographical location and, indeed, the length of the article or the number of images that it contains.

As a result, the accuracy or otherwise of the results that you get becomes based in part on the extent to which you actively participate with social media.

There are of course advantages and disadvantages in this: the more that you and your network of friends and colleagues use the internet, the more accurate your results will become, while conversely the less that you use social networking (or the extent to which you value your privacy), the less accurate your information will be. Another glaring problem also manifests itself at this point: if the search is done by you, an information professional with a wide range of interests, it may become almost impossible for a search engine to narrow the criteria for search down to anything other than broad elements such as language, reading level or location. The danger here, therefore, may be that the most effective way of existing on the internet with regard to search is to create a variety of personae to overcome the 'jack of all trades, master of none' issue. Another way of approaching the problem is for the searcher to highlight or otherwise indicate individuals or organizations that exhibit the kind of authority that is needed in order to more closely focus on the subject of the original enquiry. A search engine may thus, as an intermediate step, begin to return results based on the information it has found for thought leaders - either individuals or organizations. This in turn leads to a different type of multi- or meta-search engine, one that is capable of ignoring databases and focusing instead on reputation and authority.

We should also take into account at this point that information professionals themselves, when not searching (or indeed as searchers!), can become reputable resources in their own right. This is certainly an area that experts and subject librarians can expect to take on in the next few years. The more that they (you) are able to tweet, become involved in Facebook discussions, post photographs or write blogs, the more influential and authoritative they (you) will become. Consequently their role will begin to move away from the provision of data to answer individual queries, and towards the identification of data that will be of use and value to a much wider community. That community may be a social network based around their library or university, or it may be based around a network of friends and colleagues from other institutions around the world.

We now have an intrinsic change in the way in which search works. No longer does the value of websites have a pre-eminent position; indeed, the value of the website will decrease as the reputation and authority of the individual who creates the website increases. While it is really important for those individuals to be involved in social media, the mechanism that they use, such as blogs or tweets, becomes less important - it is the type and amount of interaction that they have with other individuals that will become the new 'page rank'.

Will this new search paradigm be reflected in or embraced by existing search engines? This is of course the really big question, but we don't seem yet to be in a position to answer it. Certainly Facebook is beginning to take on the mantle of a search resource and some companies and organizations are beginning to find that their Facebook profile is as important as if not, indeed, more important than their traditional website. Facebook also has the advantage of the 'like' button and an existing infrastructure of friends and colleagues. Google, on the other hand, while it has consistently failed to understand or embrace social media, has the power of data at its disposal and, for the moment at least, a fledgling social network. However, we also need to remember the other major players: Twitter, Microsoft (in the form of Bing) and Apple with the iPhone and iPad. We may well in fact see the rise of a new type of search engine that embraces elements of all of that, but which, nonetheless, is still entirely new. As the title of this chapter indicates, however, none of this is yet certain and at the moment we are still in a chaotic environment.

Personalization, search engines and copyright: pitfalls and perils

Personalization, localization and semantic search are now the norm. Log in to Amazon and it is no surprise to see 'New for you ...' or 'Recommendations for you ...' based on previous purchases. If you buy groceries online from a site such as the UK's Ocado, when you go to the checkout the system looks at your past orders and asks 'Have you run out of ...?'. This approach to personalization based on past activity is just one of the many methods used by search engines and social media networks and, although it is debatable whether, overall, this is a good thing, the results retrieved are, for many people, better. However, the unilaterally imposed filtering does limit and seriously bias results, and there is no magic button that you can press to switch it off. Anyone who uses the internet as a means of research must understand how the networks and search tools work and when they can bypass or manipulate the search and ranking algorithms to achieve truly relevant results.

Search engines

Google is still way ahead of the pack when it comes to search, and the search engine that experiments the most with new features and search algorithms, and it is also the one that is investing most heavily in devising ways of tailoring results to the individual searcher. The evolution of Google is neatly summarized in the graphic 'Google's Collateral Damage: how the evolving algorithm shapes the web'.[1] Google's initial success was down to the main component of its ranking algorithms - the Page Rank, based on who is linking to whom and the authority of those links. The results that Google presented at that time were more relevant than those from already existing search engines and so Google gained in popularity. Since its launch in 1998, Google has added more search features and the number of 'signals' it uses to rank results have increased. All search engines have had to contend with website owners trying to use ranking algorithms to their advantage by designing pages with little content or added value and yet still managing to appear at or near the top of search results. The search engines continually endeavour to counter this by adding yet more criteria to the list, the most recent and widely publicized changes being Google's Panda update.[2]

All of the search engine owners remain reticent about the details of the signals used to rank pages. Bing has said that it uses 1000, whereas Google claims to use over 200, each of which may have over 50 variations, bringing its total to about 10,000.[3] This sounds impressive, but of greater importance is the relevance of the results that these algorithms deliver. As more signals come into play and as more adjustments have to be made to compensate for unwanted effects, the algorithms start to behave like intertwined spaghetti. Pull on one piece of spaghetti, and the whole pile could end up on the floor. Run a seemingly straightforward search, and the most bizarre results may appear.

Search engines, and in particular Google, continually experiment with new algorithms and a recent example of how badly it can go wrong has been documented.[4] This is an extreme example, and straightaway it is obvious that something odd is going on with the search. More often, though, the changes made to searches are more subtle. Variations on terms may be automatically included, for example 'Smith' may be added to the search as well as the specified 'Smyth'. For a long time Google has been very sympathetic to typographical errors, and rather than return no results it would ask 'Did you mean ...?'. Google rarely asks now and instead runs what it thinks was your intended search with a link to your original query under 'Search instead for ...'. For some searches, it will not even provide the alternative. The variations in search terms are usually highlighted in the web page extracts on the results page, but identifying the effect of personalization and social media interactions is more difficult and often impossible. The results that the search engines provide depend on:

- the country version of the search engine used and your location within that country
- the language used for the search interface
- the browser, version of browser and operating system
- whether you are using a PC, smartphone or tablet
- whether or not you are logged in to a search engine account
- web and search history, blocked sites and favoured sites lists (created by both you and the search engine)
- the type of search - for example, person, company, current news, scientific or technical query
- your social networks and level of interaction within those networks
- search engine experiments (especially Google).

In practice, this means that an identical search run at the same time by several people with differing social network connections and on different devices in different locations will come up with different results. This presents problems for those of us who help and advise others on effective search strategies. What appears on your screen may not be what is appearing on theirs. We can no longer say that a particular strategy is the best approach to dealing with a specific type of search. There are far too many variables being considered by the search engine.

Type Bing.com or Google.com into your browser and you will usually be taken to a country version of the search engine, based on your IP address. Although you will still be searching the whole of the world wide web, local content and websites will be given priority. Both Bing and Google go even further and try to work out your location, down to town or city level. If they get it wrong you can correct it, but it is impossible to switch it off. The best you can do is set your location to, for example, UK. However, extreme localization such as this encourages lazy searching. If you are looking for somewhere to eat and you have set your location to Bristol, you need only to search on the single term 'restaurants' and a list of possibilities will be displayed on a map. This is not so helpful if, for example, you are researching the distribution of McDonalds restaurants across the whole of the UK. However, the localization feature can be used to your advantage - for example, when researching an industry, person, company or services in a particular country or city. You can choose to go to a specific country version of the search engine and even change the town or city as needed. Search options, ranking algorithms and display features also differ from one country version to another. Google.com and Google.co.uk may now have accepted that coots are in no way related to cats or lions, but in the Czech Republic, Norway and Sweden cats are still offered as an alternative and Google Germany offers cows.[5]

Search engines also try to determine the context of your search and the type of information you want. If they think you are looking for a person they will give priority to social media profiles (Flickr, Twitter, Facebook, LinkedIn etc.). If the topic is a major news story, additional pages are added to the results that might not otherwise appear: after the Japanese earthquake and tsunami in March 2011 Google added links to the Pacific tsunami warning centre and the Japanese earthquake person finder to the top of the results. Type in the name of a foodstuff, and Google sometimes displays its recipe results page, which includes options for choosing ingredients. If a query uses technical or scientific terms, Google emphasizes papers from Google Scholar. Very often, the search engines get it right and the top results are good enough for most enquiries, but you may, for example, be looking for information on the history of pancakes and not for recipes! A year ago, a simple search on the single search term 'pancakes' would yield a mix of results, with at least one page in the top 10 that was of interest. Now, however, you have to consider very carefully what to include in the strategy in order to retrieve meaningful results. For instance, to get the best results for the pancake search, a more detailed strategy, such as 'pancakes origins OR history' is required.

As mentioned earlier, the major search engines now look at social media connections when compiling your results. If you are searching Bing from within your Facebook account, Bing will take into account the 'likes' of your friends. If you are logged in to a Google account Google may include, and give priority to, content from your social circle gleaned from contacts in your Gmail account, Google Reader, Google Groups, Google Buzz and other social networks mentioned in your Google profile. Not only does it search postings, tweets and websites owned by your first-level connections but it also looks at second-level connections. The problem here is that a social circle may be personal and totally irrelevant to business or scientific research.

Sometimes it seems impossible to make search engines – and Google in particular – behave, but there are some strategies that we can use, and, importantly, pass on to others to ensure that we are getting what we ask for:

1   Look very, very carefully at your results and at what the search engine is
    trying to do to your search. What is highlighted? Do the results make
    sense? Has Google, for example, automatically looked for synonyms and
    spelling variations without telling you? Use plus signs before a term to try
    to force an exact match or quote marks around a phrase (although,
    unfortunately, Google does sometimes ignore these).

2   Change the order of the terms in the search. This can radically change the
    search engine's behaviour and your set of results. Repeat one or more of
    the terms, one or more times. Again, this can significantly change your set
    of results.

3   Make full use of advanced search commands to focus the results. For
    example, try using 'filetype:pdf' when looking for a scientific paper
    because they are usually made available in this format and this will better
    focus your search.

4   Enable or disable the 'web history' option. Sometimes enabling web
    history so that results are adjusted according to your previous queries is
    helpful. However, it can bias the search results.

5   Clear cookies and your browser's cache. This has the advantage of
    removing personalization that has been unilaterally imposed on you by the
    browser, but the disadvantage is that it also removes your own settings.

6   Use a completely different search engine, for example DuckDuckGo.com,
    Blekko.com, subject-specific databases or institutional repositories.

The only way to decide how useful these approaches are is to try them out for
yourself, in different search situations, either on their own or in combination,
and choose the ones that work for you.

Unfortunately, finding the information is only half the battle. Much of what
you find will be user generated, disjointed and out of context. We need to be able
to recognize the different forms and presentations of information and how they
impact on veracity and quality. All too often we are in a hurry, and only have time
to skim through a page, thus missing essential clues.

A comment in a discussion forum viewed in isolation could be interpreted in
a completely different way than if it were read as part of the whole conversation.
A blog posting by an eminent researcher on, for example, wind turbines, may
come to one conclusion as to their efficiency, but the comments and discussion
following the article may cause him to revise his figures. Comments are often
separated from a posting by adverts, navigation bars or share buttons, and it may

not be obvious that there is a lively and important debate taking place 'below the fold' (further down the web page).

A lengthy document or a book might be split into sections or chapters and presented as separate web pages. You may be looking at a chapter that states the disadvantages of wind turbine energy generation. Even though the navigation links - often overlooked - suggest that there are additional chapters covering the advantages and conclusions, the author could be cited as being 'anti' wind power when in fact they are very much in favour of it.

A business analysis on an academic website of the strengths and weaknesses of a company may, not unreasonably, be assumed to be authoritative, especially if it is on the site of a well respected business school. But it could in fact be the basis of a student exercise to identify 'what is wrong with this analysis?'. Knowing how to back-track a URL and follow navigation links to the page in order to uncover the context is vital.

Copyright

Having found our way through the chaos that the search engines create for us and having identified the sources we wish to use, there is yet more trouble ahead. So many tools now allow us not only to store and organize links to pages, but also to keep copies of the pages themselves. The practice is commonplace in many types of business research where it is essential to be able to present on request a copy of the document that is cited in a report. The web page, although referenced in the report, may have significantly changed since the initial research and may no longer contain the data cited. Some tools go even further and enable the researcher to quickly compile a report from these copies, extracting quotes and images from the originals. Plagiarism is an obvious issue here, but so is copyright. It has now become so easy to pull together snippets of text and data from multiple sources that their copyright status may be overlooked.

Even when you have identified the type of licence associated with a piece of work, there is still the task of working out what you can and cannot do with it. Copyright that states 'All rights reserved' is clear cut, as is 'public domain'. The former means that you cannot copy, manipulate or republish the content in any way without express permission from the copyright owner. The latter allows you to do pretty much whatever you want with it. In between these two extremes there are now Creative Commons licences (www.creativecommons.org/). These were set up so that creators of text, images, videos, podcasts etc. could clearly state what people could and could not do with their content. For many users, the result has arguably been yet more confusion. Creative Commons is often viewed as a licence for anyone to do anything with the content, which is simply not the case. There are actually six Creative Commons licences,[6] each of which details the varying degrees of restriction and freedom in terms of reuse, mixing and adaptation. There is the further problem of varying licences within a work: a search for an image using the licence options on Google's advanced search screen may come up with the perfect photo, appearing in an article which seems initially to be 'free' for commercial use. Referring to the original document, you may find that it contains several images and discover that the 'free to use' licence applies to an image different from that identified in the search, which turns out to be 'all rights reserved'. And we haven't even begun to consider the intricacies of licensing issues with respect to social media such as Twitter, Twitpic and Facebook! On top of all that, you then have to consider how to cite and reference the work properly.

A poster called 'Giving credit ...' by Pia Jane Bijkerk[7] highlights the need to identify the owner of a work and the possible consequences of failing to do so. Although it refers to the use of images, the principles can be applied to all types of media and information.

Conclusion

The internet is ever changing. Search engines come and go, as do social media and personal networks, and the ways in which searches are conducted and presented to us will continue to evolve. It is indeed chaotic out there, but understanding how it all works and what drives it is the key to retrieving relevant results.

Notes

1   www.seobook.com/learn-seo/collateral-damage.php.
2   Official Google Blog: Finding more high-quality sites in search,
     http://googleblog.blogspot.com/2011/02/finding-more-high-quality-sites-in.html.
3   Dear Bing, We Have 10,000 Ranking Signals to Your 1000. Love, Google,
     http://searchengineland.com/bing-10000-ranking-signals-google-55473.
4   'Google decides that coots are really lions',
     www.rba.co.uk/wordpress/2011/02/12/google-decides-that-coots-are-really-lions/
     and 'Update on coots vs. lions', www.rba.co.uk/wordpress/2011/02/21/update-on-
     coots-vs-lions/.
5   'Google still thinks coots are possibly cats (or cows)',

www.rba.co.uk/wordpress/2011/06/07/google-still-thinks-coots-are-possibly-cats-or-cows/.

7   Documented at http://creativecommons.org/licenses/.

6   http://blog.piajanebijkerk.com/WordPress/2011/03/18/giving-credit/.

Chapter 5

Web 2.0: from information literacy to transliteracy

Susie Andretta

Introduction

This chapter is divided into two parts. In the first part literacy is discussed in terms of its 'functional' nature, as it provides the basis for social interaction, be it in print or digital worlds. The second part presents the view that there is a dynamic relationship between literacy and the information environment in which it operates. This relationship, which defines the functional attributes of literacy, is mapped onto a timeline that illustrates the shift from print to web environments. As the title of this chapter suggests, transliteracy is promoted as the literacy that is needed to function in a Web 2.0 world. This is because, as current technologies offer new 'applications of established processes of knowledge construction and sharing' (Thomas et al., 2007), the competences underpinning these processes need to be updated. Hence the need to move from information literacy to transliteracy. For those who are not familiar with it, the term 'transliteracy' was coined by Professor Thomas to describe 'the ability to read, write and interact across a range of platforms, tools and media from signing and orality through handwriting, print, TV, radio and film, to digital social networks' (Thomas et al., 2007). The two main practices of Web 2.0, namely the reorganizing and sharing of information and knowledge that are undertaken collectively (Witteman and O'Grady, 2008), are discussed here in terms of their impact on web users, turning them from consumers into 'produsers' of information (Bruns, 2008a, 2). The concept of produser is analysed later on. For now, it suffices to say that this is a compound term derived by the merging of 'producer' and 'user'. The exclusion of Web 3.0 from this timeline is deliberate, as we need to establish the functional literacy operating in a Web 2.0 environment before we can turn our attention to the functional literacy associated with the semantic, sentient, mobile and virtual environments that characterize a Web 3.0 world (O'Reilly and Battelle, 2009, 2).

Functional literacy

Whilst to be functionally literate means simply to be an 'active participant in society' (Ipri, 2011), it is not surprising that functional literacy means different things in different contexts. In its broad social function, literacy capitalizes on individuals' potential to foster the collective development of local and global communities (UNESCO, 2008, 1). Within an economic context, functional literacy is described by Hyslop-Margison and Margison as satisfying 'the human resource demands of the global corporate community' (Hyslop-Margison and Margison, 1998, 4). This, they argue, is in line with the idea that there is a correlation between literacy and economic performance, a view that was initially promoted by the Organisation for Economic Co-operation and Development in its first International Adult Literacy Survey (IALS, 1994, cited in Hyslop-Margison and Margison, 1998, 7). McGarry proposes that variations in the way literacy is described are also influenced by cultural differences: 'To be literate in the Honduras is not the same as to be literate in Hampstead, London NW3. Literacy can denote a minimal print-decoding skill; it may denote a critical awareness of the cultural assumptions, the ethical norms and the aesthetic value of the printed word' (McGarry, 1993, 83). A comparison between the official definitions of literacy in the UK and in Honduras reveals a similar emphasis on reading and writing, although in the UK to be literate also means having completed five or more years of schooling to develop competency in the 3Rs of reading, writing and arithmetic (Horton, 2007, 5). By contrast, statistical data on internet access paints substantially different experiences of the digital environment within these two countries. For example, by 2010, Honduras, with a population of around eight million, recorded just under one million internet users, about 12% of the population.[1] In the same year the UK recorded 51 million web users in a population of just over 62 million, that is, 82.5% of the total population had access to the internet.[2] It follows that functional literacy in the UK necessarily encompasses a degree of digital fluency that would not be included in the Honduran definition of this term. Readers in the UK (and other equally digitally oriented countries) may find it hard to imagine a society where phenomena like the 'Google Generation' and the 'Digital Natives' (CIBER, 2008, 5) are not the norm.

The main point raised here is that the social function of literacy is defined by the relationship to the information environment in which it operates. In practice, this means that the attributes of literacy change in response to the technological, cultural and economic requirements that literacy needs to address (Arp, 1990, 47). The second part of this chapter offers some reflections on this relationship and the ways in which literacy has evolved in response to the technological developments from print to Web 2.0 by illustrating this in a literacy timeline. Before we look at this timeline, it is important to note the following premises. Firstly, each literacy subsumes all of the attributes characterizing preceding literacies. For example, an information-literate person needs to master reading and writing before they can critically appraise the digital sources generated in a Web 1.0 environment. Similarly, a transliterate person must be information literate (i.e. able to master critical and reflective evaluation and synthesis of information) before they can actively participate in the collective repackaging and sharing of information and knowledge promoted by Web 2.0. Secondly, while the shift from print literacy to information literacy has long since come to pass (Bawden, 2008; Greenmeier, 2009), the transition from information literacy to transliteracy is yet to occur, even though the idea of Web 2.0 as the dominant information environment was acknowledged in 2004, when this term was first introduced by O'Reilly and Battelle (2009, 1).

The literacy timeline

The diagram (Figure 5.1) representing the literacy timeline consists of three dimensions: literacy, the information environment and the literacy's functional attributes. In addition to inheriting the attributes from the preceding literacy as discussed above, each literacy assumes specific attributes that are required

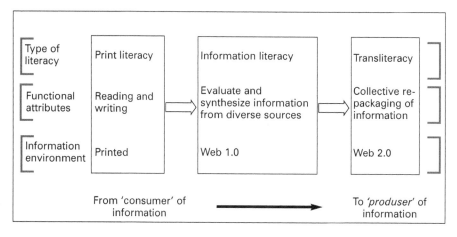

Figure 5.1 Literacy timeline: from print literacy to transliteracy

in order to function within the appropriate information environment. Reading across the diagram from left to right, one can distinguish three types of literacy: print literacy, information literacy and transliteracy, associated with the following information environments: Printed, Web 1.0 and Web 2.0, respectively.

Print literacy is described as the 'basic competences of reading, writing [...] essential to a print-oriented society where most information was authored, recorded, published, disseminated and communicated using print media' (Horton, 2007, 4). From a publishing perspective, the print-based environment is characterized by a well-established 'publication chain' (Bawden, 2008, 29) that claims author, publisher, bookseller and librarian as its main participants. From a user's perspective, Thomas et al. (2007) argue that in a pre-internet environment searching relied on the consultation of encyclopedias, indices and catalogues. Following the economic shift from 'the industrial age to the information age' (Hyslop-Margison and Margison, 1998, 7), it became clear that reading and writing alone would not fulfil the requirements of a Web 1.0 world, where ascertaining the accuracy of the information and managing access to diverse online sources have become priorities (Andretta, 2007a; Johnson, 2008; Ipri, 2011). Functioning in a Web 1.0 environment means constantly redefining the way in which we interact with large quantities of information, and the Australian Library and Information Association (ALIA) makes a convincing case for information literacy as the functional literacy suited to dealing with these challenges.

> Coping with a bewildering amount of information requires a new form of literacy, one that goes beyond the ability to read – something educators refer to as information literacy. This expanded definition of literacy means more than being able to read or use a computer. It means knowing how to find, evaluate and use the best information from an ever-increasing array of sources.
>
> (ALIA, 2003, 15)

The functional role of information literacy has also been acknowledged at an international level through the Prague Declaration (UNESCO, 2003), where it was promoted as fostering lifelong learning, and through the Alexandria Proclamation (UNESCO, 2005), where it was described as a human right, and therefore part of a global social empowerment. In addition, a more recent UNESCO project (Catts and Lau, 2008) set up to develop indicators to measure the impact of information literacy programmes nationally and on a global scale has encouraged the integration of information literacy initiatives beyond the educational scenario and into 'the broader context of work, civil society, and health and well being' (Catts and Lau, 2008, 9).

The terms Web 1.0 and Web 2.0 are used in Figure 5.1 to signify the web as if it were a software program that has developed from version one to version two (O'Reilly and Battelle, 2009, 1). Just as in a Web 1.0 world information literacy has assumed the functional role of dealing with the challenges of an information environment that is in a constant state of expansion (Lichtenstein, 2000; Bundy, 2004; Campbell, 2006), Web 2.0 requires a functional literacy that harnesses the plethora of social media and addresses the needs of diverse digital communities (Thomas et al., 2007; Andretta, 2009a).

A functional literacy in a Web 2.0 environment needs to prepare us for the changes in the nature of work and education that we have witnessed in the last decade (Institute of Museum and Library Services, 2009). For example, the 'job for life', with its local geographical character, has been replaced by career-hopping on a global level (ibid., 11), which is estimated by the US Bureau of Labor Statistics to involve four to six career changes over a lifetime (Baty, 2011, 5). The job requirement has also changed from routine to creative and non-routine, shifting from the 'mastery of one field [to the] simultaneous mastery of many rapidly changing fields' (Institute of Museum and Library Services, 2009, 11). This level of creativity and the ability to deal with uncertainty brought about by rapid changes require a functional literacy that focuses on interpersonal and communication skills in addition to competences in critical thinking and synthesis (Davidson, 2011, 35). Parallel to these work-related changes, the educational model has gone through an equally radical transformation from '[i]nstitution-centred where the attainment of a formal degree is the primary goal [to] [l]earner-centred which is self-directed, and where lifelong learning is the primary goal' (Institute of Museum and Library Services, 2009, 11). In other words, learning occurs 'across the lifespan', presumably to deal with the emerging trends of career-hopping and non-routine working practices. Lifelong learning that enables one to address 'unexpected and unfamiliar' conditions (Andretta, 2007b, 2009b) needs to be embedded in the literacy that enables us to function in a Web 2.0 environment. Dealing with the unknown is a particularly crucial functional attribute when we consider the claim that most of the jobs that will be offered at the end of this decade do not yet exist (Baty, 2011, 5).

A point that needs to be stressed here is that Web 2.0 is a 'platform provider', rather than a 'software provider' like Web 1.0 (Institute of Museum and Library Services, 2009, 13). O'Reilly and Battelle (2009) explain this claim within the context of web companies that survived the dotcom bust by using the 'the network as platform' (ibid., 1). In practice, this strategy involved creating web applications that 'literally get better the more people use them, harnessing network effects not only to acquire users, but also to learn from them and build on their contributions' (ibid.). In contrast with the 'network as platform' strategy, also known as the perpetual beta state of Web 2.0 applications (Witteman and O'Grady, 2008), in a Web 1.0 environment the network is used to provide access to applications, so focusing on provision of the 'software', rather than the network, as a service (O'Reilly and Battelle, 2009, 1). This marks a significant shift in the role of the web, which, in Web 1.0, consisted of static html pages that described a particular aspect of the world, while in Web 2.0 the web *is* the world (O'Reilly and Battelle, 2009, 2). At the root of this platform-provider strategy are two main features of Web 2.0, described by Witteman and O'Grady (2008, 106) as 'community and information reorganisation'. These two features have changed the nature of content development and sharing from 'centralized and top-down' to 'decentralized and bottom-up', leading to web users' demands for 'personalized, customized and on-demand experiences [...] collaborative, crowd-sourced decision-making (e.g. online consumer reviews) and free open sources products (e.g. Google Docs)' (Institute of Museum and Library Services, 2009, 13). In the literacy timeline shown in Figure 5.1 the outcome of these changes is illustrated by a shift from 'consumer' to 'produser' of information which spans the length of the literacy timeline. Bruns argues that in the setting of user-led creation associated with a Web 2.0 environment the term 'producer' is outdated because it reflects 'industrial modes of production' (Bruns, 2008a, 2) found in the print environment. The concept of produser, derived by merging producer and user, is adopted instead to convey the active engagement in 'the collaborative and continuous building and extending of existing content in pursuit of further improvement' (Bruns, 2008b).

The fact that we are all potential 'produsers' of information has substantial implications for the way we interact with and share information and knowledge. For example, Witteman and O'Grady (2008) argue that the appraisal practices that establish credibility in terms of the 'authority' of the source and the 'expertise' of the author are unsuitable in a Web 2.0 environment. They contend that we should be adopting quality-control strategies that are based on Web 2.0

criteria such as 'reputation' in order to measure 'collective [...] trustworthiness (in the sense of reliability) based on the referrals or ratings from members in a community' (Witteman and O'Grady, 2008, 109). This is easier said than done, as applications that operate on reputation have received a mixed response from academic and research communities. Reactions to Wikipedia, for example, reflect the views of those who question its use as a reference resource for scholarly work (Doucet Rand, 2010; Luyt and Tan, 2010), and the views of those who are cautiously optimistic about the degree of credibility Wikipedia enjoys amongst researchers (Chesney, 2006). Perhaps a more revealing insight into the mistrust of Wikipedia as a 'valid' source is illustrated by lecturers who actively discourage the students from using this resource to support their academic work. Anecdotal evidence for this is based on a recent personal experience of a Media Studies lecturer warning his first-year students that he would not accept essays citing Wikipedia as a source. Instances such as this are of particular concern because they illustrate that resistance to the contribution that Web 2.0 and social-media applications can offer occurs in disciplines that should have vested research interests in these phenomena, such as Media Studies.

In summary, the way that information and knowledge are organized and accessed in a Web 2.0 world is democratic because it harnesses a collective intelligence (Bruns, 2008b; O'Reilly and Battelle, 2009) and promotes a culture of open access and decentralized knowledge creation, and the freedom to share and discuss information using diverse forms of communication (Witteman and O'Grady, 2008). Some advocates of information literacy do account for some of the communicative aspect of Web 2.0 by promoting an active participation in the 'creation of information through traditional publishing and digital technologies (e.g. blogs, wikis)' (SCONUL, 2011, 11). Others (Bawden and Robinson, 2002; Bawden, 2008; Johnson, 2008) argue that digital literacy, thanks to its wide remit, promotes interaction with various media alongside the ability to engage at the level of meaning and context (Bawden and Robinson, 2002, 298). However, neither information literacy nor digital literacy can address the participative nature of Web 2.0 without challenging traditional academic and publishing conventions where authority-based quality-control practices prevail. Transliteracy, on the other hand, realizes the Web 2.0 practices of collaborative content development by combining a functional literacy that is expressed through linear and non-linear messages and that targets diverse audiences with the creative but at the same time reflective engagement in multiple communication channels and across a range of media. To put it simply, the prefix 'trans' in transliteracy stands for effective communication 'across media', especially non-traditional Web 2.0 publishing, and 'beyond literacy', using different languages (e.g. visual, oral, audio or textual) to convey the appropriate message to a targeted audience (Andretta, 2009a). Gilster's notion that digital literacy 'is about mastering ideas, not keystrokes' (1997, cited in Bawden, 2008, 28) is worth bearing in mind when we consider the type of functional literacy which would suit a Web 2.0 world and acknowledge that, whatever name we give to this literacy, its overall function should be to strive for critical engagement with content and context, rather than to focus on the mechanical interaction with the technology.

Conclusion

This chapter has presented a case in support of transliteracy as the appropriate functional literacy for Web 2.0. The premises presented to justify this claim are summarized as follows. Firstly, that the functional attributes of literacy are determined by its relationship with the information environment in which it operates. Secondly, that changes in the information environment necessarily lead to new interpretations of literacy so that, just as information literacy was seen as suitable to address the requirements of Web 1.0, and as the successor of print literacy, transliteracy is seen as the appropriate successor of information literacy because it enables one to operate effectively in a Web 2.0 world. In practice, becoming transliterate means taking the opportunities to exert our individual and professional rights as produsers, actively engaged at the level of meaning and ideas, while at the same time addressing the challenges of defining our educational practices within an information environment that is in a perpetual state of beta.

Notes

1   See www.internetworldstats.com/am/hn.htm.
2   See www.internetworldstats.com/eu/uk.htm.

References

Andretta, S. (2007a) Information literacy: the functional literacy for the 21st Century. In
    Andretta, S. (ed.), *Change and Challenge: information literacy for the 21st century*,
    Adelaide: Auslib Press, 1–14.
Andretta, S. (2007b) Phenomenography: a conceptual framework for information
    literacy education, *Aslib Proceedings*, **59** (2), 152–68.

Andretta, S. (2009a) Transliteracy: take a walk on the wild side. How the 21st century library can bridge the divide between oral, visual, print and digital worlds, *World Library and Information Congress: 75th IFLA General Conference and Assembly*, 'Libraries Create Futures: building on cultural heritage', 23–27 August 2009, Milan, Italy, www.ifla.org/files/hq/papers/ifla75/94-andretta-en.pdf.

Andretta, S. (2009b) Facilitating Information Literacy Education (FILE). In Brine, A. (ed.), *Handbook of Library Training Practice and Development, Vol. 3*, Ashgate Publishing Ltd, 49–75.

Arp, L. (1990) Information Literacy or Bibliographic Instruction: semantics or philosophy?, *RQ* (Fall), 46–9.

ALIA (Australian Library and Information Association) (2003) *Information Literacy Forum Advocacy Kit*, www.alia.org.au/advocacy/literacy.kit.pdf, 1–31.

Baty, P. (2011) Wise Up to the Modern World, *Times Higher Education*, 28 April–4 May, No. 1996, 5.

Bawden, D. (2008) Origins and Concepts of Digital Literacy. In Lankshear, C. and Knobel, M. (eds), *Digital Literacies. Concepts, policies and practices*, New York: Peter Lang Publishing, 17–32.

Bawden, D. and Robinson, L. (2002) Promoting Literacy in a Digital Age: approaches to training for information literacy, *Learned Publishing*, **15** (4), 297–301.

Bruns, A. (2008a) *Blogs, Wikipedia, Second Life, and beyond: from production to produsage*, New York: Peter Lang Publishing.

Bruns, A. (2008b) The Future Is User-led: the path towards widespread produsage, *The Fibreculture Journal*, **11**, DAC Conference, http://eleven.fibreculturejournal.org/fcj-066-the-future-is-user-led-the-path-towards-widespread-produsage/.

Bundy, A. (2004) Zeitgeist: information literacy and educational change. Paper presented at the 4th Frankfurt Scientific Symposium, Germany, 4 October.

Campbell, J. D. (2006) Changing a Cultural Icon. The academy library as a virtual destination, *Educause Review*, January/February, 16–30.

Catts, R. and Lau, J. (2008) *Towards Information Literacy Indicators*, UNESCO, www.uis.unesco.org/template/pdf/cscl/InfoLit.pdf.

CIBER (2008) *Information Behaviour of the Researcher of the Future*, CIBER, University College London.

Chesney, T. (2006) An Empirical Examination of Wikipedia's Credibility, *First Monday*, **11** (11), http://firstmonday.org/htbin/cgiwrap/bin/ojs/index.php/fm/article/view/1413/1331.

Davidson, C. (2011) So Last Century, *Times Higher Education*, 28 April–4 May, No. 1996, 33–6.

Doucet Rand, A. (2010) Mediating at the Student–Wikipedia Intersection, *Journal of Library Administration*, **50** (7–8), 923-32.

Greenmeier, L. (2009) What Drove Tim Berners-Lee to Imagine this Game-changing Model for Information-sharing and Will Its Openness Be Its Undoing? *Scientific American*, 12 March,
www.scientificamerican.com/article.cfm?id=day-the-web-was-born.

Horton, F. W. (2007) *Understanding Information Literacy: a primer* [Online], UNESCO,
http://unesdoc.unesco.org/images/0015/001570/157020e.pdf.

Hyslop-Margison, E. J. and Margison, J. A. (1998) *The Organisation for Economic Co-operation and Development: functional literacy and corporate agendas*, ED420843,
http://eric.ed.gov/ERICDocs/data/ericdocs2/content_storage_01/0000000b/80/25/f3/68.pdf.

Institute of Museum and Library Services (2009) *Museums, Libraries and 21st Century Skills*, www.imls.gov/pdf/21stCenturySkills.pdf.

Ipri, T. (2011) Transliteracy at ALA Annual 2011. *Libraries and Transliteracy* (blog), 27 April, http://librariesandtransliteracy.wordpress.com/.

Johnson, G. M. (2008) Functional Internet Literacy. Required cognitive skills with implication for instruction. In Lankshear, C. and Knobel, M. (eds), *Digital Literacies. Concepts, policies and practices*, New York: Peter Lang Publishing, 33-45.

Lichtenstein, A. A. (2000) Informed Instruction: learning theory and information literacy, *Journal of Educational Media and Library Sciences*, **38** (1), 22-31.

Luyt, B. and Tan, D. (2010) Improving Wikipedia's Credibility: references and citations in a sample of history articles, *Journal of the American Society for Information Science and Technology*, **61** (4), 715-22.

McGarry, K. (1993) *The Changing Context of Information*, Library Association Publishing.

O'Reilly, T. and Battelle, J. (2009) *Web Squared: Web 2.0 five years on*,
http://assets.en.oreilly.com/1/event/28/web2009_websquared-whitepaper.pdf.

SCONUL (2011) *The SCONUL Seven Pillars of Information Literacy: a research lens for higher education*,
www.sconul.ac.uk/groups/information_literacy/publications/researchlens.pdf.

Thomas, S., Joseph, C., Laccetti, J., Mason, B., Mills, S., Perril, S. and Pullinger, K. (2007) Transliteracy: crossing divides, *First Monday*, **12** (12),
www.uic.edu/htbin/cgiwrap/bin/ojs/index.php/fm/article/view/2060/1908.

UNESCO (2003) *The Prague Declaration 'Towards an Information Literate Society'*,
http://portal.unesco.org/ci/en/files/19636/11228863531PragueDeclaration.pdf/PragueDeclaration.pdf.

UNESCO (2005) *Alexandria Proclamation on Information Literacy and Lifelong Learning*,

http://portal.unesco.org/ci/en/ev.php-
URL_ID=20891&URL_DO=DO_PRINTPAGE&URL_SECTION=201.html.
UNESCO (2008) Table 1a and 1b - Literacy,
http://unstats.un.org/unsd/demographic/products/dyb/dybcensus/V2_Notes1.pdf.
Witteman, H. and O'Grady, L. (2008) eHealth in the Era of Web 2.0. In *Proceedings of the Virtually Informed: the internet as (new) health information sources, final conference of the project Virtually Informed - The Internet in the Medical Field,* University of Vienna, Vienna, 25-26 January, 104-20.

Chapter 6

Informed learning in online environments: supporting the higher education curriculum beyond Web 2.0

Hilary Hughes and Christine Bruce

Introduction

As boundaries between physical and online learning spaces become increasingly blurred in higher education (HE), how can students gain the full benefit of Web 2.0 social media and mobile technologies for learning? How can we, as information professionals and educators, best support the information literacy (IL) learning needs of students who are universally mobile and Google focused? This chapter presents informed learning as a pedagogical construct with potential to support learning across the HE curriculum, for Web 2.0 and beyond.

Informed learning (Bruce, 2008) responds flexibly to the dynamic information-learning environment of HE, embracing the opportunities of learning and teaching with new and emerging media. It supports a holistic learning approach whereby students consciously engage in a process of *using information to learn specific content or practices.* By promoting enquiry and problem solving, and the adoption of discipline- or context-specific knowledge and practices, it enables learners to develop the flexibility and confidence to use information in constantly evolving information environments. In this way, informed learning shifts the focus of IL education from mastering information skills to using information critically, ethically and creatively to learn within the wider context of students' disciplinary learning.

After outlining the principles of informed learning and how they may enrich the HE curriculum, we explain the role of library and information professionals in promoting informed learning for Web 2.0 and beyond. Then, by way of illustration, we describe recent experience at an American university where librarians simultaneously learned about and applied informed learning principles in reshaping the IL programme.

Informed learning for the online-intensive HE information-learning environment

The contemporary HE information-learning environment is online intensive and dispersed. Learners and educators are culturally and socially diverse and often physically remote from their institution's home campus. They have access to an ever-widening range of Web 2.0 resources from myriad international and local sources, way beyond the controlled environs of their institution's learning management systems (LMS) such as Blackboard and Moodle. Since Web 2.0 media are in a constant flux of evolution and extinction, students need to develop the confidence and flexibility to take the changes in their stride. However, while contemporary learners (of all ages) are increasingly IT savvy, they tend to demonstrate quite limited critical and strategic approaches and tend to rely on familiar, popular tools such as Google (Head and Eisenberg, 2010; Hughes, 2009; Lorenzo and Dziuban, 2006). This apparent *information literacy imbalance* (Hughes, 2009; Hughes, Bruce and Edwards, 2007) signals the need to foster deeper IL learning among students. In response, *informed learning* offers information professionals and educators a set of principles for developing critical, ethical, creative and reflective information use and learning.

Informed learning (Bruce, 2008) is a pedagogical construct that supports active learning and enquiry across the curriculum in HE. Informed learning reflects evolving theory and practice in IL education. It involves a shift of focus from information skills and competencies to students' experiences of using information as they engage with academic or professional content and practices relevant to their area of study. In the context of constantly advancing online media and changing interfaces, teaching about digital skills or the functions of particular databases is of limited long-term value to learners; thus, with informed learning, information skills represent 'building blocks' rather than intended outcomes.

In contrast to skills-based IL education, informed learning focuses on how people *use information to learn*. This is understood to be a complex experience, which at one level may be represented as *seven faces of informed learning* (Bruce, 1997; 2008). In other words, learners may experience IL in differing ways, which include using information tools to search for information, as well as extending their knowledge base, creating new information and using information wisely. Informed learning is a holistic approach where students learn simultaneously *about* particular subject(s) whilst learning about, or becoming aware of, *how* they use information. It takes account of learners' varied experiences to ensure the relevance of learning activities and assessment to diverse contexts. The design of informed learning places equal attention on what is learned and how working with information contributes to the learning process. Thus, students learn specific academic and professional content or practices, whilst becoming aware of their experience of information use.

Principles of informed learning

The theory and practice of informed learning is explained in detail elsewhere (Bruce, 2008; Bruce and Hughes, 2010). To summarize, the key principles are that:

1   Informed learning builds on learners' own experiences of using information to learn.
2   Informed learning promotes the simultaneous learning of discipline or professional-related content or practices, and learning about the experience of using information.
3   Informed learning is about changing learners' experiences in order to be reflective learners, helping them to develop new and more complex ways of working with information.

Educators could ask students to reflect on their experiences of information use as part of the learning process, and introduce them to new ways of using information to learn as part of that process. Students could be encouraged to embrace other forms of information use, such as using technology for communication and awareness, or using information for the benefit of others.

Taking the example of a nursing course, an educator could translate the above principles into the following goals for an enquiry-based project about common medical conditions:

1   In the initial stage of the enquiry the students will use a personal blog to document information gained previously through informal family experiences and formal practicum experiences in a community health centre.
2   Students will work in small groups to create a series of wikis on different medical conditions in order to organize, share and evaluate information gained from a range of online sources.

3   Students will use their personal blogs to reflect on their information use
     and learning experiences throughout the enquiry process, focusing in
     particular on new Web 2.0 strategies or sources that they could use to
     create a social network for sufferers of a particular medical condition. They
     will make informed decisions about which tools to use and the kinds of
     information and interactions to include in order to best meet their
     intended users' needs.

In this way, informed learning principles lead to an educational focus on:
understanding students' existing experiences of using information; building
into the curriculum relevant experiences that will encourage them to adopt the
desired approaches to information use; building reflection on those experiences
into the curriculum; and, where possible, enabling them to apply their
experiences to novel contexts (adapted from Bruce, 2008, 12-13). When
developing curriculum, the principles can also inform the development of
specific learning outcomes that combine subject learning and experiencing
information use. To continue the nursing example, students' learning outcomes
for the enquiry project could be expressed as follows:

On completing this unit of work, you will have:

- experienced information literacy in different ways by using information in diverse
  online settings to learn about liver disease; for example, via the information
  portals of professional health services, the blogs of voluntary support groups or
  the interactive display of a research foundation
- used information effectively in a range of contexts and employed transferable
  approaches to learn about the varying information needs of the parents of
  children and the carers of elderly relatives with liver disease
- discerned different ways of thinking about the application of information use to
  problems, by participating in a web-based debate on liver transplantation and
  alternative treatments
- considered information as subjective and transformational in character by
  reflecting on how you would inform and advise a relative diagnosed with liver
  disease
- explored the socially distributed character of information literacy by engaging in
  and reflecting on online forums dedicated to supporting people suffering from
  liver disease.

Informed learning in practice

To explain how informed learning might be applied in practice, Bruce, Hughes and Somerville (2011) describe a possible enquiry-based team project to select an 'ideal study abroad destination'. In that scenario, first-year university students use information critically, ethically and creatively in different forms and ways to learn about a variety of geographical locations and cultural and educational practices and to make a wise decision about the personally relevant matter of where to go for their study abroad programme.

The following two examples, which feature recently implemented units of study, further demonstrate the viability of informed learning for diverse educational settings. While both examples incorporated informed learning principles, they were very different in terms of learners, disciplinary content and context.

Personalized Language Development (in 2009) was part of the Master of TESOL programme at Queensland University of Technology (Bruce and Hughes, 2010). The principal aim of the unit was to enable learners, teachers and researchers of English as a second or foreign language to develop fluency in academic English and familiarity with scholarly research conventions. The students embarked with their colleagues on an 'informed learning journey' in which they learned how to use scholarly information whilst developing knowledge on professionally relevant topics. Throughout this process they reflected on and shared their experiences of using information to learn, both face to face and online via blogs.

Learning in the 21st Century (in 2010) was a first-year experience course (unit of study) at University of Colorado, Denver (Hughes, Basile and Bruce, unpublished). In this course, students learned about basic learning theory whilst exploring their own learning styles and needs and conducting a simple research project. The disciplinary focus of the unit was 'learning'. Informed learning elements were woven explicitly through the course syllabus and were implemented through weekly class activities and assessment. From the outset, students were encouraged to consider themselves as informed learners who were undertaking an informed learning journey through the course, and beyond. The students' informed learning included making decisions about which information types and sources would best meet their needs, whether print, digital, personal interaction or sensory. In addition to attending on-campus classes, they visited other educational sites, such as the Natural History Museum and a nursing simulation laboratory, in order to experience differing learning technologies and contexts. Importantly, they also engaged with various Web 2.0 media, including Google and Google Scholar (for sourcing information), Google Docs (for organizing and communicating information), blogs (for reflecting on their information use and learning), Flickr and YouTube (for presenting information to classmates). Again, they documented and shared their learning through informed learning maps and 'treasure chests' in various formats, including blogs and wikis, and handmade artefacts. In their learning maps the students presented written and graphical reflections on their informed learning journey. In their treasure chests they collected useful information of various types, gathered during their informed learning journey. These included: references, links to websites, journal articles, video clips, photos, feedback from mentors, museum pamphlets; one student included an encouraging letter from her grandmother, written 10 years previously.

The above examples were not specifically Web 2.0 projects but, rather, informed learning experiences that incorporated Web 2.0 elements. Both were situated principally in a traditional classroom. In contrast, the informed cyberlearning case study presented in Chapter 13 demonstrates informed learning principles applied to a wholly online context.

Informed learning and Web 2.0 (and beyond)

The nature of information literacy in Web 2.0 environments is under discussion, with the suggestion of information literacy 2.0 being a subset of a broader information literacy framework (Špiranec and Zorica, 2010). However, informed learning does not distinguish between 'traditional information literacy' and digital, mobile or Web 2.0 literacy. The principles of informed learning remain constant across learning environments and disciplines. They are applicable to the use of all technologies, both existing and emerging, from the pen to the iPad, embracing Web 2.0 and beyond.

The Web 2.0 galaxy offers a vast array of learning tools and environments that support participative engagement, multi-tasking and mobile learning. In order to flourish in this rapidly evolving Web 2.0 galaxy, where new applications are constantly being born and others are morphing or becoming extinct, both educators and learners need the well developed problem-solving and critical capabilities that informed learning aims to develop.

A possible challenge for informed learning educators is to determine which Web 2.0 applications are most conducive to particular learning outcome(s). Different Web 2.0 tools lend themselves to different learning experiences. For example, Facebook might be a suitable option for sounding out popular sentiment on a topical issue, whilst Google Scholar would be a more productive source of research data. Table 6.1 suggests possible Web 2.0 options for enhancing particular informed learning experiences. The left-hand column outlines *the seven faces of informed learning*, or different ways in which learners may experience information use (Bruce, 2008). The middle column indicates the nature of each of these experiences for informed learners. The right-hand column identifies possible Web 2.0 options for supporting these informed learning experiences. (The table shows an extremely limited representation of Web 2.0 options; and the tools listed are often relevant to more than the one

Table 6.1 Experiences of informed learning with Web 2.0		
Experiences of informed learning	**Experiences of informed learners with Web 2.0** *Individually or collaboratively ...*	**Possible Web 2.0 options**
1. Information awareness	Scanning, exploring and sharing information in Web 2.0 and other online environments	Google, Facebook, LinkedIn
2. Sources	Sourcing information of all kinds (including text, graphics, audio and video) in Web 2.0 and other online environments to meet learning needs	Google Scholar, YouTube, Flickr
3. Process	Engaging with Web 2.0 and other digital media to learn, for example, through enquiry, problem- or resource-based learning	Zoho Projects, Ning
4. Control	Organizing information in Web 2.0 and other online environments, making and managing connections between information and learning needs, for assignments and projects, both independent and collaborative	Google Docs, Dropbox, Delicious, Zotero (for citation)
5. Knowledge construction	Developing personal understandings of knowledge domains, via Web 2.0 and digital environments, through critical and creative thinking processes	Inspiration (concept mapping), Wordpress (blogging)
6. Knowledge extension	Creating and communicating new knowledge in Web 2.0 and online environments, innovating and creating new insights and new solutions to problems as outcomes of learning activities and assessment	Wikispaces, Posterous, Glogster, Weebly (website), Second Life, Prezi
7. Wisdom	Using information wisely and ethically in Web 2.0 and other online environments, applying knowledge developed through learning and assessment activities to further social and educational well-being	Open source journals, Creative Commons, online forums and support groups

category of experience shown here. For more extensive Web 2.0 selections for educators, see O'Connell, n.d.)

Putting together such a table raises four important considerations. First, while certain Web 2.0 tools might be more useful than others for particular informed learning experiences, the variety and accessibility of social media ensure that informed educators and learners are limited more by their imaginations than by the tools. Second, Web 2.0 tools are integral to the informed learning process; they mediate information use and learning, just as books, documentaries and Bunsen burners do. Third, Web 2.0 media can be transformative through their ubiquity and mobility, and their ability to support informed learning any place, any time. They facilitate communication between information-using learners and provide a participative context where information can be shared, consumed and produced (Bruns, 2008). Thus, Web 2.0 represents both a virtual learning space and a suite of online resources for learning. Fourth, returning to the principle that informed learning promotes the simultaneous learning about subject and the experience of using information, it is notable that we can learn about Web 2.0 as an information environment whilst using Web 2.0 tools to learn in an academic field, as illustrated by the case study in Chapter 13.

Librarians' roles in informed learning

The idea of informed learning as a way of thinking about both learning and IL requires the dual lenses of interest in content (discipline and professional expertise) and process (information-use experiences that are ultimately also embedded in context). Typically, discipline experts adopt one lens and information professionals or librarians adopt the other. The challenge of informed learning for both academic teachers and information professionals is to bring these lenses together for students through learning design and implementation. The intended outcome is a combination of discipline-based learning and awareness of information use in the learning process.

Ideally, library and information professionals would work together with discipline teachers, either in a professional development capacity, encouraging discipline teachers to embrace informed learning, or as members of a collaborative teaching team. This was the case in the previously mentioned Queensland and Denver examples, where a librarian was part of both unit teams and collaborated with the teachers in planning and presenting research-based activities. Fundamentally, informed learning is a way of thinking about IL education that is embedded or integrated into the curriculum. The language of informed learning places emphasis on the importance of information use in the learning process and makes it possible for librarians to communicate important dimensions of their potential contribution in the educational environment with discipline-centric colleagues. As outlined below, the current Auraria informed learning project at the University of Colorado Denver (USA) provides a real-life example of how this might be achieved.

The Auraria informed learning project

Librarians at the Auraria Library have adopted informed learning as a basis for revitalizing their IL programmes and strengthening partnerships with academic teaching colleagues. In order to bring about these changes, the librarians undertook first to extend their knowledge and expertise. The planning and implementation process is supported by a continuing professional development programme, with the librarians themselves engaging in informed learning as they develop familiarity with the principles, practices and literature of informed learning.

The Auraria informed learning project is strongly collaborative. It arose from the shared professional and research interests of Dr Mary Somerville (Auraria Library Director), Professor Christine Bruce (Queensland University of Technology) and Dr Hilary Hughes (Queensland University of Technology). The practical implementation of the project began during Hughes's period as Fulbright Scholar-in-Residence based at the Auraria Campus during August–December 2010. It was launched through an introductory workshop on the 'Six frames of informed learning' presented by Bruce and Hughes. Since the initial goal was to enable the librarians to become conversant with informed learning principles and practices, Hughes led a series of workshops, guided readings and discussions over the next four months. These activities resulted in significant practical outcomes, which include: frameworks for collaborative planning and implementation of curriculum-based informed learning; a revised policy document and planning process in the form of an Informed Learning Blueprint; and the creation of new promotional and instructional materials. The framework shown in Table 6.2, which was used for professional development purposes at Auraria Library, provides a glimpse of the introductory stage of the planning process for informed learning.

Table 6.2 Planning framework for informed learning			
(a) Key concerns			
Why?	University and library mission, professional excellence, system improvement		
Where?	Library as place, learning space, physical setting, social environment, virtual space		
Who?	Stakeholders: students, clients, teaching and administrative staff, library staff		
What?	Reports, strategic plans, curriculum documents, architectural plans		
How?	Learning and assessment activities, teaching approaches, orientations, workshops, projects, research, collaborative partnerships		
(b) Assessing student information and learning needs			
Why?			
Where?			
Who?			
What?			
How?			
(c) Planning informed learning			
	Library as resource	Library as space	Library as service
Why?			
Where?			
Who?			
What?			
How?			
(d) Supporting informed learning			
	Library as resource	Library as space	Library as service
What will I do to help other people learn?			
What do I need to learn?			

Regarding the four parts of the framework:

(a) Outlines fundamental considerations for informed learning design: *Why? Where? Who? What? How?*
(b) Focuses on the context and informed learning needs of students using Auraria Library. The five questions prompt the librarians to gather, process, organize and communicate essential information about Auraria Library users as informed learners. Depending on the level of enquiry and timeframe, this stage may take several hours, weeks or months.
(c) Involves a change of perspective to focus on three key roles of the library in informed learning: as a resource for learning (or collection of myriad resources); as a space for learning and for social interaction; and as a

service (or multiple services) to support learning for a diverse range of information users and learners.

(d) Focuses on the informed learning processes of both library users and the librarians themselves. The learning process is inextricably linked with the library's three roles as resource, space and service. This section emphasizes that the librarians themselves need to be informed learners in order to support the information use and learning of library users.

The framework supports an ongoing process of enquiry and reflection, which informs planning, decision making, implementation, problem solving, evaluation and ongoing development of informed learning.

An essential element of the Auraria Library project is reaching out to teaching colleagues and learning advisers to promote the opportunities and benefits of collaboratively developing curriculum and teaching. Faculty members noted for their innovative approach to learning and teaching are invited to participate in regular informed learning development meetings with librarians. A practical expression of this collaborative process is the previously mentioned first-year experience course, for which a librarian led two classes and became a 'cool' library contact person for the students.

Web 2.0 media are integral to the Auraria Library project. For example, an informed learning wiki has become the central organizing and productive focus for the project and virtual home of the Informed Learning Blueprint. In undertaking the informed learning planning process outlined above, attention is constantly paid to digital resources, virtual spaces and online learners. Online surveys and polls are used to assess student and staff learning needs and outcomes, as well as to coordinate meetings. Twitter and an online 'Ask a librarian' helpline are being used to communicate with the library's informed learner patrons. Skype enables team cohesion and communication.

The Auraria Library experience and the framework (see Table 6.2) offer a model for library practitioners at other institutions who are seeking to reshape or enrich their IL programmes. While informed learning is ideally curriculum wide, it is realistic for librarians to work with like-minded teaching colleagues to gradually build a community of informed learning practice. Informed learning principles can be gainfully applied at the level of a particular lesson or unit of study. Successful outcomes can then be showcased more widely as a way of spreading the message and drawing in further collaborative partners. For example, the first-year experience class at University of Colorado Denver was the subject of a faculty development seminar at Auraria Library in April 2011. In order to demonstrate the collaborative potential of informed learning, the co-teachers (Dr Carole Basile and Dr Hilary Hughes), the first-year coordinator (Dr John Lanning), a librarian (Karen Sobel) and a student peer mentor (An) all contributed to the panel discussion. Notably, the transformative learning outcomes were represented by two students, Jordan and Anthony, who described how the unit had helped them to better understand the different ways in which they (and other people) learn and so to tackle personal challenges such as developing self-discipline for their study and finding greater direction in their lives.

Benefits of informed learning for Web 2.0 and beyond

Informed learning underpins a holistic learning approach that responds to contemporary social, cultural, technological and pedagogical trends. Through its combined emphasis on information use, discipline content, learning processes and reflection, it enables students to develop understandings and practices in order to succeed as lifelong learners and global citizens in an increasingly dispersed society. Informed learning empowers students to reap the benefits of emerging mobile technologies that allow engagement at any time, in any context (Johnson et al., 2011). Through ongoing exploration and reflection, students become able to venture safely and confidently into and between familiar and fresh online environments.

With Web 2.0, communicating and publishing is relatively easy, through social software such as blogs, wikis, Twitter and Facebook. While this leads inevitably to an over-proliferation of information of widely varying quality, the advantage of Web 2.0 for informed learners and educators is that Web 2.0 media encourage curiosity and creativity in environments that are becoming increasingly familiar and hospitable to contemporary learners. It makes sense for educators to engage learners with Web 2.0 media in ways that make most sense to them.

The multiplicity of information sources and forums in the online environment can be both liberating and bewildering for students. Informed learning places particular emphasis on developing a critical approach that will allow students to discriminate information of varying quality and relevance, and to identify information that responds to specific needs at appropriate levels. In addition, informed learning promotes reflective information use and learning, whereby students can build upon previous experiences in future contexts.

The Web 2.0 environment is unpredictable and serendipitous. Students need to be alert to risks and opportunities, and to attend to their rights and responsibilities. Informed learning promotes ethical information use that upholds citizens' rights to freely access and publish information. It fosters respect for text in all forms (words, images, sounds) through an understanding of intellectual property and the legal implications of copyright. Importantly, an informed learning approach can raise awareness of varying cultural sensitivities towards original and shared work and differing academic conventions around the world. In this approach, students are encouraged to use Web 2.0 tools such as Delicious and Zotero and to adopt Creative Commons practices. Informed learning can also be a context for equipping them with strategies to preserve their privacy and safety online.

Both Web 2.0 media and informed learning can support HE institutions in producing graduates who are both independent thinkers and team players. Web 2.0 media afford high levels of social interaction and multi-tasking, as demonstrated throughout this book. Informed learning provides a basis for enhancing the quality of these interactions and supporting productive collaboration. Students can learn to work in virtual teams to carry out design projects. Educators can meet colleagues from down the corridor and around the world in webinars or Second Life to develop their knowledge and practice. Librarians, lecturers, ESL teachers and learning advisers can come together online or face to face to plan and implement new curricula that incorporate the creative online strategies.

In online environments, as elsewhere, effective learning and teaching builds on a sound conceptual basis and a holistic commitment. From a pedagogical perspective, informed learning, by focusing attention on the processes of information use, minimizes the mentality and chance of 'copy and paste' that can occur in online learning. Informed educators model ethical uses of information and base learning activities and assessment around enquiry and problem solving. They generally focus on academic integrity rather than plagiarism, adopting an educational rather than a punitive position.

Intercultural fluency is particularly critical at a time when revolutions are brought about through Web 2.0 media. Informed learning responds to the social and cultural diversity of contemporary HE populations. It is essentially inclusive by encouraging learners to share their diverse cultural, linguistic and professional knowledge (Bruce and Hughes, 2010). This inclusive approach enables students not only to develop familiarity with a wider range of information sources, but also to become aware of different social and political contexts that affect the ways in which people access, use and value information around the world. In this way, students of all backgrounds, domestic and international, benefit through widening their information horizons.

Conclusion

Educational technologies and learning spaces are constantly evolving. Like the evolution of other technologies before, Web 2.0 media and their future evolutions have the potential to transform learning and IL education. Like earlier technologies, we need to allow Web 2.0 to help us better meet learning objectives, and also to influence the nature of objectives that are possible. Web 2.0 is yet another information and learning environment, one in which we want our students to be both comfortable and experienced as they engage with information to meet academic, professional and personal needs. Informed learning is offered as a framework to assist this process, providing ways of thinking about learning design that will allow learners to use information of all kinds and in different technological spaces, through Web 2.0 and beyond.

References

Bruce, C. S. (1997) *Seven Faces of Information Literacy*, Adelaide: Auslib Press.

Bruce, C. S. (2008) *Informed Learning*, Chicago: College and Research Libraries, American Library Association.

Bruce, C. and Hughes, H. (2010) Informed Learning: a pedagogical construct for information literacy education, *Library and Information Science Research*, **32** (4), A2–A8.

Bruce, C., Hughes, H. and Somerville, M. (2012) Supporting Informed Learners in the 21st Century, *Library Trends*, **60** (3). In press.

Bruns, A. (2008) *Blogs, Wikipedia, Second Life and beyond: from production to produsage*, Digital Formations 45, New York: Peter Lang.

Head, A. and Eisenberg, M. (2010) *Truth to Be Told: how college students evaluate and use information in the digital age*, Project Information Literacy Progress Report, 1 November, The Information School, University of Washington, http://projectinfolit.org/pdfs/PIL_Fall2010_Survey_FullReport1.pdf.

Hughes, H. (2009) International Students Using Online Information Resources to Learn, Doctoral dissertation, Queensland University of Technology, http://eprints.qut.edu.au/29348.

Hughes, H., Basile, C. and Bruce, C. (unpublished) Turning the First Year Experience into an Informed Learning Journey.

Hughes, H., Bruce, C. S. and Edwards, S. L. (2007) Models for Reflection and Learning: a culturally inclusive response to the information literacy imbalance. In Andretta, S. (ed.), *Change and Challenge: information literacy for the 21st century*, Adelaide: Auslib Press, 59-84.

Johnson, L., Smith, R., Willis, H., Levine, A. and Haywood, K. (2011) *The 2011 Horizon Report*, Austin, TX: The New Media Consortium, http://net.educause.edu/ir/library/pdf/HR2011.pdf.

Lorenzo, G. and Dziuban, C. (2006) *Ensuring the Net Generation Is Net Savvy*, ELI paper 2, Educause.

O'Connell, J. (n.d.) Toolkit A–Z for Education, http://sites.google.com/site/ptcweb2/toolkit-a-z.

Špiranec, S. and Zorica, M. B. (2010) Information Literacy 2.0: hype or discourse refinement? *Journal of Documentation*, **66** (1), 140-53.

Part 2

Case studies

Chapter 7

Reinventing information literacy at UTS Library

Sophie McDonald and Jemima McDonald

Introduction

At the University of Technology, Sydney (UTS) Library we are reinventing our information literacy (IL) programme and developing a dynamic new approach to engaging with clients. We realize that the information landscape of our clients is changing, and mobile devices have created a convergence of physical and digital information practices. At the same time, Web 2.0 has led to a more social approach to the way information is found, stored, used, created and shared. We have responded by reshaping our IL programme through experimentation and play, addressing the move towards active learning by developing a dynamic programme of generic and specialized IL workshops, both face-to-face and online. We have moved beyond just teaching clients how to find journal articles in a database, and now cover topics such as Google Skills, Collaborative Tools, Finding Images and Mobile Searching. Our IL programme supports a range of learning styles and provides formal and informal instruction through a diversity of access points. This allows for planned or just-in-time learning, extending beyond the classroom into flexible, personalizable, 24/7 physical, digital and mobile spaces.

Making it visual

On our library website we provide multiple access points for clients to engage with online IL, enabling self-directed or just-in-time learning. We have developed an open content system, called InfoSkills Bank, to house learning objects and allow greater discovery of and access to handouts, lesson plans, podcasts, vodcasts and screencasts. InfoSkills Bank objects have been added to our Endeca discovery layer so they are found alongside other catalogue items. Discovery layers are now commonly used to enhance library catalogues with extra content and features. For example, a search for Academic Search Premier will find the link to the database as well as a screencast on how to use it. An icon has been created to identify screencasts easily in the catalogue and it's also an option within faceted browsing.

We all know what it's like to attend a class and think we know it all, only to find when we return to our own computer that we seem to have forgotten everything! Feedback after classes indicated that, even after hands-on sessions, students were struggling with database searching. So in an effort to provide ongoing support after the initial class, we decided to create a screencast for every key database on which we deliver instruction to our students. So much of library instruction is text based: we wanted to make our IL much more visual. We limit our screencasts to no more than 3 minutes so they can be easily absorbed. The content we create is then uploaded to InfoSkills Bank. We also link to online tutorials that we discover on the web and that we consider will be useful for our clients. We upload selected InfoSkills Bank tutorials to YouTube (Figure 7.1), which allows us to easily embed them in web pages and access them on mobile devices. We can send links easily to students on and off

Figure 7.1 InfoSkills Bank on YouTube channel (Source: University of Technology, Sydney)

campus, and we can embed them in the university's learning management system, Blackboard.

Librarians are using Audacity, Adobe Captivate, Camtasia, Jing Pro and other software to create learning objects. We are self-taught in these tools. One member from each of our three teams is identified as a main creator, and they then train other staff. We have been cascading these skills since about 2003. As we increase the range of our skills and learn from each other we have created podcasts, screencasts and vodcasts that address the multiple literacies our clients need. An important development in our learning over the last twelve months is how to design screencasts for a smaller screen and how to deliver content specifically for mobile devices. Uploading our files to YouTube means that they can be viewed on mobile devices, and we make the viewing experience on a small screen more enjoyable by using more zooms and keeping the screencasts clear and succinct.

One way in which clients can access screencasts on their mobile devices is via the QR codes we have around the library, which connect to contextual support at the point of need. For example, we created a series of instructional videos showing how to book a room, ask for assistance at the Research Help Desk, use the printers and more. Clients can scan the QR code on our self-service loans machine, for example, and watch a short video on how to use it via the free university WiFi network. Like many libraries, we've observed that QR codes have not had a huge uptake, mostly due to the barriers involved in needing the right device, WiFi access, a QR code reader and the right conditions for a good scan. However, the ability to scan physical objects with a mobile device and connect to digital information is a trend that will continue as technology changes.

Making it social

Clients can access our IL content through social media sites such as Facebook, Twitter and YouTube. This has allowed us to connect with clients informally and become part of their online communities. In a recent survey of UTS Library clients, 36% of respondents said that they get their library news from Facebook or Twitter. The content we share is a combination of text, links, video, podcasts and screencasts. By utilizing the immediacy of social media, librarians can be aware of a need and offer a solution within a very short period of time and engage more directly with clients. For example, by monitoring mentions of UTS Library in Twitter we were able to respond to a client who mentioned they were at UTS Library and needed help finding information for their microbiology assignment. We responded by suggesting which database to try and recommended our instant messaging chat if they needed further assistance. They retweeted our suggestion to their followers and tweeted back with thanks. On Facebook we share photos of our events, such as the Library Fun Day and the staff edible books contest.[1] We also created a Facebook quiz 'Your secret library self' to engage our students using humour. We are lucky to have staff with great senses of humour, and they really shone in their categorizations of library 'types'. More than 300 people have now done the quiz. Strategically, developing the quiz is a precursor to running more activities in Facebook with a stronger focus on gaming and IL.

The informal nature of this range of communication allows librarians to present a casual, friendly tone on behalf of the library, thus challenging traditional notions of libraries and librarians. Creating a social media presence has enabled the development of an online community of library clients who comment, share and tweet with us, about us and each other. There are no guidelines for these activities and they depart significantly from the traditional roles we have shaped for ourselves over generations of dealing with library clients.

Making it fun

Since 2009, we have been increasing our support for first-year students and seeking to ease the transition to university by making the library a fun and friendly place to be. We have focused much of our time firstly on the annual Library Fun Day held during orientation week, and secondly on supporting our new students in our virtual learning environment (VLE), Blackboard. In 2011, approximately 500 students attended Library Fun Day, which boasted free food and drink, games, prizes, a treasure hunt, a trivia quiz, a murder mystery and a technology 'petting zoo'.[2] Some of these activities were just for fun and some introduced IL skills in subtle ways. The treasure hunt required participants to form small groups of two or three and navigate through six 'stations', photograph each one and be first back in order to claim a prize. Clues were given on paper or by QR code and volunteers were at each station to assist participants. The stations were: find the research help desk, find a book in the catalogue, find the same book on the shelf, take our 'librarian or not' test, become our fan on Facebook and find the printing/copying room. In just 15 minutes most groups were able to navigate all of the stations and cover everything normally taught in a one-hour introductory information literacy class. Feedback from participants was positive, and the winners received movie or iTunes vouchers. The treasure hunt was such a success that it has been used as a model for first-year IL sessions for several hundred new nursing students for two years in a row. It helped to make them feel more relaxed about the library and library staff. Students worked in pairs in a fun and collaborative way. Staff noted that there was much giggling and enthusiasm for the course; students also showed strong ownership of their results, being upset if they got something wrong. Library staff enjoyed participating in the training because the students were obviously engaged and having fun. Small prizes of chocolate helped the competitive juices to flow.

We have also used treasure hunts with high school students as part of the University's Widening Participation Strategy, which aims to encourage students from lower socio-economic status schools to attend university. We took the treasure hunt online last year and hid clues around the library website. This year we have more fun planned, including a self-guided library treasure hunt with daily prizes.

We will continue to experiment with ways of using gaming to make our IL programme more dynamic and fun. We need to call on our 'inner teenager' and put ourselves in the shoes of a new student, which is sometimes quite difficult for those of us removed in age from our clients by several decades. First-year students are being overwhelmed by an enormous amount of serious information, so we have a better chance of having a positive impact if we can entertain as well as inform.

Students are begging for library workshops to be more interesting, and the success of our treasure hunt demonstrates that games can be used effectively in academic libraries. What is also important here is the shift away from the didactic model of IL and towards a collaborative approach using game-based learning.

Making it useful

Below is a brief overview of some of the workshops we offer in order to help develop digital and IL skills:

- *Google Skills 1* covers advanced searching of Google and Google Scholar, followed by an introduction to Google Books and Google Docs.
- *Google Skills 2* covers the use of RSS feeds to support research by setting

up feeds to the tables of contents of journals and feeds of searches in databases.

- *Make Me Famous* introduces researchers to ways of publishing strategically within high-impact journals. The class also covers how to promote your worth as a researcher by understanding the h-index and other measures.
- *Get Connected* helps researchers to connect with colleagues near and far by using databases and sites such as academia.edu and Twitter to share work more extensively.
- *Collaborative Tools* teaches how to use Diigo and Google Docs to make collaborating on projects faster and easier.
- *Mobile Searching* is a 30-minute intensive workshop helping students to connect to the UTS free WiFi network and learn to search for books and journal articles on a mobile device.
- *Finding Images* covers how to find and use images ethically for teaching, learning and research by exploring Flickr, Google Images and library databases. The workshop also covers Creative Commons licensing and the ethical reuse of images.

Conclusion: making it happen

As IL instructors, it is our challenge to make IL more fun and engaging for our clients. IL is about more than finding journal articles in a database. It now includes being a content creator, collaborator, expert evaluator and ethical reuser of all sources of information. In order to transfer these skills to future clients we need to experiment and play with new technology and become experts ourselves. Web 2.0 has enabled IL to become more fun, and with so many 2.0 initiatives to play with, developing engaging IL programmes should be easy. However, we must consider the context in which our clients are working and embed our training in ways that support their learning, teaching and research needs. There is much speculation about the future of libraries and IL. However, there can be no argument that technology such as mobile devices, e-books and cloud computing, amongst others, will continue to change the way we find, create and use information. What won't change is the move towards fun, collaborative and game-based learning. At UTS Library we will continue to experiment with new ways of delivering IL by learning from each other and trying things in response to changing client needs.

Notes

1   See www.facebook.com/media/albums/?id=93282252430#!/
    UTSLibrary?sk=photos and
    www.flickr.com/photos/utslibrary/sets/72157624967118828/.

2   See www.flickr.com/photos/utslibrary/.

Chapter 8

Using games as treatments and creative triggers: a promising strategy for information literacy

Susan Boyle

Introduction

How do librarians build creativity into information literacy (IL) and keep students engaged so that they learn and retain valuable, transferable IL skills? As teaching librarians, we should be exploring whether there are more creative IL teaching approaches that we can adopt in order to foster effective teaching and engagement, and to cultivate more opportunities for creative thinking about information-seeking concepts amongst students. Teaching librarians want to empower students with lifelong research skills, in a context where many higher education students are becoming more disengaged. Facilitating creativity and innovation is also now expected in the educational setting (Barrett and Donnelly, 2008).

In this chapter, some dimensions of educational games will be explored. New game ideas, specifically designed for face-to-face IL sessions, will be presented, with an illustration showing games used with Irish nursing and midwifery students. Finally, the chapter will explore Library 2.0 and 3.0 initiatives that may assist teaching librarians to encourage the widespread adoption of IL games.

The objective of this chapter is to prompt more teaching librarians to:

- become IL games advocates
- consider creating their own customized games for IL
- share and evolve their games and game-design skills for IL face-to-face sessions or smart learning environments, with the help of Library 2.0 and 3.0 initiatives
- use games to become leading innovative practitioners in higher education and thus promote the value and expertise of librarians.

Games as educational treatments in IL

This section will cover how games treat disengagement, trigger creativity and innovative thinking, cultivate effective learning and provide inherent benefits and retention and knowledge transfer properties. It will also detail some of the challenges in using games and the overall benefits of games for librarians and libraries.

Games treat disengagement

Librarians involved in IL delivery look to best practice in education so as to draw on pedagogical tools and solutions appropriate for IL. Student disengagement is a growing challenge in higher education generally, and with IL in particular. The new generation of students is characterized as having low boredom thresholds (Fink, 2003) and there is evidence that some lectures are ineffective, especially for these learners (Smith, 2007). As Barrett and Donnelly (2008) state: 'Pedagogy should be focused on arousing student imagination and engagement.' Games that have an educational intent provide a platform for active learning, where students can discover IL concepts in an engaging way. Fink (2003) suggests that we need to create more significant learning experiences for students and believes that replacing lecturing with more active learning can address boredom. Games stimulate the imagination and encourage excitement and engagement through active learning. So it is not surprising that games are being used more and more in a growing list of applications, from military and health to commercial sectors (Ulicsak and Wright, 2010). Games may also help to negate the 'learning hostage' (Smith, 2007) effect, where a student feels trapped in a learning session and less inclined to absorb the learning messages. With targeted, break-out games, students are less likely to feel like learning captives. I believe that educational games are useful and engaging learning devices for IL when they are used to treat issues with which the students themselves identify difficulty. I refer to these as 'treatment games', which remedy a specific IL symptom.

Games trigger creativity and innovative thinking

Student engagement in IL is critical for achieving good overall learning outcomes, but creativity is also gaining significance in the educational mix. Creativity in graduates is becoming a highly sought-after quality - the Revised Bloom's Taxonomy (Anderson et al., 2001; Overbaugh and Schultz, n.d.), for example, rates creativity highly. Employers are placing higher value on creative attributes when they recruit graduates into the workforce (Huhman, 2011; Page, n.d.). Games are triggers for creativity: according to Fuszard, they 'encourage creative behaviour and divergent thought' (Fuszard, 2001). Creativity cannot be reduced to merely being creative (Kleinman, 2008). Similarly, game play is not creativity, but games that educate students can be creative starting-points for divergent thinking because they:

- break from the routine
- give students the time and space for experiential learning
- induce creative 'flow states' (deep absorption in a discovery learning activity)
- provide challenge through peer discussion.

More exposure to positive 'flow states' may trigger students to make new connections and move towards innovative behaviour (Webb Young, 2003).

Effective learning and the inherent benefits of games

In addition to the engagement and creative and innovative potential of games for IL students, games may improve effective learning. According to Fuszard, games help to depolarize the weak and strong students: they 'reduce the gap between quicker and slower learners' (Fuszard, 2001). During game play, students also gain from active discovery, receive immediate feedback and develop new kinds of comprehension, which are all beneficial properties in IL (Ulicsak and Wright, 2010).

Apart from content learned via active games, students develop other team, communication and problem-solving skills during game play. Fuszard maintains that games even 'have a special role in building students' self confidence' (Fuszard, 2001). The relaxed, fun learning quality that games evoke means that they can help to build student confidence, and possibly also reduce anxiety about IL concepts.

Teaching librarians seek to align their teaching to best-practice IL standards so that graduate attributes can successfully be achieved. Explicit scoring mechanisms can be used in educational games to see how effective the learning is; for example, 'the number of correct answers and possibly time taken to complete the game are measures' (Ulicsak and Wright, 2010) of scores achieved. Students will continue to achieve best-practice IL outcomes as long as the IL learning objectives remain integral to the game play.

Using games to enhance retention and knowledge transfer

Games have other interesting properties – Jaffe, for example, maintains that 'educational or instructional games expect benefits for all participants that last beyond the game itself' (Jaffe, 2007). Ameet Doshi (2006), moreover, suggests that by including a gaming element in library teaching, 'the potential exists to excite this millennial generation about information literacy and to infuse them with lifelong library skills'. So games may impact on the retention of IL concepts amongst IL students. Furthermore, Chow suggests that games also assist students to transfer learned knowledge by helping them to 'reach the level of generality that will allow for more suitable follow-up application' (Chow, Kelly et al., 2011). These retention and knowledge transfer benefits can therefore enhance the delivery of IL.

Challenges with games

The use of games is not without challenges. Games rely on the teaching librarian's pro-activity, attitude to change and flexibility with regard to innovative methods. Games take time to design and develop and tweak, which can add to the teaching librarian's workload. As game facilitators, they are also challenged; they have to work out and enforce timings, monitor play to ensure that it remains educational and provide appropriate debriefing (Jaffe, 2007). Introducing a treatment game to students too early in the session will make it too challenging; too late, and it may not be challenging enough. The positive support of the teaching librarian is also significant in cultivating a creative learning environment (Barrett and Donnelly, 2008). Without this timing and support, games will not be effective learning devices.

One of the key pitfalls with designing games for IL students is ensuring that they remain educationally appropriate. The key is to think '*EDU-tainment as opposed to ENTER-tainment*' (Smith, 2007). Not all IL learners will feel comfortable with games, so it may be better to use games as treatments (Boyle, 2011) as and when required, rather than as a complete replacement for traditional methods.

Games in face-to-face sessions are also more challenging to facilitate with larger groups; location affects whether or not a game is appropriate. It helps if the game can migrate to the online environment in order to accommodate larger student numbers. In the future, IL games could migrate to smartphones, to satisfy Web 3.0 demands.

Benefits of IL games from the perspective of librarians and libraries

It is in librarians' best interests to deal with the challenges, because there are attractive benefits to games, not just for students but also for teaching librarians and libraries. Incorporating treatment games (Boyle, 2011) into sessions can be an effective use of the librarian's time.

Using games ensures variety and helps us to meet millennial students' evolved learning expectations and preferences, so that they can feel more 'connected' rather than 'fragmented and isolated' (Fink, 2003). Games provide creative triggers in IL and may also be a useful tool for bridging the generation gap between teacher and students (Jennings and Cashman, 2008).

Clearly, games provide an innovative and creative route for libraries and librarians to explore. Rossiter (2008) suggests that when we do something differently, this can bring people back in to the library. Perhaps using games can help to present libraries in a more modern and innovative light, and update their image.

Case study: IL treatment games for nursing students

In University College Dublin, I was prompted to design a customized treatment game for my sessions with final year nursing students, as part of a four-year undergraduate IL programme (Boyle, 2009).

These students required a refresher on searching techniques, and the traditional lecture-style approach to this concept was not fully effective. I decided to explore whether this topic could be tackled in a more engaging way. I focused on the learning objective and the 'search techniques matching pairs' game grew from there. The game design form (Figure 8.1) shows the design steps.

'Search techniques matching pairs' game play

In the 'matching pairs' game, the students are arranged in small groups of up to seven players. Each group is given a set of playing cards (see Figure 8.2). Students then have 10 minutes to discuss the task and arrange the cards into matching pairs. One set of cards name the different search techniques. The other set of cards detail the corresponding function and the benefit of using the particular search technique.

Before the game is played, I introduce the concept and link the game to the learning benefit. I explain how the game will help students to get more relevant

Game design form – Matching pairs game
Student group: Can be offered to stage 1 students or as a refresher for higher stage students. Alternatively can be incorporated into a problem-based learning (PBL) fixed resource session to address a specific need or in a problem clinic triage session to address particular IL symptoms.
Learning objective: To understand searching techniques.
Learning outcome: Students will be familiar with the different search techniques and know what each of them achieves.
Name of game: Matching Pairs
Aim of game: Match the search technique to what it does.
Playing time: 10 minutes
Game format: Special cards
Game description: Students in small groups discuss which search tool goes with which search function and arrange the cards into matching pairs.
Game rule: Students are not allowed to consult other materials during the game.
Instructor guidelines: Arrange students into small groups. Explain purpose of the game and link the game to learning objectives for the students. Follow game with correct play and tasks that require students to use the learning obtained from the game. Include question on the game in the assessment.

Figure 8.1 Game design form for the 'search techniques matching pairs' treatment game, explaining the steps for designing the game

results when they search for information on their projects. I walk the room during game play and offer positive encouragement to struggling students, as well as to those who have matched some, but not all, pairs correctly. After 10 minutes, I go through the correct answers ('correct play') with the students, providing them with immediate feedback. I then have the students carry out searching exercises in nursing databases which require them to use the learning obtained during the game, using a worksheet I have compiled; I find that this links the game learning to practice. The feedback from students is positive (Figure 8.3).

The word cloud in Figure 8.3 displays what some final year and postgraduate nursing students have said about the 'searching techniques matching pairs' game. The comments imply a deeper understanding, reflective practice, effective content learning, critical thinking, knowledge transfer, retention and understanding of broader applications.

A teaching librarian's reflections on the 'matching pairs' treatment game

Once I had reassured the students and made the learning from the game obvious, I found that they became very willing game players. As a facilitator, walking the room during the game, I observed peer learning, discovery learning,

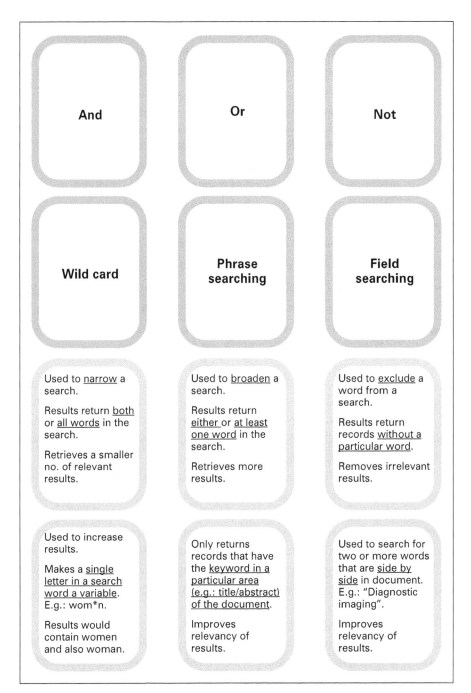

Figure 8.2 Playing cards used in the 'search techniques matching pairs' game

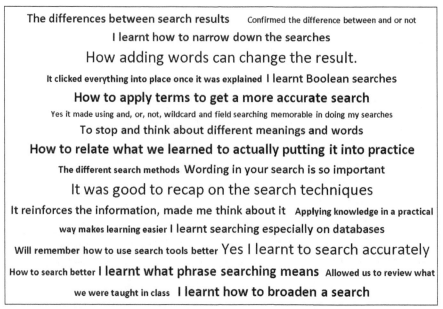

The differences between search results Confirmed the difference between and or not

I learnt how to narrow down the searches

How adding words can change the result.

It clicked everything into place once it was explained I learnt Boolean searches

How to apply terms to get a more accurate search

Yes it made using and, or, not, wildcard and field searching memorable in doing my searches

To stop and think about different meanings and words

How to relate what we learned to actually putting it into practice

The different search methods Wording in your search is so important

It was good to recap on the search techniques

It reinforces the information, made me think about it Applying knowledge in a practical

way makes learning easier I learnt searching especially on databases

Will remember how to use search tools better Yes I learnt to search accurately

How to search better I learnt what phrase searching means Allowed us to review what

we were taught in class I learnt how to broaden a search

Figure 8.3 Feedback from nursing students about what they learned by playing the 'search techniques matching pairs' game

flow (Barrett and Donnelly, 2008) and even animated discussion about the search techniques. Following the game, students interacted more readily with me and were curious to see if they had the correct matches, or, if not correct, welcoming instant feedback. Their confidence and satisfaction visibly improved and questions, interest and engagement all increased.

At the Web 2.0 2010 summit in San Francisco, Mary Meeker stated that 'humans want everything to be like a game' (Meeker, 2010). The body of literature on the benefits of game-based learning is vast. This evidence, along with student feedback, my personal experiences of the benefits of games in learning and feedback at library conferences (LILAC, CONUL and HSLG) has prompted me to design two further gaming treatments for IL symptoms: 'bin or basket' and 'sticky databases'. I hope to use these treatments in future IL sessions.

'Bin or basket' game

The 'bin or basket' game requires players to place a variety of librarian-selected screenshots of websites illustrating good and bad information quality into a bin or basket, depending on their appraisal. Playing time is 10 minutes (Figure 8.4). Students are arranged in small groups and are required to provide reasons for

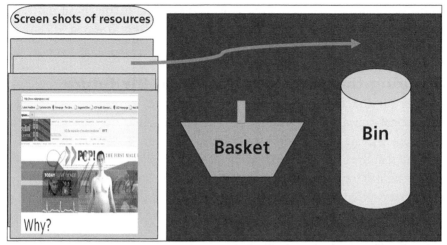

Figure 8.4 'Bin or basket' treatment game (Source: RYT Hospital Dwayne Medical Centre, 2011)

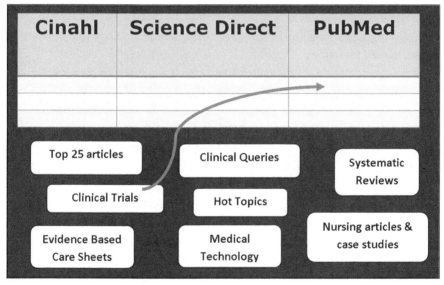

Figure 8.5 'Sticky databases' treatment game

their choices. The aim of the game is to improve the students' ability to differentiate good from poor-quality resources.

'Sticky databases' game

In the 'sticky databases' game, small groups of players have 10 minutes to attach topic contents to the correct database in a chart (Figure 8.5). The aim of the game is to familiarize students with the specialist content of different databases, so that they will pick the appropriate databases to search when they face any research question.

Ensuring that IL games flourish in the future

Despite all the engaging, creative, retention and learning benefits that educational games offer for IL, librarians and libraries, they have not yet reached the tipping-point and become mainstream. Westera and Nadolski (2008) contend that the use of games in education is still limited. Treatment games are not a blanket replacement for traditional IL methods. However, they are appropriate as remedies for certain IL symptoms. For the use of these games to become more widespread, more librarians need to add them to their teaching toolkits and become better at:

- designing customized IL treatment games that address specific learning objectives
- scanning, upskilling and adapting to changes in technology that can be harnessed for games
- sharing and collaborating to create best-practice rubrics for games use in IL
- collaborating to design and carry out impact studies of games in IL.

Gaming and Library 2.0 and 3.0 tools

Library 2.0 and 3.0 tools provide significant opportunities to assist teaching librarians interested in advancing games in IL:

- by establishing an international creative commons for IL game design to act as a collaborative space for sharing treatment game ideas as well as experiences of using and overcoming challenges with games in IL
- by keeping up to date with emerging technologies that could enhance educational games via, for example, Twitter or other viral information tools
- in the future, IL games may be developed and pre-loaded onto smartphones and iPads for enrolling students in the same way that iPads are now being 'furnished with a suite of learning apps' (Fallon, 2011). We will probably also see IL games incorporating location-aware technology
- gaming librarians may use Library 2.0 and 3.0 tools to collectively create standards for games in IL, improve game assessment and collaborate in more comprehensive impact studies of games in IL.

Conclusion

If teaching librarians can harness the educational power and engaging, creative and innovative properties of treatment games to reach IL learners, the future will be promising. IL students will have enhanced learning experiences and libraries will benefit from the innovative profile that games will generate. Technology and education are changing, but, with the help of Library 2.0 and Web 3.0 tools, teaching librarians will, it is hoped, reach a tipping-point (Gladwell, 2003) for shared, customized, librarian-designed treatment games and thus increase the evidence base of their impact in learning. This will help to propel IL forward to a valuable future, presenting librarians positively as creative leaders in innovative methods. Futurists anticipating tomorrow's IL may then describe us as creative and innovative 3.0 librarians.

References

Anderson, L. W., Krathwohl, D. R. et al. (2001) *A Taxonomy for Learning, Teaching, and Assessing: a revision of Bloom's taxonomy of educational objectives*, Longman.

Barrett, T. and Donnelly, R. (2008) Encouraging Student Creativity in Higher Education. In Higgs, B. and McCarthy, M. (eds), *Emerging Issues II: the changing roles and identities of teachers and learners in higher education*, Cork: NAIRTL, 115-30.

Boyle, S. (2009) Exploring and Extending Information Literacy Support with Nursing and Midwifery Students, *Journal of the European Association for Health Information and Libraries*, **5** (3), 18-21.

Boyle, S. (2011) *Creative Problem Clinics: information literacy triage*, Pecha Kucha presentation, LILAC 2011.

Chow, A. F. and Kelly, C. W. et al. (2011) Deal or No Deal: using games to improve student learning, retention and decision-making, *International Journal of Mathematical Education in Science and Technology*, **42** (2), 259-64.

Doshi, A. (2006) How Gaming Could Improve Information Literacy, *Computers in Libraries*, **26** (5), 14-17.

Fallon, J. (2011) School Replaces Books with iPads, *Irish Times*, (30 May).

Fink, D. L. (2003) *Creating Significant Learning Experiences: an integrated approach to designing college courses*, New York: Jossey-Bass, a Wiley imprint.

Fuszard, B. (2001) Gaming. Fuszard's Innovative Teaching Strategies in Nursing. In Lowenstein, A. J., Bradshaw, M. J. and B. Fuszard (eds), *Fuszard's Innovative Teaching Strategies in Nursing*, Gaithersburg, MD: Aspen Publishers, 112-20.

Gladwell, M. (2003) *The Tipping Point: how little things can make a big difference*, Wheeler Publishing.

Huhman, H. (2011) Five Types of Employees Companies are Seeking, *Glassdoor.com*
    (blog) (13 June), www.glassdoor.com/blog/types-employees-companies-seeking/.

Jaffe, L. (2007) Games Amplify Motivation in Education. In Bradshaw, M. J. and
    Lowenstein, A. J. (eds) *Innovative Teaching Strategies in Nursing and Related Health
    Professions*, Sudbury, MA: Jones and Bartlett Publishers, 161–72.

Jennings, D. and Cashman, D. (2008) Mature Cynics and Fledgling Eclectics:
    elaborating instructional design for the net generation. In Higgs, B. and McCarthy,
    M. (eds), *Emerging Issues II: the changing roles and identities of teachers and learners
    in higher education*, Cork: NAIRTL, 23–35.

Kleinman, P. (2008) Towards Transformation: conceptions of creativity in higher
    education, *Innovations in Education and Teaching International*, **45** (3), 209–17.

Meeker, M. (2010) Internet Trends. Web 2.0 Summit, San Francisco.

Overbaugh, R. C. and Schultz, L. (n.d.) Bloom's Taxonomy,
    www.odu.edu/educ/roverbau/Bloom/blooms_taxonomy.htm.

Page, L. (n.d.) Joining Google, www.google.com/intl/en/jobs/joininggoogle/index.html.

Rossiter, N. (2008) *Marketing the Best Deal in Town: your library – where is your purple
    owl?*, Chandos Publishing.

RYT Hospital Dwayne Medical Centre (2011) POP! The first human male pregnancy,
    www.malepregnancy.com/.

Smith, F. A. (2007) Games for Teaching Information Literacy Skills, *Library Philosophy
    and Practice*, (April).

Ulicsak, M. and Wright, M. (2010) *Games in Education: serious games. A Futurelab
    literature review*, www.futurelab.org.uk/projects/games-in-education.

Webb Young, J. (2003) *A Technique for Producing Ideas*, McGraw-Hill.

Westera, W., Nadolski, R. J. et al. (2008) Serious Games for Higher Education: a
    framework for reducing design complexity, *Journal of Computer Assisted Learning*,
    24, 420–32.

Chapter 9

Changing the conversation: introducing information literacy to a generation of smartphone users

Kristen Yarmey

Background

Smartphones, or mobile phones with computer-like capabilities, have rapidly grown in mobile phone market share since the introduction of the Apple iPhone in 2007. To date, librarians' responses to the growing adoption of smartphones have largely centred on providing mobile access to existing services and resources. The past few years have seen significant increases in libraries offering text messaging reference (e.g. Kohl and Keating, 2009) and building mobile websites or apps (e.g. Bridges, Rempel and Griggs, 2010; Seeholzer and Salem, 2011). Less frequently, however, have librarians considered the effects of smartphones and other mobile devices on students' achievement of information literacy (IL). Godwin and Parker (2008) and Cvetkovic and Lackie (2009) have presented a variety of discussions about IL for the millennial generation, though none has specifically examined smartphones as an emerging technology. Godwin (2010) focused on using mobile devices to deliver IL instruction. Walsh (2011) compared competency-based models for IL to relational models, finding the relational models more adaptable to mobile information use. A wealth of research addresses mobile search (e.g. Kamvar et al., 2009) and mobile learning (e.g. Kukulska-Hulme and Traxler, 2005; Ally, 2009), though the findings are not often applied to IL instruction. Thus, while librarians acknowledge that patrons increasingly use mobile devices and strive to provide useful services for them, the profession has not yet fully investigated whether and how these new devices change the ways in which users search, find, evaluate, process and use information, particularly information external to library collections. Such research can lead to evidence-based improvements in IL instruction.

Process

My continuing research at the University of Scranton seeks to identify and make explicit the relationships and interactions between smartphones and student IL, with a goal of improving my approach to introductory IL instruction. I began by exploring the functionality and capabilities of the Apple iPhone and various Android smartphones, studying the culture and behaviour these devices enable and seeking to understand how smartphone users engage with information. Using the Association of College and Research Libraries (ACRL) *Information Literacy Competency Standards for Higher Education* (2000) as a framework, I mapped relationships between expected learning outcomes and smartphone functionality, pinpointing areas in which smartphone use could either help or hinder students' achievement of IL (Yarmey, 2010).

Several potential barriers to the achievement of IL were identified, including increasing complexity in the organization and dissemination of information (e.g. understanding the difference between native apps and mobile websites, or identifying the original source of information provided by an app) and, as a result, increasing complexity of information evaluation (e.g. how do you evaluate an app?). Furthermore, several novel IL needs emerged from this research. For example, the ACRL standards address only text-based searching, but smartphones offer several methods of search. Students with smartphones can use a variety of input types - including photographs, quick response (QR) codes, barcodes, sounds, spoken words and geographic locations - to retrieve customized information relevant to their current situation.

Based on this conceptual mapping, in October 2010 I conducted a survey to better understand the campus mobile environment and to observe if and how current college students would display information-literate behaviour when engaging with information on their smartphones (Yarmey, 2011). The survey was administered via e-mail to a random sample of University of Scranton students aged between 18 and 24 and consisted of 35 questions, mostly multiple choice.

Survey results depicted a growing culture of mobile information access. Out of the 333 students who responded to the survey, 229 (69%) reported owning a smartphone (defined as an 'internet-capable mobile phone'), indicating that the devices indeed had a significant presence at the university. Though only 35% of the phone-owning students had 'high end' smartphones (iPhones or Android phones), an additional 45% intended to upgrade their device within the next year. Still, already over 80% of the smartphone owners had used their phones to search for information at least once, and more than 60% browsed the web on their phone at least once a day, if not several times. Other survey questions probed the students' mobile behaviour, investigating how they searched for information and what kind of textual content they would consider reading on their phone.

Overall, the survey results indicated that, whether individual searches were conducted on desktop computers or on phones, the capabilities of smartphones were influencing the information landscape of our campus and affecting students' perception of, expectations of and behaviour towards information. As a result, my current work involves applying lessons learned both from the survey data and from my earlier analysis of the ACRL standards to my IL instruction, in order to determine what content would most effectively introduce students to basic concepts of IL.

Challenges

The University of Scranton's Weinberg Memorial Library, like many of its peers, bases its IL programme on the ACRL standards. While the Weinberg Library's programme is multi-faceted, one way in which librarians guide students towards IL is through guest lectures to freshman seminars, which are semester-long, one-credit courses required of all first-year students. Every year, the library invites the professors of each freshman seminar to bring their students to the library for a 50-minute, 'one-shot' IL session.

Each instructional librarian has their own lesson plan for these sessions but, as of 2008, most address several of the ACRL learning outcomes by following this general outline:

- students watch a 15-minute video tour of the library
- the librarian orally introduces and describes the library's services
- the librarian demonstrates a search of the library catalogue
- the librarian demonstrates a search in one or more subscription databases, choosing content relevant to the students' majors.

In some classes, the seminar professor asks the students to complete a library-related assignment (such as preparing a brief bibliography), but most classes have no such assignment.

As the Weinberg Library's liaison to the university's science departments, I taught my first set of these sessions for freshman science students in 2008.

While no formal assessment instrument was employed, informal feedback was discomfiting. Students expressed little interest in participating and sometimes struggled to recall services or concepts that I had introduced earlier in the session. Without an immediate academic research assignment to complete, the class content, centred on library resources, seemed irrelevant to them. What did seem relevant, on the other hand, were the mobile phones many kept eyeing. In pilot sessions run in the 2010-11 academic year, guided by my research on smartphone owners' attitudes towards information, I experimented with several conceptual shifts in my teaching.

Emphasis on services over location

The original one-shot sessions were designed for a desktop world, in which students had to come to where we (the librarians) and our desktop computers sat. Instructional librarians told the students that many library resources could be accessed from anywhere, but the length of the library tour video, combined with the requirement that students come to the library for the session, gave the opposite impression and emphasized the physicality of the library building, a place you had to go in order to benefit from its services. For smartphone owners, however, 'the proliferation of mobile technology has driven a demand for - and indeed an expectation of - being able to do whatever we want to do, wherever we happen to be. The library as a place ... has possibly now been overtaken by the library as a service' (Schachter, 2011, 32). For my pilot sessions I went to seminar classrooms, rather than inviting the classes to the library. My visit to the class served as visible evidence that librarians were not confined to a single building. I stripped out the library tour video and took care to emphasize the accessibility of library resources, conveying that the library was not simply a physical building but a suite of services, available from anywhere.

Attention to informal learning

The Weinberg Library's IL sessions historically focused purely on academic information, with sample searches demonstrating how students could use library resources for course assignments. While my survey found that students are in fact interested in using their phones for academic purposes (Yarmey, 2011), it also shed light on the informal learning and information seeking that often occurs on smartphones. Many respondents described using their phones to follow their interests, from politics and financial news to sports. Mobile information access seemed to be 'woven into all the times and places of students' lives' (Traxler, 2010, 151), and much of their searching and information use occurred outside of the classroom. According to the Scranton survey, only 29% of students with smartphones who used their phones for information seeking reported doing so while in class (either 'sometimes' or 'frequently'). If librarians want students to embrace IL as a lifelong skill we cannot limit ourselves to academe when introducing IL concepts to them. Traxler (2010, 157) agrees, arguing that mobile devices cause the 'simple dichotomy' between 'formal' and 'self-motivated learning activities' to break down. With this approach, the learning outcomes of a one-shot session shift. Instead of centring on the library's offerings, the session becomes an opportunity to discuss lifelong skills such as critical evaluation. By grounding my pilot sessions in general information use, I could more naturally guide the students towards an understanding of why library resources are so essential for academic work and lay a foundation for more library-centric instruction in the future.

Searching outside the library

In the traditional one-shot sessions, much class time was spent conducting sample searches of library resources, including the library catalogue and one or more subscription databases. The sessions did not reflect the reality of college student life, in which the library is often at the 'periphery of undergraduate student information seeking' (Hahn, 2010, 286). OCLC's 2005 report *Perceptions of Libraries and Information Resources* found that 89% of college students started their information searches by using a search engine, compared to only 2% who began with the library website. In the Scranton smartphone survey, though a large majority of students with smartphones were using their phones to engage with information, only 25% of them expressed interest in mobile access to the library catalogue and databases. In my pilot sessions, I started the class where student mobile and desktop searches most often begin: with Google. We discussed the importance of choosing the right tool for a search and understanding a given tool's limitations and potential biases. This discussion related directly back to student smartphone use, in that many students reported using apps to search for specific types of information. When asked on the survey what motivated them to install and use a certain app, most students cited recommendations from friends or rankings in an app store. More than half of the app users said that they did consider whether or not the app creator was an authoritative source, but only 38% said they paid attention to how often the app was updated. Encouraging students to think critically about their choice of search tool, rather than simply showing them library search interfaces, addressed their mobile information use and introduced a lifelong skill.

Instilling the habit of evaluation

Students with smartphones interact with a constant flow of information as they receive text messages, scroll through their Facebook feeds and browse the web for news throughout the day. The ability to quickly and astutely filter out relevant, authoritative and trustworthy information from dynamic media formats has become essential to student success. Smartphones, however, do not necessarily facilitate the critical evaluation of information. Small screen sizes and often slow connection speeds discourage the exploration of multiple sources. As of 2009, compared to desktop searchers, mobile searchers were 'less likely to scroll past the first few search results, less willing to click on search results ..., [and] willing to spend more time on the search results page before clicking their first link' (Carpineto et al., 2009). In the Scranton survey, only 15% of the students with smartphones looked beyond the first five results of a search when searching on their phone. More than 25% of the students admitted that they did not question the reliability of websites that they visited on their phones, and only 7% reported visiting a mobile site's 'About Us' page to investigate its source. Concurrently, anecdotal feedback from faculty members indicated that student research assignments frequently cited 'content farm' sites like eHow and Ask.com, which commonly appear at or near the top of Google search results (Roth, 2009). To address these concerns, in the last of my pilot sessions I initiated a conversation with students about website evaluation, using several familiar content farms as examples. We discussed their advertisement-driven business models and the students considered how the content creators for such sites are incentivized to cover a topic speedily and simply, using a maximum of frequently searched keywords, rather than to provide a deep understanding of a concept. The discussion aimed to reveal to students that the most convenient information available might be misleading, and gave me an opening to introduce more reliable sources that were easily accessible and not nearly as inconvenient to use as the students had thought.

Assessment

I assessed my pilot sessions informally, observing student behaviour and checking comprehension and recall of important concepts at the end of the class. Student feedback in most pilot sessions was unexpectedly and vocally positive. Although I used the same discussion-based teaching style as in my earlier, traditional IL sessions, students were much more engaged, both answering my questions and asking their own. One student raised his hand at the end of class to tell me that while he had heard talks about library resources before, their usefulness had never 'clicked' for him until our discussion. Feedback from professors was also positive; the instructor whose class served as my last pilot session reported back to me that his students' use of sources had significantly improved after our meeting. In 2011–12, as I teach another set of incoming students, I plan to conduct more formal assessment to further test the effectiveness of this content in a one-shot introduction to IL.

References

Ally, M. (ed.) (2009) *Mobile Learning: transforming the delivery of education and training*, Athabasca University Press.

Association of College and Research Libraries (2000) *Information Literacy Competency Standards for Higher Education*, www.ala.org/ala/mgrps/divs/acrl/standards/standards.pdf.

Bridges, L., Rempel, H. and Griggs, K. (2010) Making the Case for a Fully Mobile Library Web Site: from floor maps to the catalog, *Reference Services Review*, **38** (2), 309–20.

Carpineto, C., Mizzaro, S., Romano, G. and Snidero, M. (2009) Mobile Information Retrieval with Search Results Clustering: prototypes and evaluations, *Journal of the American Society for Information Science and Technology*, **60** (5), 877–95.

Cvetkovic, V. and Lackie, R. (2009) *Teaching Generation M: a handbook for librarians and educators*, New York: Neal-Schuman Publishers.

Godwin, P. (2010) Information Literacy Gets Mobile. In Ally, M. and Needham, G. (eds), *M-Libraries 2: a virtual library in everyone's pocket*, Facet Publishing.

Godwin, P. and Parker, J. (eds) (2008) *Information Literacy Meets Library 2.0*, Facet Publishing.

Hahn, J. (2010) Information Seeking with Wikipedia on the iPod Touch, *Reference Services Review*, **38** (2), 284–98.

Kamvar, M., Kellar, M., Patel, R. and Xu, Y. (2009) Computers and iPhones and Mobile Phones, Oh My!: a logs-based comparison of search users on different devices, *WWW 2009: Proceedings of the 18th International Conference on World Wide Web*, Madrid, 801–10, www.google.com/research/pubs/archive/35252.pdf.

Kohl, L. and Keating, M. (2009) A Phone of One's Own: texting at the Bryant University reference desk, *College and Research Libraries News*, February, 104-6.

Kukulska-Hulme, A. and Traxler, J. (eds) (2005) *Mobile Learning: a handbook for educators and trainers*, Routledge.

OCLC (2005) *Perceptions of Libraries and Information Resources*, www.oclc.org/reports/2005perceptions.htm.

Roth, D. (2009) The Answer Factory: demand media and the fast, disposable, and profitable as hell media model, *Wired*, October, www.wired.com/magazine/2009/10/ff_demandmedia.

Schachter, D. (2011) A Resurgence in Our Relevance, *Information Outlook*, **15** (1), 32.

Seeholzer, J. and Salem, J. (2011) Library on the Go: a focus group study of the mobile web and the academic library, *College and Research Libraries*, **72** (1), 9-20.

Traxler, J. (2010) Students and Mobile Devices, *ALT-J: Association for Learning Technology Journal*, **18** (2), 149-60.

Walsh, A. (2011) Mobile Information Literacy: mobilising existing models? In: *Handheld Librarian* **4**, 23-24 February, http://eprints.hud.ac.uk/9470.

Yarmey, K. (2010) When Students Go Mobile: smartphones and information literacy in higher education, *Pennsylvania Library Association Bulletin*, **65** (4).

Yarmey, K. (2011) Student Information Literacy in the Mobile Environment, *Educause Quarterly*, **34** (1), www.educause.edu/EDUCAUSE+Quarterly/EDUCAUSEQuarterlyMagazineVolum/ StudentInformationLiteracyinth/225860.

Chapter 10

Tweets, texts and trees

Andrew Walsh

Within Computing and Library Services at the University of Huddersfield we have been enthusiastic adopters of and experimenters with Web 2.0, social learning technologies and mobile learning opportunities over recent years. These have often found their way into our teaching, directly into our face-to-face inductions and information skills sessions and more generally into our online information literacy (IL) materials.

Let's start with the basics ...

We spend a great deal of time carrying out face-to-face inductions for our new students and we try to see as many as possible for inductions, but could never hope to see everyone. We also accept that they may well forget a large part of the information we give them, however much we try to make it interesting. So, in 2008, we produced a separate mini-site within our web pages called 'The Basics' and incorporating much of the basic information that we impart in inductions, but including many more Web 2.0 ideas than appeared in our standard web pages at that time. These web pages (Figure 10.1) pulled into one place a lot of our early ideas about using Web 2.0 for our online teaching materials.

Behind the pages was one simple idea that underpins a lot of the design – we wanted to move away from static, text-heavy pages to pages that looked fresh and encouraged exploration and interaction with the content. Though there was a core of basic textual content, this was enriched with podcasts, videos and interactive tutorials. Each page included a facility for leaving a star rating, or comments, embedded into it. Making 'The Basics' look as though the content was regularly changed was difficult. We wanted to achieve this without dedicating much time to actually changing the content. We knew that although we had time available to set

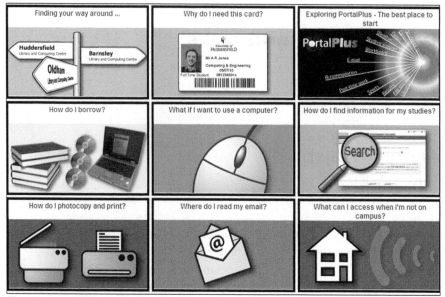

Figure 10.1 'The Basics' (University of Huddersfield)

up the pages initially, realistically speaking it would be difficult to find the time to repeatedly update existing content. Instead of planning to change the main content, we decided to cheat by using another Web 2.0 tool! On each page we embedded a Twitter feed, setting up a library Twitter account (@hudlib). This meant that we could spend small amounts of time tweeting and then reuse the content in many places. As long as we tweet regularly, the pages have new content and look as though they are constantly changing.

We have applied the lessons learned from 'The Basics' to our main pages, with similar features now cropping up regularly on the 'normal' Computing and Library Services (CLS) web pages. We have included the ratings and comments feature on many pages, enabling interaction to be embedded into these pages for the first time. The best Web 2.0 feature that we have moved from 'The Basics' to our normal pages, in my opinion, has been our short cut to making the pages look more dynamic. We have embedded our tweets into every CLS page and our blog feeds into various subject pages (Figure 10.2). We continue to update the pages occasionally rather than regularly, but, because we reuse content, our users would never know that!

Figure 10.2 Example subject page (University of Huddersfield)

Now we get mobile ...

As more of our staff and students buy and use internet-enabled handheld devices, such as smartphones, we have seen opportunities to move on from user involvement and user-generated content online, to user involvement via mobile phone. We have brought mobile learning into our teaching practice, starting with some basic technology that practically all our users can take advantage of by using their mobile phones – text messaging.

It seems strange that up until recently people could talk to us face-to-face, phone us on various numbers, fax us, e-mail any number of addresses, post us a letter or fill in a web form to ask questions, but couldn't send us a text message (SMS), even though many of our users seemed permanently attached to their mobile phones. We brought in a Text a Librarian service (users text LIBRARY plus their question to 81025) to remedy this. We have expanded what we offer via this route to include popular services such as text NOISE, whereby people can report inappropriate behaviour in the library and have a library warden come straight to that area.

Following the introduction of this basic service, we have been able to use the same underlying text messaging portal to experiment with teaching via SMS. We asked first-year students to sign up to a pilot project in which we sent out a series

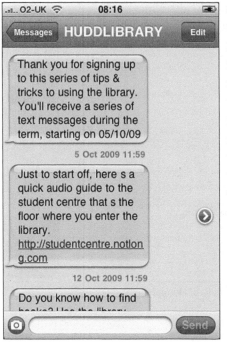

Figure 10.3
Using SMS for student induction (University of Huddersfield)

of text messages during the autumn term (see Figure 10.3). These messages covered the same basic material that we talk about during inductions. The big difference was that we could deliver the text messages closer to the point of need, rather than during the first week, when students were bombarded with more information than they could possibly hope to assimilate. In the first week of term we provided information on borrowing books from the library. Our normal loan period is two weeks, so we followed this up in week three with information on renewing loans or extending the loan period. We didn't mention electronic resources until towards the end of the first term, when we expect students to start needing to use these resources.

We've sometimes used interactive handsets (often called clickers) in our teaching, but we have found them awkward to set up, especially when teaching outside our own library teaching rooms, so they perhaps haven't been used as often as we would like. However, we have successfully turned mobile phones into clickers by using Web 2.0 systems. After experimenting with various ways of doing this we've found that Poll Everywhere (www.polleverywhere.com) works well with smaller classes (at the time of writing it is currently free for groups of up to 30). We can ask the class questions and have them respond using their own mobile phones (or computers) via Twitter, text message or the web. The results are pushed straight into PowerPoint. As a free Web 2.0 tool, Poll Everywhere is a really viable alternative to normal clickers.

Though we've taken advantage of some quite basic mobile phone functionality, such as text messaging, we've also experimented with things that work best with higher-end phones. Our expectation is that the high-end phones of today will become the low-end phones of tomorrow, and the same functionality will become easily accessible to the majority of our users. Our experiments have included using QR

(Quick Response) codes to deliver information-skills materials, and thus help people at their point of need. QR codes can work with practically any camera phone, but work best on smartphones with a decent data connection through WiFi or 3G.

QR codes are matrix codes that encode data in two dimensions rather than the one dimension used by standard barcodes. They use a freely available international standard, meaning that many free QR reader applications are available to download onto mobile

Figure 10.4
QR codes (University of Huddersfield)

phones, as well as free services and applications for creating the codes. QR codes were originally created for stock control by Denso Wave, a manufacturer of car parts, in which context they are read by an application on a mobile phone that is then prompted to carry out a specific action. They can be used to display text, to automatically phone a number or send a text message or, most flexibly, link to a mobile-friendly web page.

To support IL, we have used QR codes around the library to connect to useful materials (Figure 10.4), such as mobile-friendly videos, from the places where students may need them. So, for instance, on our print credit machine we link to a video hosted on YouTube (which is sophisticated enough to deliver content in a mobile-friendly format), showing how to use the machine. From our printed law collection, we link to material on how to search for legal information online. Library users can find the information where and when they need it, rather than it just remaining hidden away on our main web pages.

We have also used free online Web 2.0 services to create mobile-friendly quizzes, and we provide links to quizzes, videos and further help from many printed help sheets, turning them from flat pieces of paper into interactive, enriched content – creating 'paper 2.0' through small, free-to-produce codes and people's own mobile phones.

Gaming in the library ...

We like to bring an element of fun and games into our IL teaching when we can, whether through using crosswords, treasure hunts or light-hearted videos, but we haven't really brought games, along with the technology and social nature of Web 2.0, into the core of our service. We're currently changing this, working with a creative company called Running in the Halls (www.rith.co.uk) to create a social online game based around using the library's resources. Called Lemon Tree, it brings ideas of gamification right into the heart of library activities.

There are many applications, often available as smartphone apps, that turn everyday tasks into chances to win points, badges and other virtual rewards and share them with your social networks. Location-based networks typify this idea and have exploded in popularity recently, with networks such as Foursquare (http://foursquare.com) and Gowalla (http://gowalla.com) allowing you to 'check in' to various locations, share the activity with friends, become 'Mayor' of a location or win badges for different types of activity. A more extreme version of this gamification of everyday activity is Epic Win (www.rexbox.co.uk/epicwin/), which allows you to create a 'to do' list and 'play' that list as if it were a game, gaining rewards for completing each task.

Lemon Tree (Figure 10.5) takes these ideas of virtual rewards and inbuilt social networks and turns common interactions with the library into a game.

Users are able to link Lemon Tree to their library record, winning points and badges for activities such as taking out books, leaving comments about books and borrowing a range of items. They build their own social network within Lemon Tree, but the system also links to existing networks such as Twitter and Facebook. Lemon Tree feeds back into our systems as well, so comments that a student leaves

Figure 10.5 Lemon Tree (Reproduced by permission of Running in the Halls)

about a book will appear in our library catalogue for everyone to see, regardless as to whether or not they choose to play and interact with Lemon Tree.

We're bringing our existing online information-skills materials into this social game as well, offering Lemon Tree rewards for watching certain clips or completing an online tutorial, adding a layer of fun on top of our 'normal' material. We hope people will interact with the information-skills materials because they want to, because they need the learning they contain. They may, however, choose to watch a video or complete a tutorial just to gain the same badge their friend has, or to beat them on the leader board – but provided they are learning the skills, we are happy!

The rewards that users can gain through Lemon Tree are developing as we see what works and what our users enjoy, with a massive range of options possible. We are particularly interested, though, in engaging those people who we know come into our library but borrow very few books and rarely access our electronic resources. If we can make it fun for them to use the information resources that we have, and increase their usage, then Lemon Tree will have been a success for us.

Where we are now ...

After early pilots, trials and experiments, Web 2.0 is no longer seen as cutting edge in our library service. Instead it is incorporated into most of our activities, old and new. When introducing new services, such as the new reading list software we are currently developing, we don't consider 'should we' allow user-generated content, we consider 'how will we' enable that content.

Feeds from our Twitter account and team blogs now feed into our standard web pages and comment boxes appear on many of the same pages. Instead of telling our users to turn their mobiles off, we say 'switch them to silent'; encourage them to text us with questions or to complain about noise; and use them in our IL teaching. We're encouraging people to contribute their own content, which is surely the essence of Web 2.0, and get rewarded (virtually) for it through Lemon Tree. Whether it is tweets, texts or (lemon) trees, Web 2.0 services and ideas are embedded in how we now operate. We just couldn't imagine going back.

Further reading

For more information on some of our Web 2.0 and mobile learning developments outlined above, see:

Walsh, Andrew (2010) QR Codes – Using Mobile Phones to Deliver Library Instruction and Help at the Point of Need, *Journal of Information Literacy*, **3** (1), 55-65, http://eprints.hud.ac.uk/7759/.

Walsh, Andrew (2010) Supplementing Inductions with Text Messages, an SMS 'Tips and Tricks' Service, *ALISS Quarterly*, B (3), 23-5, http://eprints.hud.ac.uk/7393/.

Acknowledgement

All images reproduced by permission of A. Walsh/University of Huddersfield.

Chapter 11

Referencing in a 2.0 world

Stacey Taylor

Introduction

Referencing is part of an integrated approach to the digital and information literacy continuum that we are working on in our school and is a part of every assessment task. Let me put this into context. The Monte School is an independent Catholic secondary school in Sydney, Australia, with 1100 girls aged between 12 and 18. We work within the dual curricula of the New South Wales School Certificate and the International Baccalaureate Middle Years Program (MYP) for years 7-10 and offer the International Baccalaureate Diploma Program (IB DP) in addition to the New South Wales Higher School Certificate (HSC) in Years 11 and 12.

We have been an International Baccalaureate (IB) school for five years and in this time the information literacy landscape has changed dramatically within our school. The need for absolute adherence to referencing systems has become apparent because IB DP assessment tasks are marked externally (all over the world) and the marking criteria award marks for accurate referencing. The other important factor in managing referencing is that we have recently become a '1:1' school, with all students having their own Mac notebooks. This provides us both with opportunities, such as a guaranteed set-up for bibliographic tools on students' computers, and also with an expectation that students will use their own computers to complete the tasks they are set.

The school has had a school-wide referencing system for at least 10 years and in the past students were encouraged to use a computer program to create their bibliographies. We used a program called 'Citation' and recommended the Harvard method of referencing. However, we found that most databases we subscribed to didn't have a Harvard option for creating citations from articles. When we started looking for suitable tools we found that Harvard was often unsupported, so we chose to move to the similar APA (American Psychological Association) method.

We use the 'guided inquiry process' to work through assessment tasks with students and have developed some strong partnerships with teachers (particularly in the senior years curriculum) which allow us to work in the 'zones of intervention' (intervention at critical points) with students working on extended assessment tasks for both the HSC and the IB DP. Helping students to develop referencing skills and showing them options for organizing resources is part of this process.

In order to make the referencing process more user friendly for junior students, we use the online tool EasyBib. (www.easybib.com). In the first instance, junior students are instructed in using EasyBib to create both their bibliographies and in-text citations. While EasyBib is a free web tool, because we use the APA style we pay a subscription to have APA available as an option within it. The students are given an access coupon code when they register, and this allows them to work on their bibliographies over a period of time.

Students are instructed both in the classroom and virtually; a Jing video on how to reference is offered via our learning management system (Moodle). We are therefore able to provide instruction at all times, so that when students are rushing to complete their assessments they have access to information at the point of need.

EasyBib

EasyBib (Figure 11.1) is a simple-to-use tool that relies on Web 2.0 capabilities to deliver citations for resources automatically. Students can enter a URL or ISBN and EasyBib returns a citation for that resource using WorldCat data. It also allows students to create a manual entry using set fields. EasyBib has a range of templates for over 50 resource types. Because our students have a subscription to the service, EasyBib also stores their bibliographies so that they can work on them over time. We encourage students to start working on their bibliographies when they begin their assessment tasks.

EasyBib also creates in-text citations (called the 'parentheticals') from each resource, which students copy and paste into their work. This has simplified this part of the process, which our students have often found difficult.

Because EasyBib is a web-based product students can access their bibliographies wherever they are, which has advantages if they are using more than one computer. The subscription fee paid by the school is small and enables

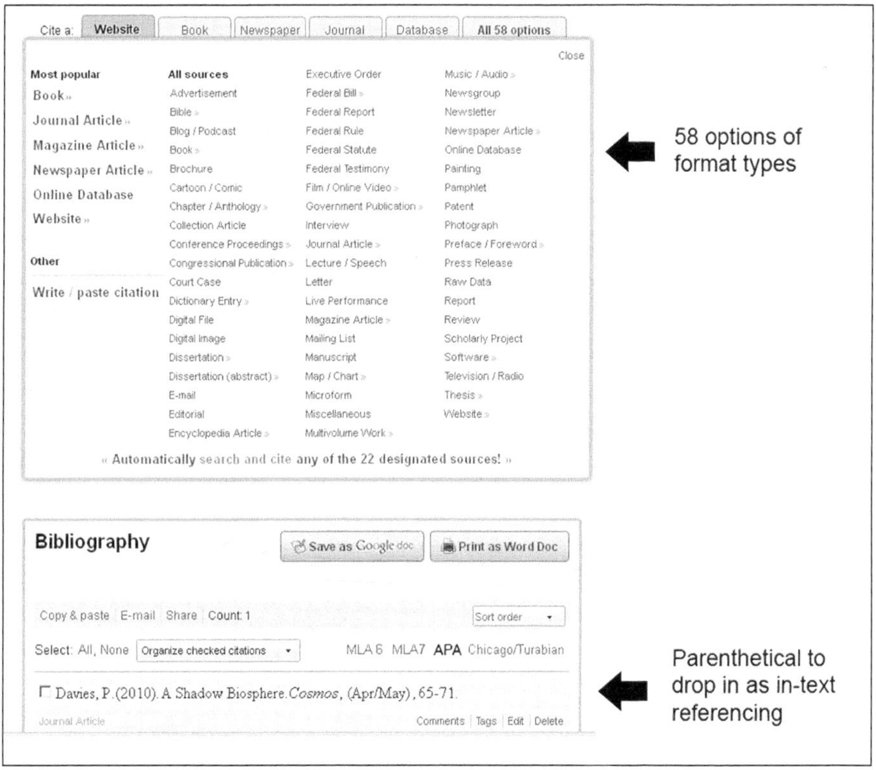

Figure 11.1 EasyBib (Reproduced by permission of EasyBib)

students both to use the APA style and to store their bibliographies. We explored a number of bibliographic products, such as Noodletools and MS Word functionality, but chose EasyBib because it was simple for the students to use.

The digital and information literacy continuum builds skills from basic bibliography creation to in-text citation from Years 7 to 10. Referencing has changed since the times when many teachers were studying and they may not be familiar with the latest tools, so we ensure that they are informed. Teachers are offered training via PowerPoint presentations and Jing videos so that they can advise students. These support materials are created by the library staff to ensure that the students understand referencing structure. Library staff are often asked to deliver referencing lessons to students at the point of need, when assessment tasks are being undertaken. Referencing lessons need to be offered to students on more than one occasion, reinforcing skills that may be practised infrequently.

Zotero

A more complex and more powerful tool used to support referencing is Zotero (Figure 11.2). We reserve this for use with senior students who are engaged in long and substantial assessment tasks that run over many weeks or even months.

Zotero was originally a Firefox browser extension but is now available in standalone form. It is a free, web-based product and payment is required only when storage needs increase. Most senior school students will not need to pay for storage. Zotero sits at the bottom of a Firefox web browser page, ready to capture any web resources that are of interest. With a simple click you can capture an image of the page and Zotero also pulls in all the metadata attached to that web page, automatically populating your bibliographic citation. Zotero not only works with websites but can also handle citations from articles within databases, and book citations can be managed manually.

The organizational aspects of Zotero, however, are its main strength. Captured citations can be sorted into relevant folders, tags can be attached to individual resources and notes can also be attached. This makes it a powerful tool for students to use in the research stages of an assessment, allowing them to capture resources, tag them and make notes as they work. Moreover, Zotero

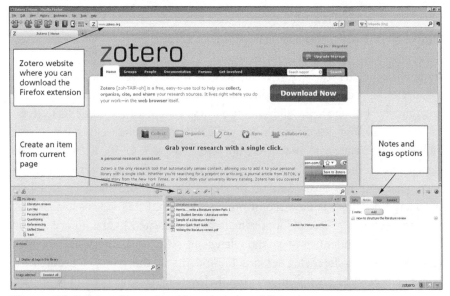

Figure 11.2 Zotero (Reproduced by permission of Zotero)

can be used to generate bibliographies, reports and annotated bibliographies and can form the basis of a literature review.

Other functionality places Zotero firmly in the Web 2.0 field. It can create shared libraries (stores of referencing data) that can be managed by library staff and shared with teachers as well as the general public. Zotero has increased in functionality in the time we have been using it and now also has an embedding functionality, which allows the creation of in-text citations within MS Word.

How Zotero is used with senior classes

We have a few HSC (the final two years of school) classes that we work closely with on long research tasks. One such class is the Community and Family Studies class. We use a guided enquiry approach with these students and will see them for at least four classes to work on various information literacy skills. Students are required to develop their own questions on a social issue and then do some primary and secondary research to answer them. Part of this process requires students to complete a literature review. We look at examples of literature reviews and show students how to create one. We also show them how to use Zotero (which has previously been installed on all their computers). We explain the benefits of starting their bibliographies early and how to capture, tag and take notes within Zotero.

The IB DP has an extended essay requirement that all students undertake. It is a 4000-word assessment, answering a question that the students develop themselves within any subject they study. The scope of the essay is wide, with a timeframe for completion of about nine months. Zotero provides the students with a means of organizing resources over this extended period. By adding tags to their resources, students can search for relevant resources at any time. We have not yet used the referencing functionality available within MS Word with students, but will be doing so in the near future.

Zotero has great functionality and I have been using it myself to organize resources for the various projects I am involved in. I can share resources if I need to, and find the notes field particularly useful as a memory aid. I believe it is important to use the tools that students are using, in order to identify any areas with which they may have difficulty. For example, Zotero has a synchronization function that allows students to access resources from different computers. This was the only area that was sometimes problematic, but it has improved and now works fairly seamlessly.

Conclusion

Most of our students will go on to tertiary education and it is important that they have a good grounding in using these tools. We aim to ensure that all our students attain the maximum marks possible for citation management and work hard to make this happen. We use a school-wide approach to facilitate this process as much as possible. We make ourselves available to students who have referencing questions and assist teachers in developing referencing skills with their classes. There is certainly growth and development in the tools available in this area, and in two years' time we may find something that works better for our students, but for now at least they are using tools that are appropriate and effective. Our students' better-developed referencing skills provide strong evidence of this.

Chapter 12

Moving information literacy beyond Library 2.0: multimedia, multi-device, point-of-need screencasts via the ANimated Tutorial Sharing Project

Carmen Kazakoff-Lane

Introduction

Providing information literacy to today's students is a bewildering exercise. People who once came to a library for information and assistance now turn to the internet; want to access educational content at their actual point of need; tend to be increasingly turning to multimedia as their preferred educational medium of choice (Pew Internet and American Life Project, 2010, 3, 5); and are accessing web information using a wide array of devices including laptops, smartphones and tablets. Librarians working with students understand that the ability to use Web 2.0 search or communication technology does not mean that students understand how to access reliable information or use it in appropriate ways – and given the complex information environment, there is a multitude of information literacy skills that need to be taught. But how does one do so in this diaspora? One initiative, the ANimated Tutorial Sharing project (ANTS), is attempting to address this by providing librarians with a means to support 24/7 point-of-need library instruction. It is also working to develop content that is available in the many useful formats required by people who access the internet using a wide range of devices.

ANTS: background and purpose

The ANimated Tutorial Sharing Project is an initiative that enables librarians to collaboratively build, update and share large numbers of useful multimedia tutorials. It has its origins in a meeting held by the Distance Education Librarians of the Council of Prairie and Pacific University Libraries (COPPUL) in May 2004.

At the time, the Distance Education Forum was discussing ways to provide information literacy to remote students. It had created a one-shot information literacy tutorial in 2000 that had received minimal usage, and the group wanted to look at screencasting as an alternative means of providing instruction. The forum thought that the technology was promising, as it enabled librarians to easily construct learning objects that included audio, text, images, quizzes, etc., that would appeal to individuals with different learning styles, and test their knowledge. The ease of creation also pointed towards the opportunity to create short point-of-need tutorials that could teach people how to do specific things, such as search a particular database. The group liked the idea of point-of-need tutorials but was aware of a few downsides: firstly, the large number of learning objects needed to support point-of-need instruction for specific e-resources and, secondly, the tendency of vendors to change interfaces frequently meant that these educational resources would quickly become dated. As the only conceivable way to build and maintain enough learning objects was via inter-institutional collaboration, the forum asked its Information Literacy Group to look into what was needed for co-ordinated development to occur. The output of this group's work was the ANTS project, which was released to COPPUL librarians in February of 2006 and opened to librarians beyond COPPUL in October of the same year.

When ANTS was released in 2006, the project had identified two important goals:

1 'To create a critical mass of Open Source Tutorials for online resources used by libraries everywhere' (www2.brandonu.ca/Library/COPPUL/index.html).
2 'To rationalize development of Learning Objects and thereby eliminate duplication of effort across institutions.'

In order to support these goals, the ANTS team put in place the foundations needed to support both collaborative development of screencasts and file sharing by providing participants with:

• information about the project on a website (www2.brandonu.ca/library/coppul/)
• access to a wiki that listed tutorials identified for development and tracked who was working on each one via postings and RSS feeds (http://wiki.uwinnipeg.ca/index.php/COPPUL_Tutorials – no longer active)

- accounts at the University of Calgary's Institutional Repository where they could upload their files, access others' files and receive immediate notification when new content was added to the collection (https://dspace.ucalgary.ca/handle/1880/43471)
- a tutorial, 'How to upload files and metadata to DSpace' (www.ucalgary.ca/lib-old/libcon/viewlets/dsub2.html)
- guidelines for tutorial development designed around best practice and ways to make file sharing easier (http://acts.twu.ca/Library/antsguidelines2008.htm).

Members of the ANTS team also went out to market the project and returned with feedback indicating, firstly, that people wanted the content at a video-hosting site like YouTube and, secondly, that it would be beneficial to also include embedding code with each screencast. The team thought it might be able to address these issues and at the same time improve workflow by consolidating sites. Although the project was unable to locate one site that did everything required, it did identify a number of sites with excellent resolution, a host of value-added services, syndication technology and one site (www.wetpaint.com) that would enable the project to consolidate the wiki and web page. The team then determined that it would move forward with a new wiki (http://ants.wetpaint.com) as well as utilize two new video-hosting sites that collectively met all of ANTS needs and enabled the project to advance its goal of providing people with point-of-need instruction. As the new sites (ironically) added to ANTS workload, the project brought in several new team members in the autumn of 2007 to support the work at various sites.[1] The project also expanded its goals to include:

- making library-related learning objects ubiquitously available to online learners and thereby enhancing librarians' ability to reach out and educate online users where they are online (http://ants.wetpaint.com/page/ANTS+and+LION+TV)
- providing library screencasters with guidance, so as to build up the number of potential contributors to the project (http://ants.wetpaint.com/page/Keeping+Up+to+Date+%26+Getting+Help).

With the launch of these new sites, ANTS evolved into ANTS 2.0, with a central focus on enhancing collaborative screencasting among libraries and ensuring that the content created was more visible and easy to use than it was before. What ANTS could not foresee was the changes that would occur at each of their sites - and how these changes would position the project to provide contributors with a wide array of multimedia files that could be used to provide people with seamless access to videos, regardless of the device or browser in use. This opportunity also comes with challenges, however, so both will be addressed later.

Supporting point-of-need access via collaboration, syndication and file conversion at ANTS 2.0

With the incorporation of new sites and team members, ANTS evolved into a project that continued with the production of large numbers of learning objects, while at the same time making this content more broadly available in a wider range of useful formats. How it does all this is best explained by discussing how the project operates, and in particular what happens at the contributor phase, and to contributor files once they have been accepted.

The contributor phase is what enables libraries to build and maintain large numbers of learning objects. It begins when library screencasters come to the ANTS wiki, where they are given instruction in how to participate and told to visit ANTS wiki lists to learn what is in need of development.[2]

When volunteers visit the ANTS wiki lists, they learn if content has been created for a specific tutorial, if it is in need of development or if someone is currently working on content. If a screencast they wish to create has not been produced, they volunteer to do it by posting their name beside 'Under Development' for a specific tutorial. Similarly, if their idea for a tutorial has not even been identified for development, they simply add it to the list and then put their name beside it. This way, others know that there is no need to undertake work on this product in their own institution.

After adopting a tutorial, the volunteer consults the 'ANTS Guidelines for Tutorial Development'. These were created by Bill Badke and built around effective instructional design/pedagogical concepts (e.g. keep content short, modular and well sequenced) and elements that make collaborative screencasting and file sharing possible (e.g. omit references to local link resolvers, use standard colours and fonts, etc.). They work to make the final content both educationally useful and easy for others to adapt if they wish to do so.

After reviewing the guidelines, a contributor spends time developing their content. Upon completing it, they return to the ANTS wiki and are (1) told to get an account at DSpace where they can upload their content and (2) given videos instructing them how to upload files and metadata and informing them of their need to sign a Creative Commons, Attribution, Share-Alike, Non-Commercial Licence.[3]

This Licence states that the creator of a learning object is the copyright holder, but that as the creator they agree to give others the right to reuse, redistribute, revise or remix their content, thus making their content an Open Educational Resource (OER). Contributors get their accounts and upload the source code (for those wishing to make modifications to the tutorial), the published video, as well as information about their creation. They can also use their account to sign up for notifications any time new content is added to the collection. At this point the contributor phase of the project ends and the project enters its second phase, of work with contributor files.

The first thing that occurs is that all contributor files are taken from DSpace and migrated to a second home at Screencast.com (www.screencast.com/users/ants). Screencast.com was selected as one of our new video-hosting sites in 2007 because:

- it is the only site that not only accepts – but welcomes – interactive ShockWave Flash (SWF) files
- it provides embedding code for all videos
- it displays videos at a good resolution so viewers can read text typed into a search box (which was not the case for YouTube at the time)
- it streams these videos at a good rate.

It continues to provide the project with an excellent home for video files with several sharing/feed options. It has also proved to be the most stable of all of ANTS video-hosting sites.

Aside from Screencast.com, ANTS also migrates contributor files to a second site, identified for adoption in 2007: BLIP.TV. The ANTS team uses the site to produce the Library Information literacy Online Network or LION TV (http://liontv.blip.tv), where viewers can find embedding code, feeds, numerous sharing options and videos that both display and stream well. Like Screencast.com, all content for the project comes from DSpace; but, in order for this content to work at LION TV, it first has to be converted to an MPEG 4 file by an ANTS team member.

As part of the uploading process the team member:

- uploads the MPEG 4 file
- indicates that contributor content falls under a specific Creative Commons Licence
- places all information about the production (taken from the metadata at DSpace) into a Description of the Episode
- indicates that the file should be converted to a m4v file (which is used by iPods and iPhones)
- tells LION TV to send ANTS content to several internet brand sites.

The first place to which LION TV originally sent content was the ANTS Internet Archive page.[4] This site accepted our files, placed the LION TV description of each episode beside each video, and created an open source OGG Vorbis video file from our MPEG 4 files. Unfortunately, the option of using LION TV to automatically migrate files to the Internet Archive is no longer available, due to changes that occurred at BLIP.TV.

The second site to which LION TV sends content is the ANTS Facebook syndication site.[5] This site does not host our video files. Instead, it contains the LION TV description of each episode and links the viewer to the video at LION TV. The third site to which contributor content goes is YouTube.[6] This was created in 2009 after BLIP.TV established a partnership with YouTube that facilitated file distribution to it. BLIP.TV's partnership occurred at a fortuitous time, as it coincided with improvements to YouTube's resolution. This meant that sending content was not only feasible; it was also desirable, as content would display and stream well, contributor content would be housed on the most highly used video site on the internet and placing videos - with LION TV's descriptions - on YouTube ensured that contributor videos were well ranked by Google (which ranked YouTube videos higher than BLIP.TV's). What we could not anticipate in 2009 was what a YouTube presence would mean for our files - as Google recently announced that all YouTube files would be converted into a file standard that it had purchased and made available as open source: the Web M video file.[7] This has provided the project with access to a third video format.

Aside from these sites, BLIP.TV has been configured to send information about LION TV content to several video search engines like BlinkX or AOL video and a growing number of video search/integration sites, including Channels.com,[8] CastTV[9] and Mefeedia.[10] With each site, the likelihood of discovering contributor content increases.

Collectively, the work by contributors and ANTS team members has led to the creation of a unique project that is taking information literacy into new territory. With the ANTS infrastructure, librarians have a mechanism to sustainably develop and maintain large numbers of screencasts. With its syndication technology, embedding codes and sharing features, librarians can look to a time when large numbers of learning objects are accessible to users at their point of need - be it on internet brand sites or on important local sites. With its file conversions, contributors are being given access to a wide range of file formats that support viewing on different devices/browsers. Finally, ANTS is helping to move information literacy beyond Library 2.0 by supporting the development of videos that work well on mobile devices because:

1   Its guidelines encourage the development of short, modular, well-sequenced content that works well for both online and mobile users; that is more likely to be viewed in full (Brown-Sica, Sobel and Pan, 2009, 90); is more educationally effective (Oud, 2009, 167; Oehrli et al., 2011, 134; Mayer, 1999, 620); and that works to ensure that viewers do not have to download or stream large files on devices that would find them difficult to handle.

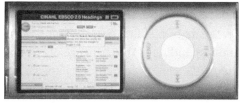

Figure 12.1
iPod Nano Playing an ANTS Video (Image: Carmen Kazakoff-Lane)

2   ANTS m4v files are designed to work on iPhones or iPod touches.

3   The resolution of ANTS MPEG 4 and Web M files enables a video to be clearly displayed on some of the smallest screens - such as an iPod Nano (Figures 12.1 and 12.2).

Figure 12.2
iPod Touch Playing an ANTS Video (Image: Carmen Kazakoff-Lane)

4   Many of ANTS videos - as well as its best practice in

screencasting – illustrate that there are ways to create interactivity without the need for Flash, which does not work on Apple technology or on the most recent mobile web browser for Internet Explorer.[11]

This support for mobile delivery of content is becoming a critical element of distributed information literacy in an age when mobile devices are becoming ubiquitous and the emergence of useful technologies – such as Quick Response (QR) codes – enables libraries to link a mobile user to an appropriate video at their point of need. One can easily see that both digital sites and physical objects (e.g. library handouts, library stacks, photocopiers) will increasingly incorporate QR codes that mobile users can scan in order to view videos that show them how to read a Library of Congress call number, make a two-sided photocopy,[12] place an interlibrary loan request, or search a database. As this becomes the case, ensuring that ANTS screencasts are suitable for handheld devices has become an important objective of the project. But meeting this and other objectives means that the project must first find ways to take advantage of emerging technologies, and second, address several ongoing challenges.

Moving ANTS and information literacy beyond Library 2.0: opportunities and challenges

Five years of building infrastructure, talking to colleagues and both evaluating and responding to the challenge of creating point-of-need content have required the ANTS team to continuously assess where information consumers are today and how best to serve them. It is an unending debate related to file standards, dramatic changes in technology, changes in user preferences and the need for a professional re-evaluation of how librarians look at serving their users – including any institutional or personal policies or attitudes that may get in the way of new ways of collaborating. This has led the project to identify ongoing opportunities and challenges associated with the objective of providing point-of-need instruction via collaborative projects such as ANTS.

Challenges

Over the course of this paper, several challenges associated with providing libraries with the ability to reach and teach have been lightly touched upon. The one repeatedly discussed is the need for any project to adapt to change, with limited resources. In particular, the ANTS project is entirely volunteer driven, with a minimal operating budget. This shoestring budget requires the project to utilize several sponsored repositories (Screencast.com and DSpace) and an inexpensive cloud site (BLIP.TV) in order to meet all its needs. While all have been good choices, overseeing them is time consuming and the cloud sites - BLIP.TV in particular - have a tendency to 'update' their product with little advance warning, resulting in sudden changes to their offerings.

Overseeing these sites has been challenging, as the ANTS volunteers are continually assessing how best to adapt to changes at them - and this would not be the case if ANTS had the resources to sponsor a site that had the file conversion, file sharing, embedding, syndication, notification and communication infrastructure of our various sites. However, one might also conclude that some cloud site changes - such as YouTube's decision to convert files to Web M - have been very positive. This leaves the project in a precarious position where, firstly, it must continually evaluate the cost/benefit of going with dynamic commercial sites versus stable institutional sites, and secondly, it will require continuous growth in the number of volunteers if the project wishes to address additional challenges - such as providing access to multiple file types.

Another major challenge that the project has identified is the need to address personal and institutional policies, directives and beliefs related to collaborative screencasting. There are several that impact on a librarian's ability or willingness to participate.

One intellectual property issue about which the project hears comments relates to actual ownership of content. Some librarians have indicated that they cannot sign a Creative Commons Licence because they do not own their intellectual property: their institution owns it. This is unfortunate because institutions of higher education - struggling to provide services - are net beneficiaries if librarians and faculty have the authority to make their content openly available. OER provides students with easy access to useful educational content and inexpensive textbooks that reduce the student debt load. Open content used by people outside of academia serves to promote awareness of the work occurring in higher education, thereby informing the general public of the importance of these institutions.

Another intellectual property issue of concern is whether or not individuals can make screencasts of a database search. In particular, many librarians have been told that it is forbidden; that it violates copyright law and would incur the wrath of vendors. ANTS has repeatedly stated that a short screen capture (e.g. two or three citations) of a specific set of results, from a specific search, at a specific point in time, does not threaten a vendor's product and in fact works to market it for them. This is why ANTS has yet to hear any complaint from any vendor and can see a need for restrictions only if a screencast were to display a complete, copyright-protected artistic work – like a painting or a poem.

One last restriction on participation in collaborative screencasting relates to one's approach to screencasts as a whole. In particular, the profession is in the midst of a debate related to the value of creating screencasts 'on the fly' in order to quickly respond to users' needs (Brown-Sica, Sobel and Pan, 2009, 90) – or whether it is better to devote time and energy to creating them based on a desire to see highly polished, professional content. Those on the 'I can quickly create and dispose of content' side frequently see no value in collaborative screencasting because they see themselves as having sufficient time to provide content. Those who feel that educational videos should be constructed around important instructional design and pedagogical concepts (Mestre et al., 2011, 246–8; Oud, 2009) – and then tested for effectiveness (Mestre et al., 2011, 238–9; Oehrli et al., 2011, 129, 135; Lindsay et al., 2006, 444) – understand that developing effective screencasts takes time (Oehrli et al., 2011, 135) and hence they are more likely to be open to the idea that the only way to produce enough quality learning objects is via collaboration – provided that they value (i.e. trust) the content created by their fellow professionals.

While there is definitely a role for quick screencasts (i.e. ones that quickly show people how to perform a simple task), research in the field of cognitive psychology indicates that poorly designed multimedia learning objects can overload working memory, split viewers' attention, or include extraneous information that detracts from learning (i.e. confuses learners). However, well-designed multimedia learning objects that include narration (processed in the verbal memory system) and graphics (processed in the visual system) enable people to process more information and lead to better learning than if a single system (i.e. visual or verbal) is used on its own (Mayer, 1997, 8, 17; Mayer, 1999; Kalyuga, Chandler and Sweller, 1999, 368; Atkinson, 2002, 426). This research demonstrates that multimedia can be an effective educational tool, but, in order for it to be so, multimedia learning objects need to incorporate a wide range of instructional design concepts. In particular, content should be short, modular, well sequenced and pedagogical; it should focus on a few main points, use narration with graphics (but no onscreen text) and direct viewers' attention to relevant points/information. Content incorporating these and other important instructional design techniques facilitates learning because it ensures that appropriate information is provided in context and that the content does not overwhelm viewers. Most of these concepts have been integrated into 'ANTS Guidelines for Tutorial Development', along with concepts that work to make learning objects useful across institutions. However, these principles have yet to become widely recognized, accepted and implemented by those tasked with the creation of screencasts in libraries (Mestre et al., 2011, 250), meaning that there is currently no professional standard or established best practice that works to encourage trust in others' work and collaboration (deemed as needed, due to the time required to produce good screencasts). But the winds of change appear to favour best practice, as the Association of College and Research Libraries itself has turned its attention to this issue,[13] and in a study on how librarians design screencasts many respondents voiced the need for standards or best practice (Mestre et al., 2011, 248).

Opportunities

Just as there are several challenges associated with the move towards collaborative screencasting, there are also several opportunities. Indeed, one could not operate a volunteer-based project like ANTS if its participants did not see the promise.

One opportunity that ANTS does have relates to how librarians view open content. Many in the profession have been strong, vocal advocates for Open Access and are starting to become cognizant of its curriculum equivalent: Open Educational Resources. Given these values, it is reasonable to surmise that, as awareness of OER increases, there should be a growing appreciation of OER projects like ANTS.

Necessity is a second opportunity that collaborative projects such as ANTS have in their favour. Most librarians recognize the need for effective, useful, point-of-need instruction that assists people with a wide array of information literacy skills. Those in cash-strapped institutions also recognize that there is no way that they can create and maintain enough point-of-need educational resources on their own. That being the case, inter-institutional collaborative development of OERs offers libraries an economically feasible means of providing these educational tools: ANTS provides librarians with all the infrastructure they need to rationalize development, share files and support point-of-need content.

A third opportunity afforded to ANTS has been the introduction of HTML 5 in conjunction with file conversions occurring at our various sites. At various times our sites have provided ANTS with access to MPEG 4, WEB M, and OGG

Vorbis files, the three file types that can be used in conjunction with HTML 5 coding to seamlessly stream videos to people regardless of the device or browser used to access them (Pilgrim, 2011). Should ANTS wish to provide people with access to all three file types, the only file it would need to create would be the OGG Vorbis one. If the project could find the human resources needed to create these files and ensure that all OGG, MPEG 4 and Web M files are openly available (by using Screencast.com to house them), the project could provide all the files needed to seamlessly stream high-resolution videos (in the case of MPEG 4 and Web M files) to viewers, who would no longer need to bother with downloading plug-ins and would be able to view videos on some of the smallest screens. Given the absence of an interoperable, high-quality video standard, the provision of these files would be an important service to ANTS contributors. Consequently, ANTS is looking into whether it could support such an initiative.

The last opportunity that works in favour of the ANTS project is its willingness to bring in new people and trust them with the required work. In 2007 and 2010 we brought in people to support work at our various sites. Also in 2010, Regional Representatives were introduced into the ANTS project. These volunteers were tasked with creating an awareness of the project in their region, instructing their fellow professionals in how to create screencasts and serving as regional contacts for screencasters. Their organization is modelled on LINUX User Groups, which encourage IT professionals to get involved with Open Source software via their local interest groups. These ANTS Representatives have created poster sessions and have been accepted to speak at regional conferences. Presently, this initiative is in its infancy and needs many more representatives, but, as it grows, their advocacy and support should work to increase awareness of the value of collaborative screencasting, OERs and the facilitation role that ANTS plays.

Conclusion

Information literacy in today's world is a complex undertaking requiring libraries to be present with instruction wherever their users are – and whenever they need it. Multimedia learning objects – located on internet brand sites, library sites, institutional course sites, institutional brand sites, etc. – are one means of providing this, using a popular medium. The literature associated with multimedia learning indicates that effective educational resources need to be designed around important instructional design techniques, and every screencaster knows that this takes time. ANTS infrastructure supports collaborative development of quality learning objects and helps to ensure that content is highly visible, and its file resolution/file size makes for videos that work well on mobile devices. There are still many challenges, but ultimately the initiatives undertaken by the project are promising and could afford libraries the opportunity to reach and teach citizens in this dispersed, mobile world.

Notes

1   http://ants.wetpaint.com/page/About+the+ANTS+Project.
2   http://ants.wetpaint.com/page/Online+Resources+Identified+for+Animated+
     Tutorial+Development
     or
     http://ants.wetpaint.com/page/Information+Literacy+Tutorials+Identified+for
     +Development.
3   www.ucalgary.ca/lib-old/libcon/viewlets/dsub2.html,
     www.screencast.com/users/ANTS/folders/Database+Tutorials/media/
     49ee3fba-173b-45ec-8e13-1333bcc7ccf9,
     http://buckrambeats.com/ANTS/ANTS_optimization1_demo.htm.
4   www.archive.org/search.php?query=antssite+AND+mediatype%3Amovies.
5   www.facebook.com/pages/LION-Library-Information-literacy-Online-
     Network/26633613400?ref=ts.
6   www.youtube.com/user/1LIONTV.
7   http://youtube-global.blogspot.com/2011/04/mmm-mmm-good-youtube-videos-
     now-served.html.
8   www.channels.com/feeds/17259#/feeds/17259.
9   www.casttv.com/video/3jbb04h/academic-search-complete-ebscohost-timesavers-
     video.
10   www.mefeedia.com/feeds/211973/lion-library-information-literacy-online-network.
11   http://webcat.camosun.bc.ca/cinahl-alert/cinahl-alert.html,
     http://blip.tv/LIONTV/database-thesauri-4424664.
12   http://jasonfleming73.wordpress.com/2010/11/03/embedding-tutorials-into-
     physical-objects/.
13   http://wikis.ala.org/acrl/index.php/Online_Learning_Toolkit.

References

Atkinson, R. K. (2002) Optimizing Learning from Examples Using Animated Pedagogical Agents, *Journal of Educational Psychology*, **94** (2), 416–27.
Brown-Sica, M., Sobel, K. and Pan, D. (2009) Learning for All: teaching students, faculty,

and staff with screencasting, *Public Services Quarterly*, **5** (2), 81-97.

Kalyuga, S., Chandler, P. and Sweller, J. (1999) Managing Split-attention and Redundancy in Multimedia Instruction, *Applied Cognitive Psychology*, **13** (4), 351-71.

Lindsay, E. B., Cummings, L., Johnson, C. M. and Scales, B. J. (2006) If You Build It Will They Learn? Assessing online information literacy tutorials, *College and Research Libraries*, **67** (5), 429-45.

Mayer, R. E. (1997) Multimedia Learning: are we asking the right questions? *Educational Psychologist*, **32** (1), 1-19.

Mayer, R. E. (1999) Multimedia Aids to Problem-solving Transfer, *International Journal of Educational Research*, **31** (7), 611-23.

Mestre, L., Baures, L., Niedbala, M., Bishop, C., Cantrell, S., Perez, A. and Silfen, K. (2011) Learning Objects as Tools for Teaching Information Literacy Online: a survey of librarian usage, *College & Research Libraries*, **72** (3), 236-52.

Oehrli, J. A., Piacentine, J., Peters, A., and Nanamaker, B. (2011) Do Screencasts Really Work? Assessing student learning through instructional screencasts, *A Declaration of Interdependence: ACRL 2011 Conference Proceedings*, Philadelphia, Pennsylvania, 127, www.ala.org/ala/mgrps/divs/acrl/events/national/2011/ papers/do_screencasts_work.pdf.

Oud, J. (2009) Guidelines for Effective Online Instruction Using Multimedia Screencasts, *Reference Services Review*, **37** (2), 164-77.

Pew Internet and American Life Project (2010) *The State of Online Video*, Washington, DC: Pew Research Center.

Pilgrim, M. (2011) *Video on the Web: diving into HTML5*, http://diveintohtml5.org/video.html.

Chapter 13
Informed cyberlearning: a case study

Hilary Hughes

Introduction

Throughout, this book highlights the potential of Web 2.0 to enhance information use and learning for personal, social and professional well-being. This cyberlearning case study demonstrates the application of Web 2.0 in the mainstream higher education curriculum, whilst providing an in-practice example of informed learning, the pedagogical construct introduced in Chapter 6. The case study features the learning experiences and creative outcomes of postgraduate cyberlearning students at Queensland University of Technology in 2011. As informed learners, the students learned simultaneously about the theory and practice of cyberlearning by carrying out a virtual team project. This involved collaboratively researching a topical issue, as well as exploring and applying Web 2.0 media. To support the informed learning of their peers, they created online resources which both convey disciplinary knowledge and showcase the educational potential of Web 2.0.

Queensland University of Technology (QUT) is based in Brisbane, Australia. It prides itself on being 'A university for the real world' with a commitment to '[p]rovide high-quality, learning-centred environments that capitalize on both physical and virtual innovations' (QUT, 2011, 4). While many of QUT's programmes are offered on-campus, an increasing number are offered in blended or completely online modes. To varying degrees, learning is mediated via online technologies, both in 'formal' educational spaces such as QUT's Blackboard learning management system and subscription databases, and in the 'informal' domains of Web 2.0. The cyberlearning unit of study is fully online and enables students to explore, apply and evaluate multiple options for learning and teaching. Students are encouraged to move constantly between formal and informal online environments. In this way they gain nuanced understandings about informed learning for Web 2.0 and beyond.

Overview of CLN601 Cyberlearning

CLN601 Cyberlearning is a fully online unit of study in QUT's Master of Education (Teacher-Librarianship) degree programme. Each year the unit attracts 60-70 students, who are spread around Australia, and a few from abroad. While it is a core unit in the Teacher-Librarianship study area, CLN601 is also a popular elective across the general Master of Education and Master of TESOL programmes and it attracts some students from Master of Information Technology (Library and Information Science). Most students are practising primary or high school teachers, some are from the vocational or higher education sectors and a few are workplace educators, librarians or IT professionals. So the student group is varied in terms of educational and professional backgrounds. Students also come to this unit with varying degrees of expertise and confidence in using online technologies. Most are comfortable using popular Web 2.0 tools, while a few have well developed IT skills. For each individual, whether an online novice or a relative expert, this unit aims to offer an opportunity to extend their online horizons, on the basis that the rapidly changing online environment ensures that there's always something new to explore.

In the context of this unit of study, *cyberlearning* implies learning in online environments mediated by online technologies. The unit allows students, as informed learners, to experience cyberlearning and the online environment in many different ways. It offers them a variety of online learning activities and resources via the QUT network and the wider internet. The unit's Blackboard (virtual learning environment) site represents the students' home base or virtual campus, which offers selected study materials, communication with students and teachers, and collaborative tools and spaces. It is also a jumping-off point to the wider online universe of Web 2.0 media. Students can experience both the relative safety and reliability of Blackboard and the chaos and serendipity of Web 2.0. In addition, they gain varying perspectives of cyberlearning as members of an online learning community, as members of smaller virtual teams and as independent learners.

For the first three weeks of the semester, learning activities take place within Blackboard, in order to build a cohesive community of cyberlearners and allow students to become familiar with learning in an online environment. For many, this is their first semester after a long break from study, and some have limited knowledge of online tools and terminology and experience various anxieties. So, using standard Blackboard tools, the students are encouraged to connect with each other via online tutorials, introductory blogs and a discussion forum, thus developing familiarity and confidence with online tools and techniques in a 'safe' environment. For example, to break the ice and initiate thinking about cyberlearning, students are invited to share via a class blog 'a song title, book title or movie title that describes how you think/feel about cyberlearning and/or the online world; and tell us why you chose that title'. In 2011 their responses evoked a range of feelings, including: 'Brave new world', 'One step at a time', 'Avatar', 'Labyrinth', 'Inception', 'Asylum', 'The climb' and 'I will survive'. One student commented:

> I feel a little like Dr Who, except with a 'virtual' TARDIS. I expect to be exploring brand new (cyber) worlds, and (virtual) realities, but without a single specific destination. I'm looking forward to the journey and the excitement, and to the people I meet on the way.
>
> (Bernadette Power, *Who's Who* blog)

Whole-class web-based tutorials via Elluminate (synchronous meeting software) continue throughout the semester in order to maintain the sense of community. However, from Week 4 the students begin to work in small virtual teams and the context shifts from Blackboard to Web 2.0 as they co-create online learning resources using Web 2.0 media (as described in the following section). During the final weeks of the semester (Weeks 10–13) the students work independently as cyberlearning critics and designers, evaluating other teams' resources and then applying their learning about cyberlearning theory, resources and practices to designing a cyberlearning experience that addresses a particular learning need (formal or informal).

Experiencing informed learning in the cyberlearning unit

The cyberlearning unit incorporates informed learning principles (Bruce, 2008; see also Chapter 6 of this book). Web 2.0 provides the environment and tools for engaging with information to learn. The students learn about cyberlearning as a subject with a particular body of theory and practice relating to the pedagogy and curriculum of online learning. Simultaneously, they develop an array of information-using practices that will not only be applicable to this unit or degree programme, but may also enhance their personal, academic and professional learning outcomes. As informed learners, the students are encouraged to engage in continuous reflection (Bruce, 2008; Hughes, 2008; Moon, 2004) on their information use and learning, with a focus on critical incidents (turning points in learning) that they experience during the unit.

The virtual team project at the heart of the unit enables students to experience informed cyberlearning in varying ways as researchers, designers, resource creators and critics. Table 13.1 relates different informed learning experiences to particular aspects of the project, and elaborates further the idea of informed learning for Web 2.0 that was presented in Chapter 6.

E-moderating the virtual team

In terms of the project's learning objectives, the process of virtual teamwork is as important as the end product. The students are required to participate actively in all aspects of forming and managing their virtual team. In particular, they each take a turn as team leader or e-moderator.

Salmon's (2003) model of e-moderation guides the practical implementation of both the whole unit and the virtual team project. This five-step model supports a learning process where students gradually and explicitly: develop familiarity and confidence in the online learning environment; establish their online identities and then interact with other students in the CLN601 Cyberlearning community; exchange information and experiences online; develop common understandings and engage in collaborative online activities; explore further potential of the online environment and tools by integrating them into further learning and teaching contexts and reflecting on their informed learning goals, processes, outcomes and future possibilities. Salmon's model places emphasis on the role of the e-moderator as an educator–guide who supports the development of an online learning environment that fosters interaction, exploration and collaboration among learners.

The cyberlearning virtual team project

The virtual team project is the focus of learning and assessment in the cyberlearning unit through Weeks 3–10 of the semester. It aims to give students first-hand experience of online collaboration as well as an opportunity to explore and create online learning resources. In virtual teams, students are required to plan, research, develop and present an online learning resource on a current cyberlearning topic for adult learner-educators. Thus, students use Web

Table 13.1 Experiences of informed cyberlearners in the virtual team project	
Experiences of informed learning	**Experiences of informed learners in the virtual team project ~ collaboratively ...**
1. Information awareness	Scanning, exploring and sharing different online information sources ~ planning the online learning resource and selecting a suitable Web 2.0 platform for an online learning resource
2. Sources	Sourcing information of all kinds (including text, graphics, audio and video) in Web 2.0 and other online environments whilst ~ selecting and researching a topical cyberlearning issue
3. Process	Engaging with Web 2.0 and other digital media to learn through ~ locating, evaluating and selecting information about the topic of the online learning resource; also through exploring and evaluating the content and appropriate presentation of other teams' online resources
4. Control	Organizing information in Web 2.0 and other online environments when ~ sharing, recording and saving information and materials for the online resource; also when documenting virtual team decisions and monitoring progress
5. Knowledge construction	Developing personal understandings of knowledge domains, via Web 2.0 and digital environments, through critical and creative thinking when ~ using selected information to develop the content and format of the online learning resource; also when engaging with other teams' online resources
6. Knowledge extension	Creating and communicating new knowledge in Web 2.0 and online environments, innovating, and creating new insights and new solutions to problems as outcomes of learning activities and assessment by ~ creating and publishing an online learning resource that contains informative original content and supports interactive learning; also when interacting with other teams' resources to learn, providing feedback via an evaluative survey
7. Wisdom	Using information wisely and ethically in Web 2.0 and other online environments, applying knowledge developed to further social and educational well-being by ~ modelling ethical use of information and providing a quality online resource that enhances colleagues' learning and teaching; also by evaluating their own contribution to the virtual team and reflecting on virtual team experience with a view to enhancing their own future learning and practice

2.0 media in multiple ways, which include forming and organizing their teams, communicating and monitoring progress, researching topics, sharing information, publishing new knowledge, fostering informed learning and teaching.

The project has an authentic purpose and audience: the students are operating as cyberlearners and cybereducators when developing an online resource that they could later use or adapt in their professional teaching context. As one 2011 student commented:

> Our resource could be an opportunity for teachers to grab ideas that others have tried and have worked [on] ... [in order] to collaborate virtually – so that we no longer have to work in a bubble. I'm thinking of bringing our resource into my school, sharing [it] and inviting teachers to contribute as they discover a practical application of technology in their classrooms.
>
> (Antonietta Neighbour, Reflection)

The students are advised that, in terms of learning and assessment outcomes, the process of virtual teamwork and resource development is as important as the product itself. In addition, the emphasis is on effective application of Web 2.0 media to support learning, rather than on a display of technical wizardry. For reasons of equity, students must use freely available Web 2.0 tools, which avoids the need for expensive software (e.g. Dreamweaver), specialist skills (e.g. web design) or access to particular servers. While advanced IT skills are not required, students are encouraged to share any expertise they have with team members.

Each team member takes a turn as team e-moderator (Salmon, 2003) for one week, in order both to give each student experience of leading a virtual team, and to spread the workload and responsibility fairly between everyone. Students generally report positive e-moderation experiences, for example:

> It was what happened when each different team member took on their role as e-moderator that affected me. It was like each member got a boost of confidence as they took their turn. The members who had been a bit quieter at the start, once they had e-moderated, seemed to find their voice. The reason behind everyone taking turns at e-moderating became so much clearer to me than [its] just being a way of sharing the role. I could see it was a wonderful way of ensuring all team members not only got to feel what it is like to take on the role of the e-moderator but that it also ensures that each team member's voice is heard. In this way, it has the potential to create confidence in others.
>
> (Michelle Ferguson, Reflection)

Since students often express reservations or anxieties about teamwork, especially in the online environment, as the educator I take particular care with the team formation process. In Week 3 students do a variety of web-based quizzes in order to self-assess their teamwork strengths, ICT capabilities and learning preferences (for example: Birmingham City Council, 2011; London Metropolitan University, n.d.; Solomon and Felder, n.d.). Then, in an online survey they: summarize the results, as well as previous evaluations such as Myers-Briggs Personality Type Indicator; possibly volunteer to be their team's first e-moderator; and indicate any people whom they would (or would not) prefer to work with. Aiming to create productive team conditions, I take all this information into consideration when allocating people to teams. As far as possible, I spread people with differing preferences, strengths and limitations between the teams, in particular allocating at least one person with average or advanced ICT capabilities to each team. While team sizes vary, experience over several years shows the optimum to be five members: any more, and online communication and organization seems to become unwieldy; any fewer, and it is difficult to sufficiently develop the resource in the allocated time. Also, starting with five team members allows for re-scoping of the project if one or two people withdraw from a team. To initiate the team process, I nominate the first week's e-moderator, who, where possible, is a volunteer. This approach to team formation is by no means a perfect science and some teams gel better than others. However, this attention to creating congenial team conditions is generally beneficial, as one student comments:

> Together, we had a balance of interests and teamwork skills. As such, overcoming
> differences in location and teaching contexts was not an issue. ... Overall, it was the
> qualities of patience, trust and generosity that defined our team experience.
> Furthermore, the positivity that pulled us out of any doubt and defused potentially
> stressful technological issues allowed us to arrive at a position of pride in our work.
> I have learned that the skills needed to create an online resource are pointless if the
> skills in working with other people have not been developed. Harmonious
> collaboration will not only improve the quality of the resource, it will improve one's
> understanding of how people will use the resource.
>
> (Greg Howes, Reflection)

Once the virtual teams have been allocated, members have six weeks in which to organize themselves, research a topic, create an online resource and make it available to the whole CLN601 community by the due date. Each team is required to determine its topic and which online tools and resources to use, the only provisos being that the online resource should focus on a current cyberlearning issue, address an intended audience of adult cyberlearners (fellow students and professional colleagues), and be interactive and demonstrate the potential of online learning.

The teams have access to a considerable array of support materials on the unit's Blackboard site, including suggested weekly timelines and guidelines for e-moderators. The teams are expected to be self-managing, but can consult me, as team adviser, whenever necessary. Collaboratively, the virtual team members need to determine appropriate means of communication and to manage the project using online media of their choice. Most use a combination of standard Blackboard tools, including Elluminate web-based conferencing, and Web 2.0 media such as e-mail, Skype, a blog or wiki, or Facebook.

The online resources have to be ready for all CLN601 students to access by Sunday afternoon of Week 9. In Week 10 students independently explore other teams' online resources. This enables them to further extend their knowledge of cyberlearning theory and practices. Then, as cyberlearning critics, they evaluate two other online resources by completing an online survey that asks them to provide commendations and recommendations to the creating teams. (Once the projects have been marked, I make the students' feedback available to the respective teams.)

Assessment of the virtual team project has two main elements:

(a) Whole team assessment: assessment of the quality and originality of the online resource, with regard to application of cyberlearning principles, content, interface and suitability to learners' needs and context.

(b) Individual assessment: evaluation of two online resources; self-assessment with evidence of own contribution to virtual teamwork; reflection on virtual team experience, based around two of three critical incidents (positive or negative), discussing the insights they have gained about virtual team processes and outcomes, and how they might apply these insights to enhance their virtual teamwork in future learning or professional contexts.

Samples of online learning resources created by 2011 cyberlearning teams

The vitality of the unit stems from students' willingness to share and experiment with online learning approaches. Collaboratively, they create online resources that both reflect their own learning about a topical issue and support the learning of their peers. The most effective online resources present information in an engaging and well researched manner, stimulate the exchange of ideas and enable self-assessment. Over the last few years the virtual teams' resources have included blogs, wikis, Nings, Voicethread, Glogster, Joomla, Prezi and Animoto, often with built-in quizzes, polls, links to videos and games, newsletters, FAQs and discussion forums. In 2011 there were 13 teams. The four online resources featured in Figure 13.1 present a representative sample of the quality and variety of their work with regard to subject coverage and application of Web 2.0 media.

Mobilised **by Team A**
Mobilised is an engaging, professional-looking online resource, created using Weebly website building software. It enables educators to explore the use of mobile devices for teaching and learning in the primary (P–7) classroom. The unifying theme 'get, set, go' captures the spirit of mobile learning. The resource both informs about the topic, and showcases the potential of a very wide range of cyberlearning resources and practices, to help teachers make informed decisions. It encourages shared learning through blog, online noteboard and suggested resources.
URL: http://mobilised.weebly.com/
Promotional video: http://fabfive11.glogster.com/glog-4853/

Educators' Lounge **by Team D**
Educators' Lounge is an innovative and practical one-stop information aggregator for busy educators. The resource offers quality content in a variety of forms (texts, web links, images, videos) and handy desktop tools (calendar, clock). A range of interactive elements enable communication (though forums, RSS and the opportunity to construct a personal learning network (PLN). As an additional bonus, the embedded *Educator's Armchair* blog encourages informal interactions and information sharing.
URL: http://protopage.com/educatorslounge (close the advertisement on first visit)

Techinfoliteracy **by Team G**
Techinfoliteracy uses the Wikispaces format effectively both to support learning about information literacy and to demonstrate the potential of wikis (and a range of other Web 2.0 resources) to support innovative pedagogy. The interface is visually appealing and user friendly. It includes a variety of formats (text, graphics, videos) and enables interactive learning through a variety of polls, quizzes, discussion forum etc. Notably, it was created by a team of three, challenged by the withdrawal of two members.
URL: http://techinfoliteracy.wikispaces.com/Home

The 21st Century Library **by Team N**
An informative resource that presents the role of the school library, in particular with regard to promoting reading in online environments. It makes good use of Yola website-building software to describe and evaluate well-chosen Web 2.0 resources. It encourages a high level of interactivity. The resource is cohesively structured and user friendly, with appealing humorous touches.
URL: http://the21stcenturylibrary.yolasite.com

Figure 13.1 Examples of online learning resources created by 2011 cyberlearning teams

Reviewing the experiences of informed cyberlearners in the virtual team project

As outlined above, the virtual team project enables students to learn about cyberlearning as a subject, in terms of information environments, concepts and practices, and simultaneously to learn how to use cyberlearning resources and tools to support their learning and teaching. In the course of the project the students gain a richly productive experience of all seven faces of informed learning (Bruce, 2008). While this cyberlearning case study relates to a postgraduate unit of study within Education, the framework shown above in Table 13.1 could be applied to differing higher education contexts. As mentioned in Chapter 6, informed learning builds on collaborative partnerships between information professionals and academic teachers.

So where is the role of librarians in informed cyberlearning? Potentially everywhere! Drawing on individual strengths, they might contribute as educators, informed learning role modellers and disciplinary experts. They might collaborate with academic teachers in the development and implementation of curricula that incorporate informed learning principles; and they might act as advisers to virtual teams on project management software, on the critical and creative uses of online information and on collaborative processes. Librarians are ideally positioned to identify and signal connections between emerging technologies and learning opportunities, by modelling innovative uses of Web 2.0 in their interactions with students and educators. For example, they might profile the use of Web 2.0 tools for organizing a cross-disciplinary research project or collaboratively preparing a conference paper. The library website might feature virtual teams' outstanding resources to support others' informed cyberlearning.

Conclusion

The dynamic Web 2.0 environment enables learners to experience informed learning in differing ways. It provides ideal conditions for innovative learning approaches that foster exploration, evaluation, creation, communication and reflection. The relative simplicity of Web 2.0 tools allows learners to focus on learning processes and information practices rather than on technical problems and skills. This comment from a 2011 student encapsulates the transformative potential of informed cyberlearning:

Overall, my understanding of cyberlearning at this point is that it is dynamic, ever changing, far reaching, both global and individualized and something I want to be a part of. It is something that will always have further to go, and have more to learn. It can be the ultimate challenge for lifelong learning, as it will continue and expand well after my lifetime. Cyberlearning is a journey that will require me to follow those learning pathways that will perpetuate in a cycle from discovery and engagement to sharing with others in a truly collaborative way! It makes me feel overwhelmed, excited, daunted, in awe, unbelieving at times, frustrated, very small, confident ... and that is just at the beginning of this journey. I look forward to continuing to feel these emotions as it becomes second nature to rely on cyberlearning as a principal mode of learning!

(Jenny Saggers, Reflection)

Acknowledgements

Sincere thanks to all cyberlearning students who each year make this such a stimulating and rewarding unit; in particular, to the following 2011 students for permission to feature their reflections and online resources:

Team A: Margot Brand, Maria Mead, Filomena Morgante, Kathleen Peasey, Donna Vine.

Team D: Anna Corboy, Gregory Howes, Sarah Scavarelli, Maryann Wasmund-Ford, Jennifer Wilson.

Team G: Taryn Berghuis, Myra Lee, Bernadette Power.

Team N: Theresa Cumming, Aneel Dewan, Francesca Penfold, Kathryn Schravmade, Kerrie Shepherd

Reflections: Michelle Ferguson, Gregory Howes, Antonietta Neighbour, Bernadette Power, Jennifer Saggers.

Note

The featured online resources and reflective comments arose from the students' normal coursework and were not intentionally produced or adapted for this case study. They are reproduced with the students' permission.

References

Birmingham City Council (2011) *Multiple Intelligences*, www.bgfl.org/bgfl/custom/resources_ftp/client_ftp/ks3/ict/multiple_int/what.cfm.

Bruce, C. S. (2008) *Informed Learning*, Chicago: ALA College and Research Libraries.

Hughes, H. (2008) Incidents for Reflection in Research. In *5th International Lifelong Learning Conference*, 16–19 June, Yeppoon, Queensland, http://eprints.qut.edu.au/17586/.

London Metropolitan University (n.d.) Team Roles, http://learning.londonmet.ac.uk/bssmquickstart/r_teamroles.htm (click on the graph to start the quiz).

Moon, J. A. (2004) *A Handbook of Reflective and Experiential Learning: theory and practice*, RoutledgeFalmer.

QUT (Queensland University of Technology) (2011) *Blueprint 3: 2011–2016*,. Brisbane: QUT, www.qut.edu.au/about/university/pdf/qut-blueprint-2011-20110411.pdf.

Salmon, G. (2003) *E-moderating: the key to teaching and learning online*, 2nd edn, RoutledgeFalmer.

Solomon, B. A. and Felder, R. M. (n.d.) Index of Learning Styles Questionnaire, North Carolina State University, www.engr.ncsu.edu/learningstyles/ilsweb.html.

Chapter 14

An online course on social media for student librarians: teaching the information skills and literacies of social media

Dean Giustini

Introduction

> [W]eb 2.0 tools such as blogs, wikis and social networking sites ... have become
> important tools for equipping new library and information science (LIS)
> graduates with the competencies and skills that fit with the dynamic, changing
> information market.
>
> (Al-Daihani, 2010)

This chapter describes the development of a new online course on social media offered by the School of Library, Archival and Information Studies (SLAIS) at the University of British Columbia in Vancouver, Canada. The creation of a course on an information and communication technology (ICT) topic involves consideration of many theoretical, practical and structural matters, and it requires perseverance on the part of instructors with regard to devising content. Social media, and how library and information professionals use them to serve users, is a constantly shifting domain. The field itself is incredibly volatile. A few social media tools seem stable enough (think of Facebook, Wikipedia or Twitter), but generally speaking, new tools appear (and disappear) with regularity. Not surprisingly, it complicates the teaching of a subject when there is a lack of evidence and the components making up the whole landscape shift regularly. As a set of tools for learning, technology is rarely enough to ensure that learning will take place (Bawden et al., 2007). On the contrary, in teaching the use of specific tools, the instructor should emphasize skills and literacies over discrete tasks (Secker, 2008; Giustini, 2008).

And so it is with social media. The two learning objectives that arose repeatedly in the development of this course were: 1) the importance of exposing students to new digital formats and channels of information on social networking sites; and 2) critiquing the use of social networking tools in the provision of information services. In addition, the course makes an effort to focus attention on assessing the quality, accuracy and relevance of information found through social media. Fortunately, developing content is an iterative, dynamic process – and with each new offering, the instructor has a chance to 'get it right'. My chapter is a reflection on these scholarly matters and on what I have learned from teaching LIS students about social technologies.

Discussion of new social literacies

[A] digitally literate citizen knows how to create and publish video and images, create and run a blog, share links to meaningful and innovative content, edit multimedia files and documents, build profiles appropriately on social networking sites and adapt and incorporate new communications technologies into daily life.

(Digital Literacy in Canada, 2010)

One of the goals of the information professions is to contribute to the creation of a literate populace (Aharony, 2008). In the digital age, access to information should be a fundamental and democratic right. In the Alexandria proclamation of 2005 (IFLA, 2005), information literacy (IL) is positioned at the core of learning, as it 'empowers people in all walks of life to seek, evaluate, use and create information effectively to achieve their personal, social, occupational and educational goals. It is a basic human right in a digital world and promotes social inclusion of all nations.' Today, some types of learning are virtually impossible without proper access to the internet. Global citizens who want to attain desirable IL skills over the internet cannot do so for a myriad of reasons. In some countries with high internet use, citizens are being denied the right to access certain tools. The phenomenon of the digital media divide or lack of reliable access to the web is one thing – but prohibiting use of Twitter, Facebook and YouTube for social and political reasons is a policy that all democratic leaders should oppose.

Librarians are familiar with the classic definition of IL as 'the ability to access, evaluate, organize, and use information'; many consider it a core competency for the 21st century (Godwin and Parker, 2008). However, the basics of IL are learned by 'negotiating increasingly complex social and technological environments' (Lloyd, 2010). In the UK, JISC (Joint Information Systems Committee) opts to use the term 'i-skills', which are skills 'to identify, assess, retrieve, evaluate, adapt, organize and communicate information within an iterative context of review and reflection'. The Association of College and Research Libraries covers similar ground by listing skills along Bloom's Taxonomy – from lower- to higher-order skills. Lower-order skills may involve the use of an online index to find an article, whereas higher-order skills may involve synthesizing content in order to solve information problems. The Presidential Committee on Information Literacy of the American Library Association reaffirms the importance of 'i' skills, stating that 'information literacy is a survival skill in the information age'.

These definitions, though helpful, do not account for the digital skills acquired through daily use of the social web. The use of blogs, wikis and social networking sites (SNSs) requires an ability to find and use, critique and create, new forms of media. In a sense, these are meta-literacies, where multiple media, platforms and texts are used to convey knowledge. In a course on social media, these meta-skills and literacies are ripe for exploration (Virkus, 2008). In a broader sense, a course focused on people and digital communication should also examine whether newer forms of mass communication are similar (or dissimilar) to those of a previous generation. Further, can the topic be historicized – in other words, situated historically? Can we, by doing so, lend social media an air of legitimacy in the academy?

Of course, the literacies needed for the digital era are demonstrably different from those of the print era. Social media extend our senses and perceptions well beyond print literacy. They move us towards multimedia navigation and immersive interactions in an exploration of mass social culture. While many of the skills needed to operate in a networked environment which the social web has introduced are not new, many in fact are. As Martin suggests, literacy in this new age moves us towards an 'awareness, attitude and ability to appropriately use digital tools and facilities to identify, access, manage, integrate, evaluate, analyze and synthesize digital resources, construct new knowledge, create media expressions and communicate with others in the context of specific life situations, in order to enable constructive social action; and to reflect upon this process' (Martin, 2009, 5). The fascination, for some, is how we shape and are shaped by these social media tools.

Collaboration as literacy

The main idea behind social media is fostering collaboration and knowledge creation. The capacity to engage with others and develop a digital identity in relevant scholarly communities is critical. This notion builds on the idea of communities of practice (CoP), a term used by cognitive anthropologists to describe groups of people who have a common set of practices and tools that they use to achieve their goals (Lave and Wenger, 1991; Wenger, 1998). Lave and Wenger say that a CoP evolves organically, due to the interest members take in ideas that comprise their discipline. Through a process of sharing, a CoP forms to benefit all members (Lave and Wenger, 1991). The principles of a CoP can also be applied digitally where social media such as blogs, wikis and Web 2.0 tools are widely used to exchange ideas and learn (Wenger et al., 2009).

Making sense of and forming new connections are critical IL skills for the 21st century. It seems safe to assume that learning in the digital age is in part a move away from learning in isolation. Given the different forms of mass communication using social media, should these skills be cultivated by today's knowledge workers? Accordingly, Canadian academic George Siemens says that 'we derive our competence ... from forming connections [where] chaos is a new reality for knowledge workers ... unlike constructivism, which states that learners foster understanding by meaning-making ... chaos states that the meaning exists – the learner's challenge is to recognize the patterns which appear to be hidden' (Siemens, 2005).

A recurring issue for online teachers is how to encourage the kinds of collaboration that seem so organic and natural in the physical classroom. Ironically, despite its collaborative potential, online learning may even emphasize our 'one-ness'. Koontz (2006) suggests that instructors can use online courses to inspire, motivate and encourage learners to meet in person (see your peers via Skype or conferencing tools!). Moreover, the design of web-based learning should aim for a blend of online and offline activities so as to ensure that participants are not fixated on the computer screen.

Theoretical framework

A basic principle of teaching adults is that each learner has extensive life experience to draw upon which allows an open dialogue with the instructor ... based on his or her experience, the acquisition of new skills, knowledge and abilities will be in relation to the [learner's] experience levels.

(Knowles, 1970)

It is important to develop a sound teaching approach suitable for adult learners when your course implies acquiring new knowledge over specific skills. For a theoretical framework, I developed a hybrid model consisting of major learning theories of the 20th century. The names that informed my approach included John Dewey (1919), adult learning theorist Malcolm Knowles (1970), constructivist Vygotsky (1978) and situated cognitivists Brown and Duguid (1991). In addition, I drew on connectivism, a participative learning theory developed by Canadian George Siemens (Siemens, 2007). The main principles of connectivism are:

- Experiential learning is a process of connecting 'specialized nodes' of people and groups, ideas, information and digital interfaces.
- The 'capacity to know more is more critical than what is currently known'.
- Fostering and maintaining connections is critical to knowledge generation.
- Metaliteracies are core to the theory of connectivism; decision making is both action and learning; 'choosing what to learn and the meaning of incoming information is seen through the lens of a shifting reality'.
- Connectivist approaches to course design acknowledge the complexities of knowledge management and learning in the digital age. Course facilitators and students can leverage knowledge networks for personal knowledge generation, sharing and collaboration (Siemens, 2005).

An online course presents new ways for students to test their skills. The platform should expose them to new experiences and people, conditions that align well with constructivism (De Jaegher and Di Paolo, 2007). Constructivist ideas are central to the delivery of many online courses because they engage learners in forming their own knowledge. As with social media, participating in that process requires engagement on the part of learners (Hrastinski, 2009). As Von Glasersfeld (1995) suggests, 'knowledge is the result of active learning' and requires self-regulation. The role of the instructor therefore must shift away from transmitting knowledge and towards helping students to learn on their own. Finally, students must see that they are responsible for their own learning and self-management – especially with respect to online codes of conduct, professional integrity and honesty.

The course considers the tensions and risks introduced by open and closed communication spaces. By an open space, I refer to the openness of social media on the open web. By closed, I mean the protected, closed spaces of content management systems where discussions are not public. A related issue with media literacies is whether they should be taught in open or closed spaces. Should the instructor's goal be to teach digital survival skills in the real world, or is it more prudent to protect students from making errors there (if that were indeed possible)? As an instructor in social media, I vacillate on this point. Students have the right to request online privacy even when studying online phenomena. By asking students to blog and tweet publicly, what are my goals? Can these skills be learned privately first? This debate continues to frame my teaching as I revise the curriculum – and I am still unsure about what is optimal.

Of course, the benefit of learning in a closed space is self-evident. In a closed learning space, ideas can be fully questioned by students without fear of censure. Students know that their conversations will be (and forever are) private. In fact, providing an opportunity in private to take whatever tentative steps students need to express their own views is a part of building trust in online classes. Some professional librarians using social media are confused by the discomfort students feel about using social tools publicly. In this course, students are provided with options and permitted to build a digital identity (or request anonymity) as they wish.

Course structure and content

We shape our tools and afterwards our tools shape us.

(McLuhan, 1965)

The course consists of 13 weeks of reading, peer-to-peer sharing and knowledge creation. It is structured in six modules as follows: affordance, participation, collaboration, knowledge creation, information aggregation and immersion. The modules are organized so that the knowledge, skills and abilities that LIS students need in order to use social media effectively are built as blocks, one upon the other. In addition, this reflects the different levels of social media involvement as one becomes more expert in using the technologies fluently.

The course has been delivered several times since 2009 but its content is in a constant state of revision. Some unanswered questions that are explored (and debated by students) pertain to the broader social and ethical issues that are introduced by social media, such as:

- Are social media and other knowledge-making technologies central to the information age and our future as library and information professionals? If so, how? If not, why not?
- Librarians and information professionals are creating and sharing their

knowledge and expertise every day. Through collaboration, will the use of social media result in our field becoming more or less innovative?

- Can social movements such as the Arab Spring be attributed to the use of Facebook, Twitter and other social media? What does it mean to say that social media are 'manifest nodes of democratic power and critical to global democracy'?
- The term Web 2.0 is not very well understood. Is it time to discard the suffix or to use another phrase? Is it even possible to teach the use of social media without talking about the 2.0 suffix? What about other terminologies emanating from Silicon Valley? Should they too be questioned?
- Social media emphasize the importance of trust, security and confidentiality in the digital age. However, do they destabilize traditional views of information dissemination, intellectual property and copyright? In what ways?
- Social media align with the rhetoric of openness, transparency and freedom in democracies - what is the role of librarians in promoting democracy in society?
- The issue of power (or lack thereof) in information organizations is an interesting one for librarians. Can social media help to move us beyond our traditional role to one that is central to business, academia and community?

Student librarian assessment

Each student taking the course is required to develop an electronic portfolio to document their learning. These personal spaces are portals to individual learning and act as a counterpoint to the course's central, managed discussions. Students have the option to select from various platforms for their blogs and can maintain them after the course if they so choose. Students work collaboratively to create a wiki entry on one aspect of using social media in libraries, archives or museums. Topics cover the tools and techniques of Web 2.0; digital pedagogies for librarians; virtual worlds, mobile learning, digital storytelling, screencasting and so on. The course wiki is a platform for cases that are supported by real-life examples from libraries, archives and museums.

The course requires the completion of a major digital project. Students engage in video production and use a myriad of instructional resources. Others work independently and produce learning objects for their organizations. Activities reflect the range of student competencies with ICTs. Synchronous debate using audio or 'in world' discussions in Second Life are considered every time that the course is offered. So far, due to technical limitations, these immersive sessions have been unsuccessful. However, in 2011 we organized presentations online across several time zones and schedules. The online sessions varied in length and guest speakers were invited as required. Simultaneous hands-on instruction was scheduled and fostered a sense of community among students. Because student competencies varied, some hands-on orientation is required to aid students in learning the technical skills required by the course.

Social tools and software used

The primary tools used in the course are a content management system and a course wiki. As social media requires signing up for personal accounts on the open web, students are asked to negotiate a variety of open (or free) and proprietary (or fee-based) tools used. Student librarians select a blogging tool and, because UBC offers an excellent hosted blogging platform (e.g. WordPress), most students use it.[1] The wiki (http://hlwiki.ca) is hosted on a UBC server and uses the same software as is seen on Wikipedia. The wiki contains the course syllabus, glossary and student projects, linking to state-of-the-art entries on social media. Various tools are used to facilitate synchronous learning. Adobe Connect, a proprietary web conferencing tool, is a good tool and relatively inexpensive to use. In one class, it presented us with audio problems and course participants experienced technical problems with it. Elluminate, a more expensive web conferencing tool, was more stable but the students did not like the interface; the software crashed when several applications were viewed at once. In one class, Ustream.tv (a free service) was used with Skype.

Conclusion

The creation of any new course is an iterative, recursive process – one of framing ideas, testing and revising as you go along. For several years, I have spent time developing (and refining) course content to incorporate new knowledge and pedagogical practices. As it is a web-based course, student librarians and archivists from other library schools in North America have been welcomed. In the digital community that we create, student librarians experience the power of being digitally connected to their peers across a distributed social information space.

The process of revising a graduate-level online course on an ICT subject as fast-moving as social media has introduced many challenges. Identifying steps in planning and revision is a critical part of its success. In that regard, I have found that collaborating with teachers and information experts (i.e. my peers, colleagues and librarians) has been an essential and enjoyable part of teaching. It has been gratifying to work with students on improving the course, and I look at the end-of-term course evaluations very closely. Consequently, much work is left to be done. Social media continue to challenge library and information professionals to keep up with the new literacies of the 21st century. Despite the challenges of doing so, these social media literacies should be embraced and celebrated.

External IL websites useful for course development

ANTS: Animated Tutorial Sharing Project: information literacy tutorials created by librarians - http://ants.wetpaint.com/.

Canadian Research Libraries Information Literacy Portal (CRLIL) - http://apps.medialab.uwindsor.ca/crlil/wiki/FrontPage/.

Connexions: an open repository of educational materials and tools that offers high-quality electronic course material - http://cnx.org/.

CORIL: Cooperative Online Repository for Information Literacy: a collection of information literacy tools from Canadian librarians - https://ospace.scholarsportal.info/handle/1873/6.

EDNA: Education Network Australia: a repository of ICT innovations that demonstrate the latest tools and technologies (e.g. learning objects, RSS feeds, wikis, blogs, podcasts and other utilities) - www.edna.edu.au/edna/go.

HLWIKI Canada: Health Library Wiki Canada: a wiki at the School of Library, Archival and Information Studies at the University of British Columbia that supports social media research and learning - http://hlwiki.ca.

MERLOT: Multimedia Educational Resource for Learning and Online Teaching- www.merlot.org/merlot/index.htm.

Note

1   See 2011 blogs: http://hlwiki.slais.ubc.ca/index.php/Class_blogs_%26_wiki_2011.

References

Aharony, N. (2008) Web 2.0 in U.S. LIS Schools: are they missing the boat? *Ariadne*, **54**, www.ariadne.ac.uk/issue54/aharony/.

Al-Daihani, S. (2010) Exploring the Use of Social Software by Master of Library and Information Science Students, *Library Review*, **59** (2), 117-31.

Bawden, D., Robinson, L., Anderson, T., Bates, J. U. and Vilar, P. (2007) Towards Curriculum 2.0: library/information education for a Web 2.0 world, *Library and Information Science Research*, **31** (99), 14-25, www.lirg.org.uk/lir/ojs/index.php/lir/article/viewPDFInterstitial/49/74.

Brown, J. S. and Duguid, P. (1991) Organizational Learning and Communities-of-Practice: toward a unified view of working, learning, and innovation, *Organization Science*, **2** (1), 40-57.

De Jaegher, H. and Di Paolo, E. (2007) Participatory Sense-making: an enactive approach to social cognition, *Phenomenology and the Cognitive Sciences*, **6** (4), 485-507.

Dewey, J. (1919) Imagination and Expression, *Teachers College Bulletin*, **10** (10), 7-15.

Digital Literacy in Canada (2010) From Inclusion to Transformation, Submission to the Digital Economy Strategy Consultation, Media Awareness Network.

Giustini, D. (2008) Utilizing Learning Theories in the Digital Age: an introduction for health librarians, *Journal of the Canadian Health Libraries Association*, **29**, 109-15.

Godwin, P. and Parker, J. (2008) *Information Literacy Meets Library 2.0*, Facet Publishing.

Hrastinski, S. (2009) A Theory of Online Learning as Online Participation, *Computers and Education*, **52** (1), 78-82, http://ict.mcast.edu.mt/moodle/data/102/resources/online_learning.pdf.

IFLA (International Federation of Library Associations and Institutions) (2005) *Beacons of the Information Society. High Level Colloquium on Information Literacy and Lifelong Learning, Bibliotheca Alexandria, Egypt, November*, http://archive.ifla.org/III/wsis/BeaconInfSoc.html.

Knowles, M. (1970) *The Modern Practice of Adult Education from Pedagogy to Andragogy*, New York: Cambridge Books.

Koontz, F. R. (2006) *Designing Effective Online Instruction: a handbook for web-based courses*, Toronto: Rowman and Littlefield Education, http://chapters.rowmaneducation.com/15/788/1578863864ch1.pdf.

Lave, J. and Wenger, E. (1991) *Situated Learning: legitimate peripheral participation*, New York: Cambridge University Press.

Lloyd, A. (2010) Framing Information Literacy as Information Practice: site ontology and practice theory, *Journal of Documentation*, **66** (2), 245-58.

Martin, A. (2009) Digital Literacy for the Third Age: sustaining identity in an uncertain world, *eLearning Papers*, 12,
www.elearningpapers.eu/index.php?page=doc&doc_id=13518&doclng=6&vol=12.

McLuhan, M. (1965) *The Gutenberg Galaxy: the making of typographic man*, University of Toronto Press.

Secker, J. (2008) Social Software and Libraries: a literature review from the LASSIE project, *Program: Electronic Library and Information Systems*, **42** (3), 215-31, http://eprints.lse.ac.uk/20338/.

Siemens, G. (2005) Connectivism: a learning theory for the digital age, *International Journal of Instructional Technology and Distance Learning*, **2** (1), 8, www.elearnspace.org/Articles/connectivism.htm.

Siemens, G. (2007) Scholarship in an Age of Participation, eLearn Space website, www.elearnspace.org/Articles/journal.htm.

Virkus, S. (2008) Use of Web 2.0 Technologies in LIS Education: experiences at Tallinn University, Estonia, *Program: Electronic Library and Information Systems*, **42** (3), 262-74, www.emeraldinsight.com/10.1108/00330330810892677.

Von Glasersfeld, E. (1995) A Constructivist Approach to Teaching. In Steffe, L. and Gale, J. (eds), *Constructivism in Education*, Hillsdale, NJ: Lawrence Erlbaum Associates, Inc.

Vygotsky, L. (1978) *Mind in Society: the development of higher psychological processes*, Cambridge, MA: Harvard University Press.

Wenger, E. (1998) Communities of Practice: learning as a social system, *Systems Thinker*, June, www.co-i-l.com/coil/knowledge-garden/cop/lss.shtml.

Wenger, E., White, N. and Smith, J. D. (2009) *Digital Habitats: stewarding technology for communities*, Portland, OR: CPsquare.

Chapter 15

Transliteracy and teaching what they know

Lane Wilkinson

Introduction

University students are surprisingly adept at finding information; only, it isn't usually the kind of information that concerns their instructors. From using Wikipedia to learn about their favourite pop-singer's time in primary school, to finding health information in Yahoo! Answers, to evaluating mobile phones based on Amazon user reviews, students appeal to a range of Web 2.0 information resources in their personal lives. Yet these same students are perplexed by library resources. Keywords? Abstracts? Boolean searching? Why does it have to be so *hard*? At the University of Tennessee at Chattanooga, the instruction team at the Lupton Library has decided to address this disconnect head on and make students' pre-existing search behaviours an integral part of library instruction. Rather than focus on the differences between scholarly and popular research, we focus on the similarities. Our approach draws heavily upon the concept of transliteracy.

What is transliteracy?

The concept of transliteracy has its roots in the Transliteracies Project, an interdisciplinary collective of scholars from the University of California-Santa Barbara dedicated to studying the myriad ways in which online reading has complicated traditional conceptions of literacy (http://transliteracies.english. ucsb.edu). Shortly after the inaugural 2005 Transliteracies Conference, Professor Sue Thomas of De Montfort University adapted the concept in a more generalized form as the core area of enquiry for the Production and Research in Transliteracy (PART) group. This working group is actively enquiring into the impact of new technologies on the broader notion of literacy as a communicative skill. The PART working definition of transliteracy is, at this point, the most commonly cited one. Accordingly, 'transliteracy' is defined as 'the ability to read, write and interact across a range of platforms, tools and media from signing and orality through handwriting, print, TV, radio and film, to digital social networks' (Thomas et al., 2007).

In this sense, transliteracy is not simply about the canonical sense of literacy *qua* reading and writing. Transliteracy takes a holistic view of the increasingly proliferating means of communication at our disposal and it focuses on the cognitive abilities inherent in transferring meaning between communication systems. From the intersubjectivity of social media tools to the intertextuality of Web 2.0 mash-ups, to new frontiers in immersive storytelling, the digital environment – and especially the Web 2.0 paradigm – has led to a distribution of literacy skills across a multiplicity of media options. Transliteracy is, at heart, simply about understanding the ways in which we navigate an ever-increasing array of communication and information resources.

Transliteracy is not information literacy

Transliteracy has only recently gained currency in the library world, though it has already become something of a divisive concept. Critics of transliteracy are rightly concerned that this is just a buzzword, a renaming of existing concepts and literacies, or a challenge to information literacy. This last criticism is especially pervasive; transliteracy seems to be something already covered by information literacy. There is no contesting the fact that the core concepts of transliteracy have been in use for quite some time, but there is still some utility in separating the concept out and away from information literacy.

From scientific literacy to digital literacy, to information literacy, to transliteracy and beyond, the conversations circling the concept of literacy invoke myriad competing senses of 'literacy'. The *Oxford English Dictionary* includes the following definition of 'literacy': 'the quality or state of being literate; knowledge of letters; condition in respect to education, *esp.* ability to read and write'. This definition is instructive because it distinguishes between the *descriptive* sense of the term and the *evaluative* sense of the term. The descriptive use of the term literacy is in the canonical sense of literacy as a type of communicative skill. Traditional print literacy (the ability to read and write) is the most familiar descriptive literacy, though other medium-specific literacies are discussed in the literature, including orality, visual literacy and computer literacy.

In contrast to the descriptive literacies tied to particular technologies, the term 'literacy' is also used in a non-medium-specific *evaluative* sense of a particular condition of education. This sense of literacy includes subject-specific literacies, such as scientific, health and economic literacy. It also includes more conceptual literacies, such as critical literacy and media literacy. These non-specific literacies are not tied to any particular technology, nor are they tied to any particular subject domain.

Figure 15.1 puts the various senses of 'literacy' into a taxonomic arrangement. This arrangement is useful insofar as it clearly delineates transliteracy and information literacy. Information literacy is, at heart, an evaluative concept, which is in keeping with the definition adopted by CILIP (Chartered Institute of Library and Information Professionals): 'Information literacy is knowing when and why you need information, where to find it, and how to evaluate, use and communicate it in an ethical manner' (www.informationliteracy.org.uk).

So, information literacy is a unifying concept underlying the evaluative sense of literacy. Moreover, understanding particular tools, media and platforms is a

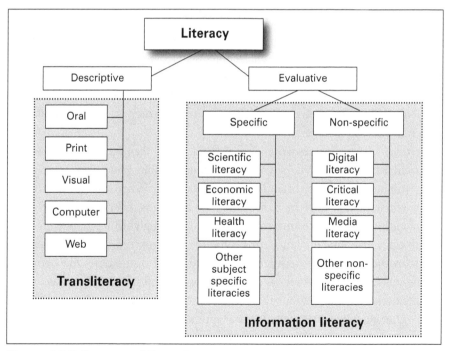

Figure 15.1 Taxonomy of literacy types

prerequisite for information literacy, but logically distinct. Hence, transliteracy serves as a unifying concept underlying the descriptive sense of literacy. To be sure, there is a great deal of overlap, but the important thing to note is that transliteracy is not a proposed replacement for information literacy; it is meant as a complementary concept. As Ipri (2010, 532) writes:

> [T]ransliteracy is concerned with what it means to be literate in the 21st century. It analyzes the relationship between people and technology, most specifically social networking, but is fluid enough to not be tied to any particular technology. It focuses more on the social uses of technology, whatever that technology may be.

Transliteracy, Web 2.0, and library instruction

Far from being a theory with no practical consequences, transliteracy can inform how librarians introduce students to library research and information literacy. In particular, three pedagogical principles can be derived from transliteracy. These are principles that, ultimately, provide a solid foundation and justification for adopting Web 2.0 technologies as an integral part of library instruction.

First, the ability to 'read and write across multiple media' requires that there *be* multiple media involved in the research process. It follows that *effective information use requires several information sources.* Library resources are not representative of the full range of information sources available and, rather than avoid Web 2.0 tools, these should be an integral part of the information literacy curriculum. The first pedagogical lesson of transliteracy is to get comfortable with non-library resources.

Second, *information resources do not stand alone, they interact.* Professional researchers have blogs. Wikipedia is increasingly reliable. Peer review takes place every minute on Twitter, Friendfeed and Facebook. When the academics are using social media and the non-academics are using peer review, the lines between information resources become increasingly blurred. Given that transliteracy is about moving *across* information resources, librarians need to focus on the interaction between them. Traditional distinctions like 'popular versus scholarly' or 'print versus online' are oversimplifications that mask more complex relationships. Rather than emphasize what makes the library *different* from other resources, the transliterate approach asks that we emphasize the *interaction* between the library and other resources.

Third, *navigating the interaction between information resources requires transferable skills.* As Holman (2011, 26) points out, the traditional focus of library instruction has been on the initial construction of a near-perfect search. Yet, she argues, the mental models of search behaviour that students bring to the classroom are shaped by publicly available resources that 'do not operate in a linear fashion and [students] learn (and search) by discovery'. Given that students have a radically different mental model of the search process, is it any wonder that students often complain that library resources do not make sense? To alleviate this disconnect, it helps to focus less on concrete search behaviours and instead on concepts that can be transferred across multiple media.

Adopting a transliterate approach

The librarians at the University of Tennessee at Chattanooga have only recently been introduced to the term 'transliteracy', though they have been following a transliterate approach to library instruction for several years. With two sessions embedded in the first-year composition programme, library instruction has moved away from mere database demonstrations and towards a model of encouraging the use of Web 2.0, teaching transferable skills and positioning the library as a complement to existing search behaviours, rather than a replacement.

Beginning in the summer of 2010, a team of library instructors gathered focus groups of first-year students and members of the composition faculty to determine how library instruction could best meet a range of information needs. These focus groups confirmed librarians' beliefs that the greatest obstacle to effective research was the students' inability to better define manageable topics. Faculty members also expressed a desire to complicate the popular/scholarly distinction and incorporate non-traditional information sources. These and other suggestions led to a radical redesign of library instruction.

In the first semester of the first-year composition programme (ENGL 1010) library instruction begins before the students enter the library, by way of a pre-class worksheet. This worksheet asks each student to research their topic using two resources: Wikipedia and the library's Points of View Reference Center (an EBSCO product). Students look for highlighted terms in the Wikipedia article, as well as important people, dates and concepts. They record these important terms on the worksheet. Students then log in to Points of View, which aggregates news, articles, blogs and more on controversial topics. There, they look for more core concepts to add to their worksheet. The completed worksheets are submitted to their professor prior to the library session, when they are returned to the students.

What makes the pre-class worksheet especially effective is the way in which it draws an implicit parallel between a familiar information resource (Wikipedia) and a library resource. The use of Wikipedia in non-academic research is well established and students are familiar with the exploratory search behaviour that Wikipedia invites. In making a conceptual link between a familiar resource and an unfamiliar resource, the pre-class activity leads students to understand that familiar search behaviours can transfer through to academic research. Rather than warn students away from Wikipedia, the library embraces Wikipedia as a tool for collecting the concepts that will eventually be used as keywords in library databases.

The first-semester library session continues with the on-site classroom experience. Wikipedia worksheets in hand, students begin with an interactive quiz that asks them to reflect on their current use of internet resources. The 'Google versus the Library' quiz presents students with a range of continually updated information needs, ranging from evaluating insect repellents to gathering opinions on famous sports figures, to identifying research on a pop-culture phenomenon. Students are presented with the information need and select whether Google or the library would be the best place to search, with 'Google' standing in for popular internet resources in general. This activity is specifically designed so that the library is rarely the best place to look for information, which gives the students a chance to discuss their native search behaviours. Students introduce issues of currency, authority, bias and reliability while the library instructor mediates the questions and answers in a Socratic fashion. The entire activity lasts 10 to 15 minutes and, by the end, the class has explored basic information evaluation skills using familiar resources.

The quiz leads to a reflection on the pre-class worksheet and a short video tutorial that draws an explicit analogy between the highlighted terms in Wikipedia and the keywords used in an academic database, specifically, Wilson's OmniFile. This PRIMO award-winning video encourages students to use familiar sources for refining their research topic. The video also incorporates discovery-based search behaviours and focuses on library database searching in general, rather than on the features specific to Wilson OmniFile. The underlying goal is to foster the transfer of skills between searching library databases and searching in non-library resources, and analogies to Web 2.0 services are abundant. The class ends with at least 10 minutes of hands-on searching in both Wikipedia and OmniFile. Some classes are also selected to take pre- and post-test assessments.

The second-semester library session for first-year composition (ENGL 1020) begins with a video discussing the 'world of information', another PRIMO award-winning tutorial. The video draws explicit parallels between popular research and academic research and situates a multiplicity of information resources within the research process. From blogs and YouTube to academic journals and databases, the popular and the scholarly are collapsed into a spectrum of equally valid research tools. The video addresses common, 'everyday' searching, such as using Twitter, YouTube and MySpace to follow a favourite pop singer, and draws an analogy with academic research, such as using professional blogs, journals and books to explore the commercialization underlying pop music. Throughout, students are reminded that their pre-existing search behaviours are appropriate (with some refinement) to academic research.

The video segues into an interactive quiz that is intended to be more challenging than the first-semester quiz. Students are asked to select the best information resource for a variety of information needs and the concepts of authority, bias, accuracy and currency are discussed in more detail. Questions have been designed such that there are no clear-cut answers, prompting healthy student discussion and debate when responses appear on-screen (Figure 15.2). The activity reinforces legitimate evaluative techniques and demonstrates that information use proceeds along the

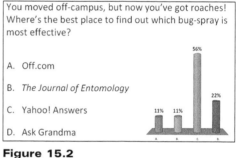

Figure 15.2
Sample question from ENGL 1020 quiz, with student responses

same lines in both the popular and the academic worlds. A short tutorial using the Academic OneFile interface to demonstrate the OpenURL link resolver follows, along with ample time to search.

Conclusion

The first-year library session is unique in that it largely does away with database demonstrations, in favour of addressing more popular resources. The transliterate aspect of this approach manifests itself in two distinct ways. First, by sharpening students' research skills with more familiar resources, the librarians are promoting transferable skills that can be applied in any information environment. Second, by removing the library from a place of privilege, students are encouraged to explore how familiar resources such as blogs or Wikipedia interact with library resources. Transliteracy is all about the moving across or between media, platforms and tools, and so encouraging cross-platform skills and resource interactions is foundational to a transliterate approach to library instruction.

In teaching the fit between information resources and promoting transferable skills, library instructors can address information literacy concepts from outside the traditional library methods of database demonstration and the focus on how the library is different. Information literacy is still the focal point for library instruction. Transliteracy just suggests a re-visioning of how and where information literacy concepts can be applied.

References

Holman, L. (2011) Millennial Students' Mental Models of Search: implications for academic librarians and database developers, *Journal of Academic Librarianship*, **37** (1), 19-27.

Ipri, T. (2010) Introducing Transliteracy: what does it mean to academic libraries? *College and Research Libraries News*, **71** (10), 532-67.

Thomas, S., Joseph, C., Laccetti, J., Mason, B., Mills, S., Perril, S. and Pullinger, K. (2007) Transliteracy: crossing divides, *First Monday*, **12** (12), http://firstmonday.org/htbin/cgiwrap/bin/ojs/index.php/fm/issue/view/255.

Primo videos available from:
www.ala.org/ala/mgrps/divs/acrl/about/sections/is/projpubs/primo/index.cfm.

Chapter 16

ANCIL: a new curriculum for information literacy: case study

Jane Secker and Emma Coonan

> You have learned something. That always feels at first as if you had lost something.
>
> (H. G. Wells)

Introduction

Recent research suggests that the information-seeking behaviour and needs of students are changing (CIBER/UCL, 2008; SCONUL, 2011 among others), driven largely by the changing experiences and expectations of 'the Google generation', who have grown up with access to the internet being the norm. While the Google generation and 'digital native' terms have been debated and widely criticized (Jones et al., 2010), it is clear that information literacy programmes over the next five years will need to adapt and respond to the needs of current students.

This case study describes a short project based at Cambridge University Library and funded by the Arcadia Programme (http://arcadiaproject. lib.cam.ac.uk), a three-year initiative designed to explore the role of academic libraries in the digital age. The project ran from May until July 2011 and sought to develop a practical curriculum for information literacy that meets the needs of the undergraduate student entering higher education over the next five years.

A new curriculum for information literacy: project overview
Aims and objectives

The project sought to develop a practical curriculum for information literacy that meets the needs of the undergraduate student entering higher education over the next five years. Specifically, the project aimed:

- to understand the information needs of future undergraduate students on entering higher education
- to develop a revolutionary curriculum for information literacy that could be used with undergraduate students entering UK higher education
- to provide practical guidance about how best to equip students with the knowledge, skills and behaviours, in terms of information use, to support their learning in the digital age
- to develop a flexible curriculum that could be used and adapted in the higher education community and used in face-to-face, blended and online learning provision.

Methodology

The authors carried out an extensive review of the literature, which forms the theoretical background to this project. A modified Delphi study was undertaken which involved consulting widely with experts in the information and education communities. The curriculum was developed and presented to the expert group and took into account findings from the literature and from the expert consultation. It was subsequently refined and a final curriculum, with a number of supporting documents, was produced.

Outputs

The project had three major outputs, which should be consulted for more detail:

1. Theoretical Background
2. Expert Consultation Report
3. The Curriculum and supporting documentation, comprising
   - curriculum overview and implementation guidelines
   - mapping to existing information literacy frameworks and standards
   - evidence toolkit for implementing the curriculum
   - six tips for transforming teaching
   - good practice in information literacy.

Outputs are freely available and can be downloaded from http://newcurriculum.wordpress.com.

Information literacy: background and context

Information literacy is often described as a key part of lifelong independent learning and as a set of skills, attributes and behaviour that underpin student learning in the digital age. Information literacy has been linked to graduate employability, and increasingly UK universities are developing strategies to ensure that their students acquire and develop these competencies during their undergraduate studies. In practice, however, our findings echoed those in previously published literature, to the effect that information literacy teaching is frequently undervalued and under-resourced in higher education institutions.

Information literacy programmes or sessions are often run by academic libraries; however, in order to be most effective, experts recognize that information literacy should be embedded within a subject curriculum and ideally taught in partnership with academic and academic support colleagues. In practice, again, the implementation often falls short of the ideal. The Theoretical Background explores this chasm in detail, concluding that it is the result of variant and conflicting perceptions, sometimes not fully articulated, of what constitutes 'information literacy'.

Definitions and terminology

Information literacy is defined by CILIP (2004) as 'knowing when and why you need information, where to find it, and how to evaluate, use and communicate it in an ethical manner'. UNESCO's (2005) definition takes a broader view that goes beyond formal learning, stating that 'information literacy empowers people in all walks of life to seek, evaluate, use and create information effectively to achieve their personal, social, occupational and educational goals. It is a basic human right in a digital world and promotes social inclusion in all nations.'

It is clear from our research that, while to some degree contested, the term 'information literacy' remains current and meaningful within the library community. However, it overlaps with numerous other terms including academic literacies, new literacies, media literacy and digital literacy. At the heart of many of these other literacies is a desire to develop critical thinking, evaluative and high-level cognitive skills in students. This is the essence of what information literacy seeks to achieve. Therefore, we hope that this study rehabilitates the term information literacy and can be a way of bringing together practitioners working in these other, related areas of literacy. Figure 16.1 illustrates what we describe as the information literacy landscape.

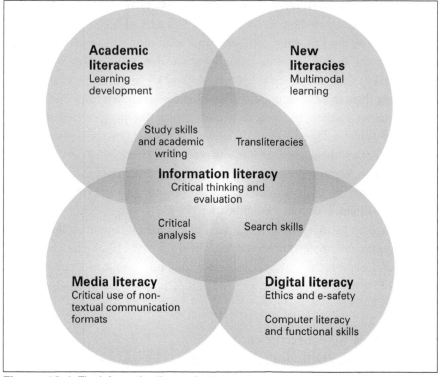

Figure 16.1 The information literacy landscape

The ANCIL vision of information literacy

The ANCIL research was grounded in a view of information literacy as fundamental to the ongoing development of the individual in both an academic and a social context. From the outset the authors decided that the curriculum design should be informed by the following principles:

* It should be holistic, supporting the whole process of study and research rather than just teaching traditional library skills.
* It should be modular, consisting of ongoing classes to meet the developing needs of students during the whole of their undergraduate careers, not just one-shot sessions.
* It should be embedded, forming a salient part of academic teaching, or run closely alongside it over the course of the academic year, and should present activities and problems directly related to students' subject context.

- It should be active and assessed, containing a significant element of active and reflective learning, including peer assessment elements.
- It should be flexible, for use and adaptation in all UK higher education institutions, and designed specifically for flexible implementation.
- It should be transformative, grounded in a broad reading of 'information literacy' that sees IL not as a set of competencies but as a fundamental attribute of the discerning scholar, and as a crucial social and personal element in the digital age.

The authors identified three key attributes characterizing this view of information literacy, which make the curriculum:

- transitional
- transferable
- transformational.

Transition is an important and recurrent characteristic of learning. It is a matter not just of a formal change of institution, e.g. from school to higher education, but also of the journey from dependent to autonomous learning. A fully holistic information literacy curriculum needs to support all stages of this journey.

The curriculum content needs to be transferable, forming a part of education and not simply being 'library training'. Information literacy fosters and develops appropriate behaviour, approaches, cognitive functions and skills around the use of information in all contexts. In essence, information literacy equips students with the capacity to generate their own strategies for dealing with new information contexts, for example when they leave higher education and enter the workplace.

Finally, information literacy should be transformational for the learner, changing their attitude, behaviour, outlook and even their worldview. Therefore this curriculum has the potential to change lives and make a real difference to society.

Findings

The project's key finding was that the way in which the teaching of information literacy is structured and implemented is as important as the topics that are covered in any new curriculum. It is essential for practitioners to model excellent practice in their teaching as they help learners to develop strategies for evaluating and managing the many forms and contexts of information.

Information literacy needs to be embedded into the academic curriculum as far as possible; it also needs to be ongoing throughout a student's academic career and adapted according to the specific requirements of the discipline being studied. The curriculum should include opportunities for students to work collaboratively and to reflect on their learning. It should be based on real needs, ideally following an audit of existing information practices. Meaningful assessment forms an important part of this curriculum. We recognize that information literacy can be difficult to assess summatively and endorse the use of innovative approaches such as peer assessment.

The curriculum is intended to be sufficiently flexible and adaptable to be implemented in any higher education institution at undergraduate level. Its implementation is likely to involve a range of different people within an institution, including librarians, learning developers, IT and e-learning staff and, most importantly, academic staff. A programme of staff development may be required in order to equip staff within an institution with the understanding and skills needed to deliver the curriculum.

In order to be most effective, the curriculum needs to have buy-in from senior management. Therefore it must be clear how information literacy relates to the strategic aims of the institution, such as graduate capabilities, employability, enhancing the student experience and improved achievement. A variety of supporting resources, including examples of good practice, an evidence toolkit and a mapping of the new curriculum to existing models of information literacy, were presented alongside the curriculum to assist with in-house advocacy and implementation.

The curriculum

The curriculum's content is divided into 10 thematic strands comprising the full range of facets encompassed by information literacy:

1 Transition from school to higher education
2 Becoming an independent learner
3 Developing academic literacies
4 Mapping and evaluating the information landscape
5 Resource discovery in your discipline
6 Managing information
7 Ethical dimension of information
8 Presenting and communicating knowledge

9 Synthesizing information and creating new knowledge
10 Social dimension of information literacy.

These strands identify the complex interplay of elements encompassed within information literacy. They are not intended to form the basis of individual teaching sessions or discrete modules, but should be combined and incorporated into the academic curriculum as appropriate to the needs of the discipline.

Strands 1 and 10, which book-end the curriculum, link reflective learning with specific transition points in the undergraduate career. Strand 1 focuses on the transition from school to higher education – a perfect time to engage students in their own learning process by giving them a vocabulary and analytical structure through which to address the significant changes in expectations, teaching styles and attitudes towards learning that occur at this point. Strand 10 deals with transferring information literacy skills, behaviours and attitudes to everyday life, in line with the principles of lifelong learning.

Strand 2, in contrast, is not linked to a specific transition point. Rather, it is informed by the idea that change occurs throughout the learning process as a natural, unavoidable and sometimes challenging aspect of learning. The content of Strand 2 is iterative and reflective, and aims to give students ongoing, scaffolded support as they develop the conceptual and intellectual infrastructure for assimilating new information over the course of their undergraduate careers. The focus in these three strands (1, 2 and 10) is on learning to learn.

Strand 3 aims to explore and develop the academic literacies of reading and writing both at the functional, procedural level – skimming and scanning strategies, recognizing and using appropriate academic idiom – and in higher-order activities such as textual interrogation and critiquing, argument construction and the understanding of a discipline's epistemological structure and values.

Strands 4 and 5 focus on dealing with subject-specific information. Strand 5 is intended to familiarize students with specialist resources of various types and content in their discipline, while Strand 4 focuses on developing awareness and understanding of the *range* of source types available and how to evaluate them for reliability, authority and their appropriateness to the student's specific purpose. The underlying purpose of these strands is to enable students to become familiar with the information landscape of their discipline.

Strand 6 focuses on practical, functional skills, many of which will be recognizable in existing library instruction courses. These remain key skills without which students will struggle to find, select, manage and process academic information efficiently. In many cases a huge range of software and online tools is available to simplify these processes. We have not stipulated particular tools to teach, firstly, because technology is moving at too fast a pace, and secondly, in order to emphasize that understanding the process itself is as important as being aware of tools or programs designed to aid the process.

Strands 7, 8 and 9 deal with the high-order cognitive and intellectual functions of information handling. These include critiquing and analysing material, synthesizing viewpoints, formulating research questions, and the ethical dimension of information use and production. These facets have traditionally been perceived as belonging to the academic province; however, as discussed in the Theoretical Background and the Expert Report which accompany the curriculum, a holistic view of information literacy holds that separating 'functional' skills and high-order abilities occludes the research process and disadvantages the student.

The strands thus fall into five broad learning categories, containing multiple levels of development:

1   Key skills
2   Academic literacies
3   Subject-specific competences
4   Advanced information handling
5   Learning to learn.

Teaching sessions are constructed by selecting an element from each category to match the overall learning outcomes of the session. In this way each session will contain:

- a practical 'take-home' skill
- a subject-specific context in which to situate and deploy the skill, including an increased awareness of academic reading and writing conventions within the discipline
- an element of advanced information handling, allowing the student to develop sophisticated and nuanced techniques for evaluating, assimilating and synthesizing information
- a reflective component, allowing the learner to assess how the new skill, insight and behaviour will affect or enrich their existing practices and attitudes.

Appendix: A new curriculum for information literacy

Learning to learn (Strands 1, 2, 10)

Developing academic literacies (Strand 3)

Subject-specific competencies (navigating the information landscape, resource discovery) (Strands 4, 5)

Key skills (e.g. searching, notetaking, referencing) (Strand 6)

Advanced information handling (e.g. evaluation, source critique, synthesis) (Strands 7, 8, 9)

Strand 1 Transition from school to higher education			
Strand content	Learning outcomes	Example activities	Example assessment
What are the expectations at higher education level in your discipline?	Distinguish between the expectations at school and HE level in your discipline. Recognize that learning at HE level is different and requires different strategies. Identify and assess the range of information formats available.	Tutor outlines contrasting expectations at secondary and HE levels. Students review examples of HE level work at school and discuss differences from their prior work. Classroom-based activity to explore and contrast how information on a relevant topic is presented in monographs, journals, reports and other formats.	Short reflective piece of writing on transition issues – students identify areas they need to address (ideally assessed by personal tutor or academic).
What are the conventions around reading, writing and presenting at higher education level in your discipline?	Develop an awareness of academic conventions at HE level. Assess your reading, writing and presenting skills and compare them to experts within your discipline.	What makes an academic journal article different from an article in a publication like *History Today* or *New Scientist*? Identify the differences in presentation, attribution, tone of voice etc.; discuss why these genre conventions are used – what purpose do they achieve? Discuss what a basic descriptive answer might be and what would need to be added to take a more analytical approach.	Rewrite a paragraph from a popular publication as though for an academic audience. (For peer assessment.)
Reflect on your current and previous information behaviour – what's different?	Assess your current information-seeking behaviour and compare it to experts within your discipline. Critique the tools and strategies you currently use to find scholarly information. Evaluate the information environment, including libraries and digital libraries as 'trusted' collections.	Using reading lists as a starting-point, identify the key types of information that are important in your discipline – discuss those you are familiar with and those you have not used before. Identify your top 3 (or 5) current information sources and evaluate their fitness for purpose in line with academic expectations – create a mind-map of your information landscape as it currently appears and share with peers.	Postcard from the edge: identify 3 new strategies, tools or sources that you found useful in class and write yourself a postcard. Class leader to send cards after e.g. 1 week.

Strand 2 Becoming an independent learner			
Strand content	Learning outcomes	Example activities	Example assessment
Learning to learn	Reflect on how to create strategies for assimilating new knowledge. Identify your learning style and preferences, including specific learning needs.	Arrange verbs from Bloom's Taxonomy on a scale into higher- and lower-order skills.	*Use activity as formative assessment.*
Affective dimension of information literacy	Critique the concept that learning changes the learner. Acknowledge the emotional impact of learning on your worldview.	Students reflect on a positive and a negative learning experience and discuss why one worked and one didn't. How did you cope with the negative experience? How did you take forward the positive?	Demonstrate an awareness of sources of support at all levels in your institution. A case study exercise to diagnose the issues: what advice would you give, and where would you refer the person?

Strand 3 Developing academic literacies			
Strand content	Learning outcomes	Example activities	Example assessment
Academic writing, rhetoric and persuasive writing	Identify appropriate terminology, use of language and academic idiom in your discipline. Identify overt and implicit techniques for influencing the reader/viewer in different arenas – in academic writing, in advertising, in the media. Develop an awareness of the epistemological structure and values in your discipline.	Assess and compare the quality of 3 short pieces of writing (one deliberately flawed). Compare writing style, structure and use of evidence across a range of papers on the same topic – students vote for best paper and discuss why it met their criteria. Analyse the structure of a key work in your discipline and break it down into component parts: does it convince you? Why?	Marks in first-year assignments explicitly awarded for academic writing abilities. The elevator challenge – pitch an argument to someone you want to convince in 2 minutes. Students vote for best elevator pitch and discuss why it met their criteria.
Academic reading, critical analysis and textual interrogation	Learn the techniques of skimming and scanning. Identify the strengths and weaknesses of source material. Evaluate the place of source material within the wider debate.	Summarize the key arguments in a monograph after being given 20 minutes to read it; discuss the different strategies adopted, e.g. using the index, reading the introduction and conclusion. Locate key information in a text which is not really about that topic, but does contain useful snippets. Discuss what it means to critique a text – i.e. not necessarily finding fault with everything; list the key evaluative criteria that you would apply to texts in your field in order to establish their relative value and contribution. Evaluate critical appraisal tools (e.g. CASP, peer review reporting, journal referee guidelines) and discuss their value and potential application in your discipline.	Timed exercise – skimming for key information: peer-assess in pairs. Write a critical review of a subject-appropriate text (part of formal course assessment).

Strand 4 Mapping and evaluating the information landscape			
Strand content	Learning outcomes	Example activities	Example assessment
Identify trusted source formats	Select appropriate resources for your assignment, discriminating between good-quality academic sources and other sources. Develop evaluative criteria for recognizing and selecting trustworthy sources of academic quality in your discipline.	Students explore a number of sources – for instance real and spoof websites (e.g. www.dhmo.org/) – and consider how they identify trustworthy sources. Compare a subject entry in Wikipedia with an entry in a non-current encyclopedia and discuss their relative values. Examine monographs, journals, reports and other formats.	Devise a list of criteria for assessing trustworthiness and credibility of source formats. Students locate a book, a journal article and a website not on their reading list and consider in pairs the relative value to their assignment of what they have found.
Who are the experts in the field? How do we know?	Identify the key experts in your field. Analyse what makes an expert in your discipline.	Choose a noteworthy author in the discipline and evaluate his/her impact through citations. Does this author qualify as an expert? Justify.	Tutor feeds back on student evaluation of expertise.
Evaluating source material and its appropriate-ness for your specific purpose	Use information sources appropriately to develop or support your argument. Develop evaluative criteria for assessing ways of using source material in your work.	Distinguish and discuss how you might use source material (to check facts, to grasp background information, to support your argument, to undermine someone else's argument ...). Look at a sample text and categorize the reasons why the author has used source material.	Marks in first-year assignments explicitly awarded for appropriate use of evidence and sources.

Strand 5 Resource discovery in your discipline			
Strand content	Learning outcomes	Example activities	Example assessment
Using key finding aids in your discipline	Identify key finding aids in your discipline – e.g. catalogues, full-text databases, abstract and indexing services. Develop strategies for using them.	Discuss the differences between academic finding aids and freely available search engines (e.g. will Google tell you what books are in the library?). List the different types of information you need to find out and match them up with the various aids – which best fits your need?	*Appropriate assessments must be developed and carried out by or in collaboration with faculty members.*
Going beyond the key finding aids	Identify subject-specific collections of information such as gateways and portals. Develop strategies for using them.	Evaluate a subject-specific resource new to you and identify how it fits into your information landscape (discuss or mind-map).	
Finding and using specialist forms of information	Identify the types of specialist information common in your discipline – e.g. datasets, statistics, archival evidence. Develop strategies for using them, including awareness of sources of expert help.	Give students some raw data and ask them to identify what subject disciplines might use it, and how. Would it be useful for your own subject? Locate sources of data that fall outside your field and discuss how they might be helpful (e.g. a historical dataset for studying literature).	
Finding and using people as information sources	Identify the strengths of people in your personal network – peers, academic staff and others – as sources of information. Evaluate the strengths of online user-generated content as sources of information.	Discuss the relative value of using social media (e.g. blogs/Facebook/Twitter) as a source of information. Choose a prominent, networked scholar and explore his/her academic research, popular profile and use of social media.	

Strand 6 Managing information			
Strand content	Learning outcomes	Example activities	Example assessment
Note taking	Distinguish between note taking (dictation) and note making (considered retention of vital points). Develop a strategy for note making – in lectures/supervisions, for your reading, in everyday situations.	Listen to short (e.g. 2-minute) podcast and make: 1) as full a transcript as possible; 2) notes of salient points. Reflect on ease and relative value of both approaches. Identify which parts of your notes reflect the original content and which are related to your own thinking. Evaluate the strategies you use to distinguish between different types of notes.	Peer discussion and assessment.
Time management and planning	Produce a strategy to manage your workload. Evaluate your own learning and working styles.	Create a plan including deadlines and a realistic timeframe for your next piece of assessed work/across the whole term. Assess your learning and working styles and identify areas of weakness.	Include plan with submitted assignment – discuss with tutor and reflect on value.
Storing information effectively	Develop and implement a plan for organizing your files (including naming and organizing folders). Decide on an appropriate information management technique suitable for your discipline/the resources you use.	Devise a system for storing a number of files prepared by session leader – including some variant versions, e.g. tutor comments on an essay draft. Explore cloud storage tools and discuss the merits of remote vs local storage, online vs paper storage. List potential hazards.	Peer assessment – students discuss, compare and rank their current strategies.
Bibliographic and reference management	Identify and use an appropriate citation style in your assignments. Construct appropriate bibliographies for your assignments. Evaluate reference management tools and strategies in the light of your own workflow.	Hands-on comparison and exploration of free and paid-for reference management software; write a review of different software for other students. Discuss the merits of different reference management strategies (e.g. software vs paper storage). List potential hazards.	Timed assessment in class – generate an appropriately formatted bibliography from a reference list supplied by class leader, using the tool of your choice.
Push services / alerting / keeping up to date	Develop appropriate strategies for current awareness in your field.	Identify and evaluate various alert services – RSS, e-mail alerts, aggregators etc.	Short reflective piece describing whether and how you will use alert services – and how you will store and organize the information they generate.

Strand 7 Ethical dimension of information			
Strand content	Learning outcomes	Example activities	Example assessment
Attribution and avoiding plagiarism	Identify the steps you can take to avoid plagiarism, deliberate or inadvertent. Use correct academic practices in quoting, citing and paraphrasing.	Discuss the need to attribute quotations, paraphrases and ideas appropriately. Identify why plagiarism might happen and categorize the types of poor academic practice that lead to plagiarism. Plagiarize deliberately and pass to another student to put it right.	Marks in first-year assignments explicitly awarded for bibliographies and appropriate attribution.
Sharing information appropriately	Summarize the key ways you can use and share information without infringing another's rights. Distinguish between collaboration and collusion. Compare dissemination practices in your discipline across a range of publication platforms (pre-print repositories, blogs, bibliographic sharing services etc.).	Students are asked to find suitable images for use in a class presentation – introduce concept of Creative Commons. Examine a number of scenarios to determine which constitute collusion.	Marks are awarded for the appropriate use of image and video sources in student presentations.
Awareness of copyright and IPR issues	Develop an awareness of how copyright and IPR issues impact on your work. Develop strategies as appropriate for working within the legal framework.	Students discuss the role of copyright laws in protecting musicians, artists and film makers. Reflect on how copyright laws have impacted on them either socially or academically. Examine a number of scenarios to determine which constitute copyright infringement.	Students work together to develop a policy or guidelines for their institution that reflects real practice and complies with legal issues. Assessment by Copyright Officer/IPR specialist.

Strand 8 Presenting and communicating knowledge			
Strand content	Learning outcomes	Example activities	Example assessment
Finding your voice	Use language appropriately in your academic writing. Analyse competing arguments and the use of evidence to justify a position.	Practise writing in first and third person. Discuss appropriate use of language for your audience. Comment critically on the views of others, so your voice is distinguished – working in pairs, swap and critique.	*Use activity as formative assessment.*
Managing your online identity and digital footprint	Develop an awareness of how you appear to others online. Decide on appropriate levels of information to communicate to different audiences (i.e. manage your digital footprint). Evaluate the suitability of different online locations/tools for your online presence.	Working in pairs, Google each other and assemble a profile of the other person, including any negative information. Consider your own profile as a 'produser' – how much of a trail do you leave by consuming information online?	*Use activity as formative assessment.*
Communicating your findings appropriately	Choose an appropriate writing style, level and format for your intended audience. Summarize the key methods of publishing research findings in your discipline (including self-publication, e.g. blogging). Assess the relationship between writing style, audience and publication platform.	Students look at how information on a topical issue in their discipline, e.g. climate change, is presented in newspapers, on websites and in academic journals and discuss the key differences.	Write different short pieces communicating the same information to different audiences for different reasons.

Strand 9 Synthesizing information and creating new knowledge			
Strand content	Learning outcomes	Example activities	Example assessment
Formulating research questions and framing problems	Use chosen information sources to articulate and analyse new problems in your field.	Discuss paradigm shifts in your field (tutor input) – e.g. impact of quantum theory on Newtonian physics. Discuss new ways of framing questions or approaching issues in the field (potentially in the context of your dissertation topic).	Assessment involves a set of marks awarded for innovation and creativity when framing problems. Students work on creating their own research questions (tutor feedback needed).
Assimilating information within the disciplinary framework	Assess the value of new information objectively in the context of your work. Develop new insights and knowledge in your discipline.	In pairs, students are given a broad topic (e.g. climate change) and asked to prepare a for/against argument. Students debate issue and a vote is taken. Marks awarded for use of evidence to support arguments.	Second- and third-year assessment is explicit about how marks are awarded for assimilation of ideas.

Strand 10 Social dimension of information			
Strand content	Learning outcomes	Example activities	Example assessment
Becoming a lifelong learner	Develop an awareness that learning is a continuous, ongoing process outside of formal educational establishments. Develop strategies for assimilating new information into the conceptual framework.	Discuss the statement 'When the facts change, I change my opinion' in the circumstance of deciding whether and how to vote in a general election. Reflect on how you have changed as a learner since school.	*Use activity as formative assessment.*
Information handling, problem solving and decision making in the workplace	Transfer the skills of finding, critically evaluating and deploying information to the workplace.	Without using any subscription resources, students search for information to answer a specific query. They carry out the same search to compare the information they can find using paid-for resources. Find information to help you handle a change-management scenario in the workplace.	*Use activity as formative assessment.*
Information handling, problem solving and decision making in your daily life	Transfer the skills of finding, critically evaluating, and deploying information to daily life.	Reflect on the best way to choose an energy supplier, using discussion and internet sources to help you. Discuss the trust value of cost-comparison websites.	*Use activity as formative assessment.*
Ethics and politics of information	Develop strategies for assimilating and analysing new information, including that which challenges your worldview.	Presentation of sensitive or nuanced information in the press – compare how the same story is reported in a tabloid, a broadsheet and in various news sources.	*Use activity as formative assessment.*

References

CIBER/UCL (2008) *Information Behaviour of the Researcher of the Future* (commissioned by BL and JISC), www.jisc.ac.uk/media/documents/programmemes/reppres/gg_final_keynote_11012008.pdf.

CILIP (2004) CILIP Definition: information literacy, www.cilip.org.uk/get-involved/advocacy/information-literacy/pages/definition.aspx.

Jones, C., Ramanau, R., Cross, S. and Healing, G. (2010) Net Generation or Digital Natives: is there a distinct new generation entering university? *Computers and Education*, **54** (3), 722–32.

SCONUL (2011) The SCONUL 7 Pillars Core Model, www.sconul.ac.uk/groups/information_literacy/seven_pillars.html.

UNESCO (2005) Beacons of the Information Society: the Alexandria Proclamation on information literacy and lifelong learning, http://portal.unesco.org/ci/en/ev.php-URL_ID=20891&URL_DO=DO_TOPIC&URL_SECTION=201.html.

Chapter 17

TeachMeet: librarians learning from each other

Niamh Tumelty, Isla Kuhn and Katie Birkwood

In summer 2010, Isla Kuhn, Reader Services Librarian at Cambridge University Medical Library, blogged about a particular type of event popular among school teachers, and wondered whether this 'TeachMeet' idea would be of interest to librarians (Kuhn, 2010). Several other librarians at the University of Cambridge responded enthusiastically and LibTeachMeet was born.

So what is TeachMeet?

First established in 2005 (Hallahan, 2010), TeachMeet is an 'unconference' organized by teachers, for teachers. These open, friendly and loosely structured events provide an opportunity for teachers to share classroom experiences and to learn from each other. The idea is that everyone is an active participant in the event – even those not presenting are 'enthusiastic lurkers', as opposed to passive 'attendees'.

TeachMeets are free to attend, but sponsorship may be sought to cover costs such as venue hire and provision of refreshments. The events themselves consist of seven-minute micro-presentations and two-minute nano-presentations. Presenters are encouraged to talk about a tool or technique they have tried themselves. Presentation topics are usually registered in advance using a wiki, but the order of speakers is selected at random on the day. There are no keynote speakers or sales pitches and participants are welcome to come and go throughout the presentations. Presentations can be in any style or format but the original TeachMeets encouraged the use of more imaginative presentation techniques than PowerPoint presentations.

Why TeachMeet for librarians?

Recent research undertaken on behalf of the Chartered Institute of Library and Information Professionals (Research by Design Ltd, 2010) found that 71% of information professionals use training skills and 50% use teaching skills in their current roles, while 63% expect to be using these skills a lot or a little more in 10 years' time. Despite the evident importance of the educational role of the librarian, educational theory and teaching skills are not included as a compulsory component of many librarianship courses in the UK, so information professionals require alternative opportunities to develop these skills. Just as many teachers work on their own in their classrooms, many librarians teach in isolation, with little opportunity to share advice and experiences. Alternative methods of training and sharing are needed and this is where the TeachMeet model can help.

TeachMeets are quick and cheap to organize, given the emphasis on informality, and offer a convenient opportunity to meet up with colleagues outside of expensive conferences or other large-scale training events. The welcoming and accessible format of these events facilitates the sharing of experiences without intimidating the first-time presenter (Figure 17.1).

The first LibTeachMeet

A number of factors combined to make the first Cambridge LibTeachMeet a success. As part of a 23 Things programme (a staff development approach to encourage the exploration of technologies) that took place in the summer of 2010, nearly 100 librarians across the University of Cambridge were blogging about a set of social media tools (23 Things Cambridge, 2010). Programme participants were actively encouraged to read each other's blogs and to comment on posts they read. This led to the development of a strong online community among staff of the University of Cambridge's many different libraries. It is therefore not surprising that when Isla Kuhn blogged about TeachMeet, a five-person organizing committee formed itself in the comments of the blog post. It is now hard to imagine that only two members of this committee had met in person before the first TeachMeet planning meeting! As the 23 Things programme drew to a close, participants began to ask how this new level of communication could be continued. TeachMeet became something to look forward to, an opportunity to continue to develop connections built during 23 Things, as well as a chance to share best practice and learn from colleagues in neighbouring libraries.

Figure 17.1 Networking at the second Cambridge LibTeachMeet (Photograph reproduced with permission of Norman Minter (photographer) and Schlumberger Research Centre)

The first planning meeting took place in August 2010. A date and time were picked, and a page was created on the TeachMeet wiki (Cambridge Librarian TeachMeet, 2010). Each member of the organizing committee blogged about the event, and the hashtag #camlibtm was used on Twitter to start raising awareness about it. By the time the 23 Things closing ceremony came around, the TeachMeet team was ready to announce the date of the first Cambridge LibTeachMeet. Bookings opened in August 2010 and began to fill even before a venue had been announced. This free event was fully booked well in advance and a self-organized waiting list formed on the wiki. There was no difficulty in finding sufficient speakers, and in fact there was just enough time to accommodate all of the volunteers.

The first LibTeachMeet took place in St John's College, Cambridge, on 27 September 2010 (Figure 17.2). Refreshments were provided thanks to sponsorship by the Cambridge Library Group and CILIP East of England. Fifty people signed up to attend (though attendance on the day was 40).

Figure 17.2 Celine Carty chairs the first Cambridge LibTeachMeet (Photograph courtesy of the Cambridge TeachMeet Team)

There were 11 presentations covering the following topics:

1 Library inductions using the Cephalonian method
2 Some informal Facebook research
3 'Getting them early': database training in inductions
4 Prezi: an improvement on PowerPoint?
5 From School to Uni: transition skills
6 Adobe Captivate video tutorials
7 The new LAT (Librarians as Teachers) network
8 'Learning Hub' (English Faculty library's blog for online help and tutorials)
9 Using Flashmeeting videoconference technology
10 Setting up a project blog
11 Solving three banner problems.

All the presentations were filmed and made available via YouTube (www.youtube.com/camlibtmvideo). PowerPoint slides were posted to SlideShare (www.slideshare.net/camlibtm), photos of the event were added to Flickr (www.flickr.com/photos/camlibtm) and blog posts and other relevant web pages were tagged in Delicious.[1]

Response to the first LibTeachMeet

Participants were invited to give their general impressions of the event at the end of the evening and the response was overwhelmingly positive: 24% of attendees enjoyed the event 'hugely' and 73% thought it was good fun (Cambridge Librarians' TeachMeet, 2010). Attendees were also asked which of the ideas presented they thought were most likely to be of use to them.

A qualitative survey two weeks later provided an opportunity for more reflective feedback and had an excellent response rate (87%). Participants were asked about their expectations prior to the event and whether they had been met. The responses were well-considered and extremely constructive (Table 17.1).

When asked if they had made use of at least one of the ideas presented, 28 of 35 respondents said 'yes', and many had explored more than one. For those who had not explored any of the ideas, the consistent explanation was 'lack of time'.

When asked if they would consider speaking at the next event, 29 out of 35 respondents said 'yes', often citing the relaxed atmosphere as a good way for

Table 17.1 Examples of feedback regarding expectations of the first Cambridge LibTeachMeet

What were your expectations?	Do you feel these expectations were met, and if so, why?
A few teaching tips.	Actually, got more out of it than that. The opportunities to chat with others were good.
I thought it might be a bit 'lecturey' and to do with teaching techniques.	No, and I was pleased they weren't. I enjoyed it and found it much more interesting than I thought I would. I liked the variety of content and presentation style, and the brevity of each presentation.
I'd been to a similar thing before – but more tech and design orientated and private sector – and from that my expectations were really quite low.	No, they were exceeded. I thought the length of time slots was very good. I felt it helped the more nervous presenters to know that this would be over in a matter of minutes, literally, which in turn seemed to relax them. The content was a good mixture and there was plenty of value to be had. Even if someone was presenting something I was familiar with, I could either learn from a different perspective or digest some of what had gone before. And also, there's nothing wrong with networking and building on the budding relationships formed during Cam23.

newcomers to get experience of public speaking. However, most respondents seemed doubtful that they had anything of interest to share: a typical response was, 'Yes, if I had something to speak about'.

The second Cambridge LibTeachMeet

The organizing team gained four more enthusiastic volunteers and planning for the second Cambridge LibTeachMeet soon began. This time, a new website was established for Cambridge LibTeachMeets and bookings were handled using Eventbrite. Feedback from participants at the first event was taken into account, and the second event took place between 6 p.m. and 8 p.m. on 29 March 2011 in Schlumberger Research Centre, Cambridge. This venue was slightly bigger, allowing for 60 participants and café-style seating arrangements. Sponsorship for the second event was provided by Schlumberger Research Centre and the Arcadia Project at Cambridge University Library.

Presentation timings were more flexible and more opportunities for networking were built into the event. The conscious effort to widen participation beyond the University of Cambridge paid off, with attendees coming from school, university, medical, public and corporate libraries and information services.

The wider range of participants resulted in a different balance of topics, from QR codes in medical libraries and the use of special collections in teaching to jigsaws (Figure 17.3) as a tool for developing essay writing skills, and 'Debunking the myth of the Google generation'. Again, the event was publicized and recorded using a range of social media services, and this time the event was full within hours of opening for bookings.

The evening began with an icebreaker, 'Human Bingo' (Figure 17.4), to encourage conversation amongst librarians from different sectors. Each attendee had to fill a bingo sheet with the names and signatures of people who worked in different types of libraries, from different countries and with different hobbies. Halfway through the presentations an opportunity was provided for round-table sessions, allowing for discussion of topics related to issues that had been raised over refreshments – but the round-table sessions were not necessary because the participants had by this stage found enough to talk about without additional encouragement! The feedback received suggests that a much better balance was achieved between presentations and networking at this second event.

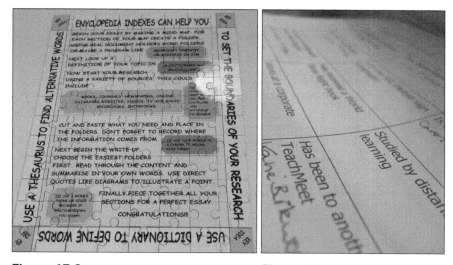

Figure 17.3
Jigsaw (Illustration courtesy of Sarah Pavey, Box Hill School)

Figure 17.4
Human Bingo (Photo courtesy of Norman Minter)

LibTeachMeet continues

Because the Cambridge events were publicized and documented using social media, news of this new teaching event spread quickly. A post on the CILIP Update blog further facilitated dissemination of the 'TeachMeet' idea (Tumelty, 2011). Even before the second Cambridge LibTeachMeet took place, University of Huddersfield librarians had held their own event. LibTeachMeets have now taken place throughout the UK, from Newcastle to Brighton and from Liverpool to London. Papers were presented at LILAC (Librarians' Information Literacy Annual Conference) (Tumelty and Birkwood, 2011) and EAHIL (European Association for Health Information and Libraries) (Kuhn, 2011b) conferences and are helping to spread the idea beyond the UK. A TeachMeet has taken place in Limerick, Ireland, and interest has been expressed in organizing similar events in Sweden and Austria. Presentations were also given more locally, in Oxford (Osman, 2011) and Cambridge (Kuhn, 2011a), and a poster session (Figure 17.5) was presented at CILIP's Umbrella conference (Birkwood, 2011). In most cases the impetus has come from academic librarians, but the museum and archives sector have adopted the idea too: TeachMeet Museums took place in February 2011. A public Google calendar has been created listing all the TeachMeets planned. While each TeachMeet will likely have its own Twitter

(lib)TeachMeet
librarians learning from each other

What is TeachMeet?

TeachMeets are 'unconferences', **informal gatherings** run by teachers for teachers since 2005. By dispensing with the organisation and hierarchy of traditional conferences they allow more time for the 'good bits': meeting new people, **learning from others' experiences** and sharing new ideas.

Typically they have **very short presentations** (7 or 2 minutes), volunteered in advance by attendees, about IT tools that they've used in the classroom. The order of presentations is chosen at random: there are no keynote speakers, and no hierarchy. They are free to attend, **informal and welcoming** and have no sponsors' pitches.

Poster presented by Katie Birkwood, Cambridge University Library
Acknowledgements, links and useful information online at:

http://camlibtm.info
Twitter hashtag: #LibTeachM

Why hold TeachMeets for Librarians?

Well, what's not to like about a free CPD and networking event?

More seriously, **librarians increasingly have to teach** as part of their daily work, and may have had little or no formal training in education. Often, like teachers in schools, they work in isolated environments where they have little chance to learn about how their colleagues are facing similar challenges. TeachMeets give librarians a chance to learn from what other people are doing, both within their own sector and from other sectors of the profession.

By presenting at a TeachMeet you get an opportunity to **hone your presenting skills** in front of an informal and friendly audience--an audience of a few librarians is much less intimidating that a lecture hall full of students!

And if you don't speak up, you still get to participate by asking questions, discussing ideas and sharing your thoughts with other attendees. The ethos of TeachMeets is that **no-one is merely a passive bystander.**

LibTeachMeets

The very first librarians' TeachMeet was held in September 2010 in Cambridge, with the theme 'techie tools and teaching tips'. It was such a success that a second was held in March 2011, and people are already asking when the third will be!

LibTeachMeets have happened in:
Cambridge (27.09.10, 29.03.11)
Huddersfield (09.02.11)
Newcastle (04.05.11)
Brighton (25.05.11)
Liverpool (26.05.11)
Leicester (14.06.11)
London (20.06.11)
Oxford (12.07.11)

LibTeachMeets are coming up in:
Stirling & Inverness (20.07.11)
Bedfordshire (21.07.11)
Sheffield (10.11.11)

See the panel on the right for tips on how to make your own TeachMeet!

What do TeachMeets look like?

Newcastle, image by toomblen
Cambridge, image by Norman Melton
Brighton, image © Sarah J tom
London, image by @HuwyThunder
Huddersfield, images by Andrew Walsh

How to make your own...

✓ Essentials: some **people** willing to help organise and a **venue** that can hold some librarians and info pros (probably between 20 and 60 of them).

✓ **Publicise a date and time** and you'll probably find that people are keen to sign up.

✓ A **web presence** - a blog or wiki and a twitter hashtag - is good to let people know what's going on and to bring information all together in one place.

✓ If you can find a little **funding** or sponsorship then that can help pay for **drinks and nibbles** - TeachMeet-ers always appreciate the presence of cake!

✓ **Speak to people** who have organised other TeachMeets. They'll be more than happy to share what they've learnt.

✓ **Use technology to make your life easier.** Online tools like Google Docs and Eventbrite make collaborative working much easier.

What do people talk about?

You can talk about anything you like at a TeachMeet, so long as it might be useful to the other people there. These are a few titles from LibTeachMeets around the country:

Effective assessment: a tough nut to crack (Kaye, Huddersfield)
Keeping the attention of your audience (Anne-Mary, Huddersfield)
Resource Discovery: two worlds colliding (Chris Keene, Brighton)
Using Skype with media students (Sarah Ison, Brighton)
Livening up library induction sessions the low tech way (Lucy Keating, Newcastle)
Lunching with Renoir: demonstrating why wikis should be more than just content (Linda Crane, Liverpool)
Library posters: engaging your students (Liz Osman, Cambridge)
Debunking the myth of the Google generation (Nicky Adkins, Cambridge)

Figure 17.5 TeachMeet poster (Courtesy of Katie Birkwood)

hashtag, at the time of writing, tweets talking about TeachMeets in general can use #LibTeachM.

Conclusions

TeachMeets are an effective and inexpensive way to enable sharing of experience and networking by colleagues locally across the various library sectors. They support continuing professional development for the organizers as well as the attendees and can be a supportive environment to encourage first-time presenters.

The genesis, development and dissemination of the LibTeachMeet idea all happened via social media. Social media tools like blogs, Twitter, wikis, Google Docs and Eventbrite have made the organization of informal networking and training events much simpler and enabled the concept to spread further and more rapidly. The success of LibTeachMeets ultimately demonstrates that a real power of social media is in enabling new and better forms of offline interaction and participation, in addition to the creation of online networks.

Appendix: Make your own TeachMeet!

Organizing a TeachMeet is fairly straightforward, but here are some key ingredients:

Teamwork

- Get a group of like-minded individuals together: there's always a bit more to do than you think, so spread the workload and increase the creativity.

Venue

- It can be held anywhere really, but ideally, the venue will not be a lecture theatre (not very conducive to mingling and conversation, and probably quite intimidating for first-time speakers). Accessibility to Wi-Fi is an advantage. A room large enough for about 60 people will probably be sufficiently big to maintain a relaxed and informal atmosphere.

Date/time

- Sometimes this is not as easy as you might think, depending on the flexibility of your target TeachMeeters.

Web presence

- Set up a blog or a wiki so that all information can be held in one central place.
- Setting up accounts on sites like Slideshare, Flickr and YouTube can be helpful for making presentations available after the event. Pick a Twitter hashtag so you can start promoting the TeachMeet.

Funding

- While attending TeachMeets should be free of charge, a small amount of funding/sponsorship to cover the cost of drinks and nibbles will always be appreciated by attendees.

Advice

- Speak with people who have organized a TeachMeet in the past – they're generally the sort of people who are happy to share their experiences.

Technology as a tool

- Use tools such as Eventbrite or Amiando to help manage the bookings. Collaborative writing tools like Google Docs or PBworks can make planning easier for the organizing team.

Source: Birkwood, K., 2011. *(lib)TeachMeet: librarians learning from each other*, www.camlibtm.info/2011/07/12/libteachmeet-at-umbrella/

Useful websites

www.teachmeet.org.uk
www.camlibtm.info

Note

1   www.delicious.com/search?p=camlibtm&chk=&context=all||&fr= del_icio_us&lc=1.

References

23 Things Cambridge (2010) The Cambridge 23 Things. *23 Things Cambridge*, http://23thingscambridge.blogspot.com/p/list-of-23-things.html.

Birkwood, K. (2011) (lib)TeachMeet: librarians learning from each other, www.camlibtm.info/2011/07/12/libteachmeet-at-umbrella/.

Cambridge Librarian TeachMeet (2010) Cambridge Librarian TeachMeet, *TeachMeet –
    teachers sharing ideas with teachers,*
    http://teachmeet.pbworks.com/w/page/28149182/Cambridge-Librarian-TeachMeet.
Cambridge Librarians' TeachMeet (2010) Quick Evaluation of the Event,
    www.slideshare.net/camlibtm/quick-evaluation-of-the-event.
Hallahan, I. (2010) TeachMeet – The Story So Far …. *The H-Blog,*
    http://h-blog.me.uk/?p=161.
Kuhn, I. (2010) teach me(et)! *Musings of a Medical Librarian* (blog),
    http://ilk21.wordpress.com/2010/07/03/teach-meet/.
Kuhn, I. (2011a) Cambridge Librarians TeachMeet,
    http://prezi.com/e9-wuhvjahw4/cambridge-librarians-teachmeet/.
Kuhn, I. (2011b) TeachMeet – Librarians Learning from Each Other,
    http://prezi.com/a7jk_zr5j6to/eahil-teachmeet/.
Osman, L. (2011) CamlibTM, http://prezi.com/pxbcuon6g428/camlibtm/.
Research by Design Ltd (2010) *Defining Our Professional Future: report to CILIP Council,*
    Birmingham, www.cilip.org.uk/get-involved/cilipfuture/Pages/default.aspx.
Tumelty, N. (2011) How to Run Your Own LibTeachMeet, *CILIP Update,*
    http://communities.cilip.org.uk/blogs/update/archive/2011/03/17/how-to-run-
    your-own-libteachmeet-160-by-niamh-tumelty.aspx.
Tumelty, N. and Birkwood, K. (2011) TeachMeet – Librarians Learning from Each
    Other, www.slideshare.net/camlibtm/teachmeet-librarians-learning-from-each-other-
    niamh-tumelty-and-katie-birkwood.

Part 3

What it means for information professionals

Chapter 18

Helping the public online: Web 2.0 in UK public libraries

Helen Leech

Background

As I write, public libraries in the UK are going through a period of change possibly unparalleled in their 200-year history. The economic situation is causing major cuts to public library budgets across the board. In addition to the usual wave of cuts to services, stock funds and opening hours, a growing number of authorities are passing the running of branch libraries to local community groups, commonly to parish councils. Along with the pressure to reduce budgets, another associated driver of change is about meeting the requirements of the UK government's policy initiative called the Big Society,[1] which is encouraging local authorities to engage more with local communities in the management and delivery of services. A third driver of change is the more subtle force of customer demand: there are some indications that online use of public libraries is rising to match physical use, as more and more people use the internet to access the library services outlined below.

All three of these factors are leading to an increasing interest in Web 2.0. Its characteristics of potential for access to and by huge user groups, opportunities to engage with communities through social networks, and user-generated content mean that it offers some useful tools for improving productivity and achieving Big Society engagement with services.

A key dilemma that public libraries are facing, as I write, is the mismatch between what customers expect to be able to do with library services online and what local authorities - the organizations that run public libraries - allow libraries to do. The most common complaint amongst public librarians is about restrictive policies - the biggest barrier to greater engagement with the public. The majority of local authorities ban their staff from using social media and this ban severely restricts both staff's understanding of the technologies and their use of them to interact with customers. However, there are signs that these restrictions are loosening up: there has been an influential report from SOCITM (2010), and some very useful work done by the Local Government Improvement and Development agency (LGID). The LGID runs the Communities of Practice for Public Service website,[2] 'a community platform supporting professional social networks across the public sector', many of which cover social media, and which many local government officers have joined.

The fact that many authorities now have Facebook and Twitter accounts seems to imply that they are less suspicious of social media, and the end result may be that library services are given more leeway to experiment. There is a strong understanding amongst public librarians that Web 2.0 and the delivery of online services is important, and there is a great deal going on, as the developments described below suggest.

Online reference resources are now offered by the vast majority of the 151 public library authorities in the UK, thanks largely to Reference Online,[3] the agreement arranged with online database suppliers by the Museums, Libraries and Archives Council (a body which is being dismantled in 2011 as part of the government's dissolution of quangos). The Reference Online agreement comes to an end in March 2012 but is likely to be continued by the Society of Chief Librarians.

Enquire is an information service that allows the public to chat, 24/7, to a librarian (after UK hours, sessions are handled by US librarians). Currently, 73 of the 151 authorities in the UK participate.[4]

E-books are arriving in UK libraries in a big way. Up until 2009, e-books in public libraries consisted of occasional subscriptions to collections of textbooks like Safari or Netlibrary. In 2009 the American company Overdrive arrived, and for the first time public libraries were able to offer the public an easy way to download popular fiction and non-fiction (plus audio-visual materials) to hand-held devices. As I write, 70 authorities (out of 151) subscribe to Overdrive and others are joining schemes run by Askews, Bloomsbury and WF Howes. Famously, Amazon in the USA announced in 2010 that sales of e-books had overtaken sales of hardbacks, and recently Amazon announced that library users in the USA can download library books to their Kindles (e-readers), something that hadn't been possible up to now (BBC, 2011).

Social media accounts are becoming common for public libraries, with the most popular applications being Facebook, Flickr and Twitter. Manchester libraries are arguably the UK's most successful users of social media, with 3800 followers on Twitter and 2100 followers on Facebook. (However, compare this with the New York Public Library's 133,000 on Twitter and 35,000 on Facebook!)

There's no good way of finding out how far these have entered the everyday in public libraries in the UK. A survey of every library authority in August 2009,[5] showed 42 using Twitter, but the number will have risen greatly since then. However, it's safe to say that social media are now recognized by the majority of library authorities as a key way to promote services.

Surveys and polls are increasingly in use. The Big Society initiative is a driver for the increasing quantity and quality of consultation activity carried out by libraries. At the same time, budget pressures are decreasing the number of authorities using well established consultation tools like the Chartered Institute of Public Finance and Accountancy's Public Library User Satisfaction annual survey and, as a result, more and more authorities are using SurveyMonkey, and the new generation of library management systems (LMS) and content management systems offer polling software.

Mobile technology and library apps are clearly going to be a boom area, but most library authorities will be slow to implement them, as their use is dependent on the latest versions of LMS software. OCLC's Worldcat mobile service has been available since 2009.[6] The county of Hampshire launched possibly the first local authority library-related app in 2010,[7] allowing users to find libraries and other leisure services; around the same time, Axiell announced the launch of its catalogue app.[8] LibraryThing launched its app[9] later in the same year, and Talis announced the launch of its catalogue app in 2011.[10] Other suppliers and authorities are following suit.

QR codes are an associated feature. The rise of smartphones is leading to increasing use of QR codes by library services to signpost information – websites, telephone numbers, snippets of information.

E-newsletters are increasingly replacing the paper versions. Using library membership databases (data protection legislation permitting), library services can reach a much bigger pool of people and can target particular groups by age or location. Hyperlinks can be embedded, and sometimes rich media too. Good examples can be found in Cambridgeshire (going to around

25,000 people), Manchester (50,000), Newcastle-upon-Tyne (50,000) and Plymouth (25,000).

RSS feeds look likely to become an important way of alerting people to and engaging them with services. Doncaster has possibly the only example in the UK of ability to create RSS feeds from a library catalogue, maybe because it has recently implemented Axiell's new Arena software. A small number of other library authorities have turned their events and news streams into feeds, a good example being Newcastle-upon-Tyne.[11]

Tagging and social bookmarking applications are being used by an increasing number of authorities for their lists of recommended websites: Suffolk, for example, is using Delicious to store bookmarks and has embedded a tag cloud into its library pages.[12] Another way that social tagging is being used is in the upcoming generation of LMS. Medialab's Aquabrowser, for example, allows members of the public to tag books, and these tags are searchable.

Book reviews – created by users – are now such an established part of the library catalogue experience that they barely justify a mention, although there is still a minority of local authorities whose LMS do not offer this functionality.

Newer Web 2.0 innovations – **mash-ups, geolocation media (such as Foursquare) and augmented reality** – have not entered the mainstream, although a scattered handful of public library staff are experimenting with these. With regard to mash-ups, Librarything for Libraries[13] functionality could be considered as a mash-up: subscribing libraries can enhance catalogue information with reviews and other data from Librarything.

What are public libraries doing in order to increase awareness of information literacy among the public?

In 2000, the government of the day put public computer terminals and internet access into every library service in the country, using funding from the Big Lottery (at the time, the New Opportunities Fund [NOF]).[14] This was followed by a wave of training for 40,000 staff in a variety of roles – net navigators, IT gatekeepers, information consultants, information navigators and educators. It was on an unprecedented scale and gave library staff confidence to work with a technology that rapidly became a fundamental part of everyone's lives, and a part of the core library offer.

Although the NOF role titles never became completely embedded into library culture, it's safe to say that the roles themselves did. Over the course of the last 10 years the internet has made major inroads into traditional library services: reference and information have largely moved online, and leisure use is following as people increasingly download music, films, audiobooks and e-books. Library staff have always had the task of educating the public in how to use printed information, such as indexes and classification systems, and now the fact that this task has moved online means that an extra step has been added: that of helping people to understand the technology that hosts the information they use. All front-line library staff have become educators.

UK Online was set up in 1999 as part of the University for Industry, with the aim of giving people the skills and confidence to go online. The majority of library services registered their libraries as UK Online centres, and many enrolled to deliver training via MyGuide, a UK Online website that led the public through the first principles of using the internet, such as how to use a mouse, and also helped them to set up their first e-mail account. Many libraries are still using MyGuide, which will be migrating to a new version at the end of 2011.

Most of the library services that opted out of delivering MyGuide have developed their own training courses for the public, often using the BBC's WebWise, a beginner's guide to using the internet.[15]

The government launched a new initiative in March 2010: Race Online 2012 (raceonline2012.org). It makes the following commitment: 'By the end of this parliament we endeavour to make sure everyone of working age should be online and no one should retire without web skills.' The Society of Chief Librarians committed public libraries to helping half a million people get online, and, at the time of writing, this target is on track.

The Big Society initiative was mentioned above. Associated with this and with the previous government's community engagement initiative, 'Communities in Control', is the rise of the computer volunteer. Some local authorities are recruiting volunteers who have more time, and in some cases more experience, than staff to help people with computer queries in the library. Kent County Council was one of the first authorities to develop the role of Computer Buddy[16].

More recently, DOTS – Digital Outreach Trainers – have sprung up, acting outside the walls of the library. At the moment, the project is limited to a handful of authorities in the north of England, funded by the European Social Fund (www.makingitpersonal.org.uk/).

What are public libraries doing in order to increase Web 2.0 and information literacy among their staff?

Knowledge of social media is recognized as a priority for librarians, and there is a huge range of training courses available from the Chartered Institute of Library and Information Professionals (CILIP), the Museums, Libraries and Archives Council (MLA), UK Electronic Information Group (UKEIG) and the Joint Information Systems Committee (JISC). CILIP's associated and local bodies regularly organize seminars and courses. CILIP's publishing arm, Facet Publishing, has published many books on the subject of Web 2.0.

In terms of other publications, the Scottish Library and Information Council and CILIP Scotland produced 'A Guide to using Web 2.0 in Libraries' in late 2009.[17]

Some major initiatives

23 Things: In 2006 Helene Blowers wrote a training course for the public libraries of Charlotte and Mecklenburg County, North Carolina, and it can still be found at http://plcmcl2-about.blogspot.com/ (Figure 18.1). It was based on a very simple concept. She set up a blog and divided it into modules. Each module or 'Thing' covered a separate technology. Staff could work through the modules from their own desks, at their own speed. The content was light and entertaining, with lots of emphasis on podcasts and videos and plenty of interactivity where staff could set up their own accounts on Twitter or Flickr and upload content. To monitor their progress through the course, participants were asked to set up a blog and record their experiences.

While the concept has been adopted widely in the USA, only Kirklees and Devon in the UK were exploring its use. In 2010 Aberdeen, Portsmouth, Suffolk and Surrey library services collaborated to rewrite the course for a UK audience. Nine library authorities and a handful of other organizations are currently rolling it out. It's not meant to be a comprehensive overview of new technologies, but rather to give staff enough confidence to handle enquiries and start thinking about using social media in their own libraries. It's free to use for anybody, and can be found at http://23things.wetpaint.com/.

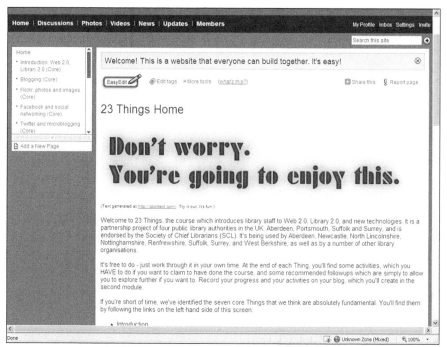

Figure 18.1 23 Things (Reproduced with permission of Helen Leech)

Enquire training: Enquire (see above, p. 206) is a service that allows the public to chat to a librarian. The chat software is called Questionpoint and is supplied by OCLC. It's an important feature on the information literacy landscape because not only has it embedded the chat software into the library toolkit, but the service aims to direct people to the information they want on the internet. If you use the service to ask for anything, from a Sudoku puzzle to a cure for cancer, the librarian at the other end will direct you to the most appropriate internet resource. This requires a high level of information literacy, and the Enquire service in most authorities is run by ex-reference desk staff, who have a great deal of experience in evaluating resources. In a similar vein, most of the companies supplying **online reference resources and e-books** offer online training in their use and promotion.

Networking opportunities

There are a number of forums and resources, places where people can learn and can gather to discuss issues, but at the moment the UK public library presence on them is not great.

- JISC runs a Web 2.0 e-mail list which is an excellent place to ask questions.[18.]
- There is an online Web 2.0 forum called Library 2.0. (www.library20.com/) that includes some useful discussion groups.
- uklibchat (http://uklibchat.wordpress.com/) is a forum run by a group of individuals, that offers an opportunity to discuss issues of the moment using organized, scheduled sessions on Twitter. Discussions so far have covered marketing and e-books.
- Twitter itself shouldn't be forgotten ... by following the right people, one can tap into a wealth of experience and knowledge.

The Communities of Practice for Public Service run by LGID (see above) includes a Social Media discussion forum,[19] which is a good place to discuss issues and find out what's going on elsewhere. One of the communities of practice was an e-books forum coordinated by the MLA – which has unfortunately become defunct following the departure of the MLA staff member who was running it.

Another opportunity is LinkedIn. There are groups on LinkedIn that provide opportunities to network with colleagues, although they tend to be American – but there is no co-ordinated group for public librarians.

A final possibility is seminars and conferences. For example, Internet Librarian International attracts many public librarians, but few from the UK – mostly, I suspect, because of the cost.

Conclusion

While there is evidence that library authorities are developing a strong individual focus on Web 2.0, it seems clear that the sector would benefit from a more co-ordinated, more national approach in order to drive adoption of Web 2.0 and prevent the duplication of effort that currently exists. There is no national strategy for Web 2.0 in public libraries, and without it development will be piecemeal, particularly in view of local authority restrictions. A national strategy could include:

- identification of the business case for Web 2.0, probably incorporating the aims of increasing customer engagement and increasing use of library services online
- strengthening staff understanding of Web 2.0 through identification of

learning opportunities

- supporting library management in implementing Web 2.0 by defining the legal and corporate risks of using Web 2.0, with suggestions for risk management
- case studies of best practice from both inside and outside the sector that could be adopted locally
- identification of opportunities for library authorities to work together using Web 2.0, for example on staff training or social bookmarking
- an online 'place', possibly an LGID community of practice, where public librarians could gather to discuss Web 2.0 issues
- incentives for library services to adopt Web 2.0, perhaps with a prize for best use.

However, it's clear that, even without a co-ordinated approach, Web 2.0 is quietly on the way to becoming a fundamental part of the library experience.

Notes

1   www.cabinetoffice.gov.uk/big-society.
2   www.communities.idea.gov.uk/welcome.do.
3   www.mla.gov.uk/what/support/online.
4   www.questionpoint.org/crs/servlet/org.oclc.home.TFSRedirect?virtcategory=10836.
5   http://librariesandweb2.wetpaint.com/page/Web+2.0+Examples.
6   www.oclc.org/news/releases/200921.htm.
7   www3.hants.gov.uk/iphone/culture-all-app.htm.
8   www.axiell.com/c/document_library/get_file?uuid=80cd3dbb-fb2d-4a6f-8f9f-c29d243b6851&groupId=10099.
9   www.librarything.com/blogs/thingology/2010/10/library-anywhere-iphone-app/.
10   www.guardian.co.uk/edinburgh/2011/apr/13/edinburgh-library-app-itunes.
11   http://community.newcastle.gov.uk/libraries/memory-bank. – *Scroll down to see their list of feeds.*
12   www.suffolk.gov.uk/LeisureAndCulture/Libraries/SuffolkReferenceDirect/listing.htm.
13   www.librarything.com/forlibraries.
14   http://research.mla.gov.uk/evidence/download-publication.php?id=705.
15   Now part of BBC First Click: www.bbc.co.uk/connect/campaigns/first_click.shtml.
16   Have a look at this video: www.youtube.com/watch?v=-RHoTq7kxtw.
17   www.slainte.org.uk/slainte2/index.html.

18   https://www.jiscmail.ac.uk/cgi-bin/webadmin?A0=LIS-WEB2.
19   www.communities.idea.gov.uk/comm/landing-home.do?id=13317.

References

BBC (2011) Kindle Gets Library Book Lending, BBC, 21 April,
    www.bbc.co.uk/news/technology-13155967.
SOCITM (2010) Why ICT Management Should Lead Their Organisations to Embrace
    IT, www.socitm.net/downloads/file/454/
    social_media-why_ict_management_should_lead_their_organisations_to_embrace_it.

Chapter 19

Change has arrived at an iSchool library near you

Judy O'Connell

Introduction

Since the start of the third millennium, the educational services of a good school library have become more important than ever – this at a time when school librarians or teacher librarians have been warned of their irrelevance, with some school libraries also having been closed. At the centre of this misguided scenario are the changes brought about by technology and the digitization of our lives, online, on devices, in a variety of formats and in a socially networked world. Our students have been born into a digital era that is significantly changing their literacy and information encounters and the ways in which they can learn. Participative new media tools have altered the shape and experience of learning and provided school librarians in the changing learning environment with new skills, new tools and new ways of working with literacy, information literacy and digital fluency in Library 2.0 (O'Connell, 2008). The iPad and other mobile devices have changed school libraries forever. While we are not yet quite sure what the implications of these changes will be over the long term, the era of the *iSchool library* has definitely arrived. In the 21st century information ecology, the school library is evolving into a school-wide, future-oriented library service, sometimes described as the iCentre (Hough, 2011) or Learning Commons (Loertscher and Marcoux, 2010). In this new library, both physical and virtual spaces are being changed. Many schools (Corbett, 2011; Subel, 2007) have transformed the library's physical space into collaborative work areas or spaces for relaxation, designed for reading; information gathering, analysis and sharing; and media creation. With improved delivery of digital content for use in new flexible learning spaces, libraries are being purposefully designed to become active agents of learning.

Our students now need help in navigating diverse information pathways within their personal and creative learning environments. They need a range of literature and information options, delivered to them via a variety of physical and virtual means – from books to all manner of media and digital objects – via a plethora of digital devices. They need to know how to juxtapose text, sound, media and social connections in real time, and how to filter, then mix and match what they see, hear and experience in order to build personal knowledge and understandings of the curriculum. For students, information literacy action happens wherever they read and interpret the world around them, not just in the classroom. Where once the bibliographic paradigm created textbook learning and school libraries, learning today requires that teachers and school librarians understand reading and information seeking in a connected world.

In this new library, the literature, magazines, information, technology, learning and teaching activities are designed to support the needs of the networked learning community, creating a partnership between teachers, students, school, home and the global community.

Meeting readers where they are

The role of the school librarian is to promote books and reading, in old ways and new ways (Gordon, 2010a). Young (2007) explains that books are *machines for reading*, in whatever form or on whatever device they come to us, allowing human conversation as both a reader and a writer. A book is an ideas machine, so reading, writing and publishing has simply moved into the digital environment.

The newest devices for reading and listening are beginning to provide options never before possible for fiction and non-fiction reading. School libraries are making use of audio and digital literature and magazines for delivery via the iPad, Kindle and other mobile devices, from sources such as Google Books, Amazon and Overdrive (www.overdrive.com) services. Fiction print collections have also been reorganized by genre, to reflect interest groupings e.g. Fantasy and Science Fiction or Mystery and Suspense. Projects and activities are also devised to promote literacy through as many different avenues as there are school librarians with imagination (see Figure 19.1 for an example).

Reading, writing, creative activities, gaming, transmedia storytelling (integral elements of the story told through different media), immersive worlds (such as Quest Atlantis, http://atlantis.crlt.indiana.edu/) and digital storytelling applications can all be adapted and adopted to meet readers where they are,

Figure 19.1 'Body in the Library': a cross-curriculum transliteracy project (Photograph: Judy O'Connell)

according to their 21st-century literacy needs. School libraries that adapt to the digital needs of their students not only continue to build a reading culture in the school but provide the divergence and convergence of media needed to provide the materials for motivation, differentiation, collaboration and connections necessary for 21st-century learning (Lamb and Johnson, 2010; Hay and Foley, 2009).

The new information environment

Print materials are no longer at the core of the reference collection, the non-fiction collection or the information search process. Students use technology to research online, anytime, anywhere. Yet, despite teachers often being critical of students' information literacy (IL) online, paradoxically, they still maintain that their students know more than they do when operating in online environments (Ladbrook and Probert, 2011). According to Herring (2011), popular assumptions about the success of IL knowledge and skills transfer are inaccurate, leading to problems in instruction.

Internet resources are easily available and present an open invitation to plagiarism. The problem, particularly at university level, is now widely discussed, especially in the media, and high school teachers have become aware of the need to help their students to understand and avoid plagiarism from the early years of their secondary education (Williamson, Archibald and McGregor, 2010). Perhaps the complication is that IL programmes in schools are trapped in past practices and unable to respond to the demands of existing and emerging digital learning environments.

Now students are involved in five interwoven, integrated kinds of learning: curriculum content, information literacy, learning how to learn, literacy competence and social skills (Kuhlthau and Maniotes, 2010). We are nurturing informed learning (Bruce, Hughes and Somerville, 2011) by refocusing attention on using information to learn, while also supporting the development of the learners' growing awareness of their experiences of information use as they go about learning.

We have a new information environment that demands more extensive IL capabilities. The purpose of, and underpinning need for, IL has evolved. The 21st-Century Fluency Project (21CFP)[1] identifies critical thinking skills as essential to living in a multimedia world and introduces *information fluency* as the ability to unconsciously and intuitively interpret information in all forms and formats in order to extract the essential knowledge, authenticate it and perceive its significance.

More recently *transliteracy* has captured the interest of school librarians as a term to explain being literate in the 21st century, where the relationship between people, technology and the social meaning of literacy is recognized in past, present and future modalities (Ipri, 2010). The emergence of social media and collaborative online communities has also led to the reframing of information literacy as *metaliteracy*, because information takes many forms online and is produced and communicated through multiple modalities (Mackey and Jacobson, 2011).

School librarians are involved with and responding to an information *renaissance* that is rewriting the world as we know it: knowledge; information bias; distributed social and personal information; public and private data; global marketing; clashing cultures; a million voices commenting on a billion issues in blogs, wikis and podcasts. Information technology has become a participatory medium, giving rise to an environment that is constantly being changed and reshaped by the participation itself, changing the flow of news, affecting tacit as well as explicit knowledge and embedding a new culture of learning (Thomas and Brown, 2011).

So now, more than ever, collaboration between teachers and school librarians is core business as students benefit from team teaching – helping them to deepen their levels of knowledge of both IL and subject content (Williamson, Archibald and McGregor, 2010, 27; Ohio Media Spectrum, 2008).

Making learning visible

Our students in primary and secondary schools need to be nurtured in *how to learn* from the multiplicity of resources at their disposal, using the best information-organization and critical-thinking strategies that we can show them.

We need to build a culture of enquiry at the heart of each of our schools. As Gordon (2010b, 79) explains, a culture of enquiry emerges as teachers become learners, and learners are self- and peer-taught, and everyone becomes a researcher. Teaching and learning in school libraries has been shifting from tool-based and skills-based instruction to constructivist user- and learner-centric approaches, and evidence-based practice has become the essential tool for improvement of practice (Bates, McClure and Spinks, 2010).

Emerging devices, tools, media and virtual environments offer opportunities for creating new types of learning communities for students and teachers. Dede (2005) described the interrelated matrix of the learning styles of neo-millennials as being marked by active learning (real and simulated), co-designed, and personalized to individual needs and preferences, based on diverse, tacit, situated experiences, all centred on fluency in multiple media, chosen for the types of communication, activities, experiences and expressions they empower. *The NMC Horizon Report: 2011 K-12 Edition* (Johnson, Adams and Haywood, 2011) (issued annually since 2009) has identified and described emerging technologies that are having a significant impact on K-12 education, reiterating the diversity of influences in the learning spaces of our schools. For school librarians, the report directs attention simultaneously to information use and to learning, and highlights the fact that 21st-century technologies are unlikely to be empowering unless they are in the hands of an informed learner.

Content

Beyond physical resources, content that was difficult to access has become accessible and searchable, such as entire historical collections of news media and photos. Libraries and museums are providing open access to a treasure trove of cultural and historical resources, providing unprecedented access for students and scholars around the world. The millions of digitized books and articles are changing scholarship and the tactics of learning. Federated search, linked-data, EZproxy, and OpenURL resolvers are all, potentially, supporting the needs of the learner by making it possible to engage in information search strategies that are automatically tailored to the task at hand.

For example, by showing our students how to connect to a database information repository (such as EBSCO, Gale or JSTOR) or to a local library service via Google Scholar, we are helping them to broaden the scope of their information seeking, while at the same time refining the quality of the information response. Alternatively, federated searching (where a query is sent to various databases in real time, using services such as Follett One Search), which best serves novice searchers with little exposure to IL training, may have a place in many schools that are still developing strong IL programmes (Abercrombie, 2008).

New developments in searching, such as Google Instant (which shows results as you type), have both enhanced and hindered the information-seeking habits of students by responding quickly to input search terms, so making the refining of searches by altering the keywords seem less relevant. Wikipedia provides instant answers. On the other hand, the computational search engine, Wolfram Alpha, allows teachers to explore complex mathematical problems without students having to calculate complex data problems for themselves, so that they can make the leap directly to the analysis and synthesis of results (Harris, 2011).

Such new search modalities require a more sophisticated response from IL programmes, where we need to teach how important it is to evaluate every information source, even those traditionally considered reliable, because of the interconnectedness of information sources and socially networked tagged repositories (Gunnels and Sisson, 2009). There is a great deal of rich content available to students and teachers that is collaboratively built and shared, including blogs, wikis, images, videos, places, events, music, books and more. Searching for content requires wise IL strategies and the embedding of tools into curriculum learning processes, in order to avoid becoming lost in the information labyrinth. Finding answers to an information query would be easy if computers could understand and collate all the information 'out there'. Finding solutions to an information problem will, however, always require metacognitive engagement with the content being found.

For educators, the promise of the Semantic Web, or Web 3.0, where meaningful connections can be established among any online pieces of information (Feigenbaum et al., 2007), will be simply to change information discovery by allowing us to ask questions rather than perform searches – no more than that.

In discussing the power and peril of Web 3.0 and the Semantic Web, Ohler (2010) suggests that knowledge construction via internet search will become much more effective in this shift from data to semantically connected resources. For example, when a student searches for *causes of the [American] Civil War*, rather than receiving a list of pages that merely contain the words *causes* and *Civil War*, they would receive information in which the word *causes* is specifically related to the causes of the Civil War. The Semantic Web (Feigenbaum et al., 2007) and RDA (Resource Description and Access) metadata standards (Oliver, 2010) for intelligent resource discovery mean that school librarians have an increasingly important role to play in nurturing information-literate engagement with content. This is because the intelligence of the connections will not help our students to learn better unless the IL strategies that we introduce them to actually ensure critical thinking and problem solving.

Content exploration and learning demands a mix-and-match approach:

- search strategies
- evaluation strategies
- critical thinking and problem solving
- networked conversation and collaboration
- cloud computing environments
- ethical use and production of information
- information curation of personal and distributed knowledge.

IL beyond Library 2.0 is an area of pivotal importance for the school librarian in terms of understanding it, becoming involved with it and presenting new methods and new information strategies for educators working within the curriculum.

Information strategy

Web 2.0 revolutionized the means at our disposal for filtering and sharing information. Whether by managing information by means of social bookmarking or RSS reads and feeds, or communicating with our school community via blogs, wikis, podcasts, YouTube or Facebook, students, teachers and school librarians have entered into digital conversations. Widgets, portals, apps, feeds, aggregators and more now provide us with our 'tools of the trade' for information curation. Global school library leader and blogger Dr Joyce Valenza of Springfield Township High School library and the School Library Journal[2] regularly provides new professional tools and strategies for school library collections, instruction, services and programmes. Valenza (2010) has published a manifesto for 21st-century school librarians, prompting deep discussion about the evolving role of the school librarian. She regularly identifies engaging new strategies for use with learners in order to promote reading, information fluency, digital citizenship, communication and creativity, providing supporting information via the school's Spartan Guides (Figure 19.2) – created using the library information organization tool LibGuides.[3]

The importance of the school librarian is intrinsically linked to effective and responsive information curation and dissemination in distributed environments within and beyond the school. Use of Web 2.0 tools has become embedded in good practice, and information curation has extended beyond the library catalogue, to library and school information management systems for bibliographic and media resources, and various organizational tools that reside beyond the school in web environments such as LibGuides, Diigo, Live Binders, wiki, Delicious, Google tools, RSS, Media Tools, Netvibes, iGoogle and many more.

But when a technology focus subverts students' conversation and their development of critical thinking skills (and their ability to evaluate and analyse the information at hand), the mental processes that change knowledge from information to concept are not learned (Bomar, 2010). With the maturation of Web 2.0 tools, nurturing IL skills and strategies has necessitated a shift towards a meta-literate approach. School librarians are rethinking what 'collection' of information means, thereby supporting personalized and collaborative information seeking. The new core *information research tools* available for students, teachers and school librarians adopting IL beyond Library 2.0 include:

- microblogging tools for information sharing by teachers, students, classes and the school community in primary and secondary schools, e.g. Edmodo, Yammer, Google+, or Twitter
- social bookmarking and tagged collections, e.g. Diigo, Flickr, Vodpod
- collaborative writing, editing, mind-mapping and presentation tools, e.g.

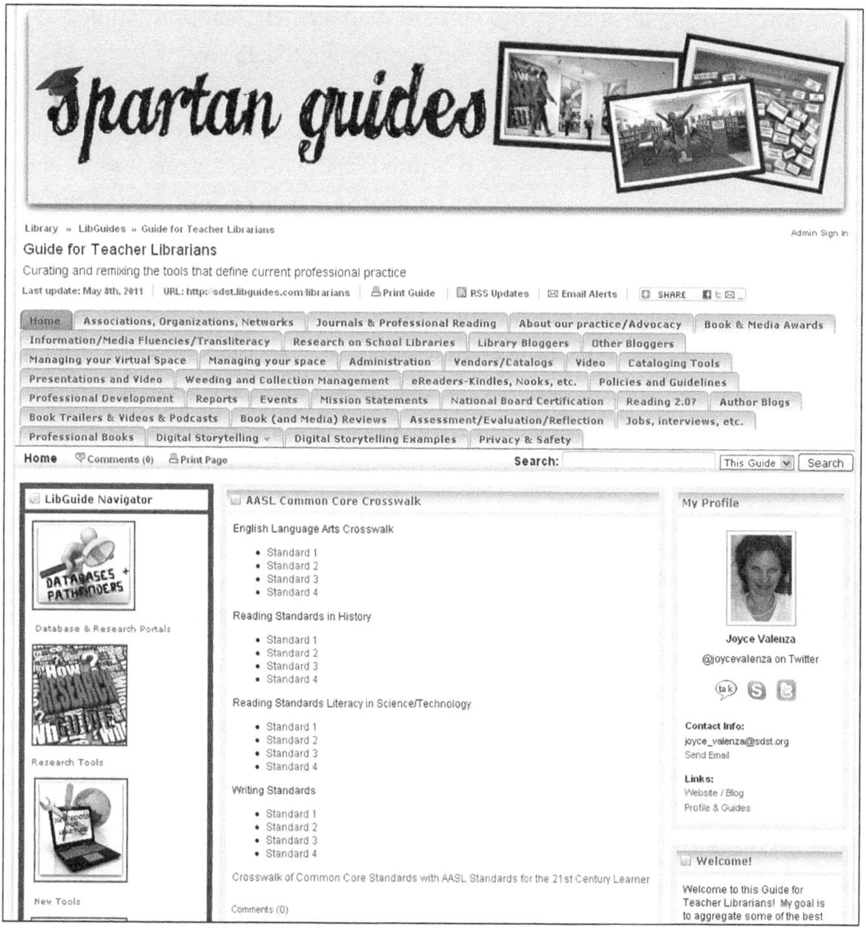

Figure 19.2 LibGuides as 'tools of trade' (Reproduced by permission of Joyce Valenza)

Google Docs, Exploratree, VoiceThread, MindMeister, Wikispaces
- research tools for online information management, writing and collaboration, e.g. Zotero, EndNote, EasyBib, BibMe, Mendeley, RefWorks
- information capture in multiple platforms and on multiple devices, e.g. Evernote, scrible.com
- library catalogues, databases, and open access repositories - all used for information collection, RSS topic and journal alerts, and compatible with research organization tools
- aggregators, news readers and start pages, e.g. iGoogle, Netvibes, Symbaloo, Feedly

- online storage, file sharing and content management across multiple platforms and computers, e.g. Dropbox, Box.net, SkyDrive.

These tools have allowed us to reframe information collection as highly flexible and collaborative information and knowledge conversations, while also facilitating information organization. Technology and online integration can facilitate critical thinking and knowledgeable actions, rather than merely permitting the access to and transformation of information as part of the IL skills set. The point is to engage our students in multiple conversations and research pathways that reflect the changing nature of scholarship in multimodal environments. As Lankes (2011) explains, at last we have a departure from information, access and artefacts as the focus. In the lens of conversation, artefacts and access are useful only in that they are used to build knowledge through active learning.

Leadership strategy

Becoming a model for lifelong learning has been the goal of every school librarian, because school libraries are in the knowledge business. By building a future-ready personal learning network, a school librarian can engage in new and emerging media to assist in promoting creative and authentic knowledge work in their schools (Cox, 2010; Harlan, 2009).

This leadership strategy allows a school librarian to be proactive within the school community and participate in many and varied learning conversations, such as:

- curriculum conversation and innovation
- project-based learning (Boss and Krauss, 2007)
- guided enquiry (Todd, 2010)
- virtual and gaming environments (O'Connell and Groom, 2010)
- digital divide, and credibility of online information
- contemporary media and open online access
- participatory evaluation of information (Flanagin and Metzger, 2008)
- digital citizenship
- internet safety
- responsible use of information (Ribble and Bailey, 2007)
- global sharing of leading practice and resources to support the 21st-century learner

- contribution to scholarly research through participatory communication and publications
- the American Association of School Librarians' (AASL) Standards for the 21st-Century Learner Lesson Plan Database (http://aasl.jesandco.org)
- Teacher Librarian Ning (http://teacherlibrarian.ning.com/)
- community entrepreneur
- bring together conversations and resources to build knowledge
- staff development to enhance student and staff learning in collaborative environments
- community outreach, supporting and motivating the evolution of the core learning mission of the school.

The future

IL beyond Library 2.0 is a story about transition to future learning – a new kind of lifelong learning that has adaptability at its core. It is a responsibility to prepare students to move from the world of school to the world of adulthood, employment, further education, vocational training and community participation. It is a responsibility to work with these students of ours, who are already immersed in creative, collaborative and socially networked environments. How we harness these environments and how we teach our students to be literate, information literate and knowledgeable in these 21st-century environments will determine our success *and* the future relevance and importance of our school libraries.

Notes

1   www.committedsardine.com/fluencies.cfm.
2   http://blog.schoollibraryjournal.com/neverendingsearch/.
3   http://sdst.libguides.com/librarians; http://sdst.libguides.com/newtools; http://sdst.libguides.com/researchtools.

References

Abercrombie, S. E. (2008) Evaluation of Federated Searching Options for the School Library, *School Library Media Research*, **11**, www.ala.org/aasl/aaslpubsandjournals/slmrb/slmrcontents/volume11/ abercrombie.

Bates, J., McClure, J. and Spinks, A. (2010) Making the Case for Evidence Based Practice, *Library Media Connection*, **29** (1), 24–7.

Bomar, S. (2010) A School-wide Instructional Framework for Evaluating Sources, *Knowledge Quest*, **38** (3), 72-5.

Boss, S. and Krauss, J. (2007) *Reinventing Project-based Learning: your field guide to real-world projects in the digital age*, 1st edn, Eugene OR: International Society for Technology in Education.

Bruce, C. S., Hughes, H. E. and Somerville, M. M. (2011) Supporting Informed Learners in the 21st Century, *Library Trends*, **60** (1).

Corbett, T. (2011) The Changing Role of the School Library's Physical Space, *School Library Monthly*, **27** (7), 5-7.

Cox, E. (2010) Building a Future-ready Personal Learning Network, *School Library Monthly*, **27** (3), 34-5.

Dede, C. (2005) Planning for Neomillennial Learning Styles: implications for investments in technology and faculty. In Oblinger, D. G. and Oblinger, J. L. (eds), *Educating the Net Generation*, www.educause.edu/educatingthenetgen.

Feigenbaum, L., Herman, I., Hongsermeier, T., Neumann, E. and Stephens, S. (2007) The Semantic Web in Action, *Scientific American*, **297** (6), 90-7.

Flanagin, A. J. and Metzger, M. (2008) Digital Media and Youth: unparalleled opportunity and unprecedented responsibility. In Metzger, M. J. and Flanagin, A. J. (eds.), *Digital Media, Youth, and Credibility*, The John D. and Catherine T. MacArthur Foundation Series on Digital Media and Learning, MIT Press, 5-28.

Gordon, C. A. (2010a) Meeting Readers Where They Are, *School Library Journal*, **56** (11), 32.

Gordon, C. A. (2010b) The Culture of Inquiry in School Libraries, *School Libraries Worldwide*, **16** (1), 73-88.

Gunnels, C. B. and Sisson, A. (2009) Confessions of a Librarian, or: how I learned to stop worrying and love Google, *Community and Junior College Libraries*, **15** (1), 15-21.

Harlan, M. (2009) *Personal Learning Networks: professional development for the isolated school librarian*, Westport, CT: Libraries Unlimited.

Harris, C. (2011) Wolfram/Alpha Figured Out, *School Library Journal*, **57** (1), 64-6.

Hay, L. and Foley, C. (2009) School Libraries Building Capacity for Student Learning in 21C, *Scan*, **28** (2), 17-26.

Herring, J. (2011) Assumptions, Information Literacy and Transfer in High Schools, *Teacher Librarian*, **38** (3), 32.

Hough, M. (2011) Libraries as iCentres: helping schools face the future, *School Library Monthly*, **27** (7), 8-11.

Ipri, T. (2010) Introducing Transliteracy, *College and Research Libraries News*, **71** (10), 532-67.

Johnson, L., Adams, S. and Haywood, K. (2011) *The NMC Horizon Report: 2011 K-12 Edition*, Austin, TX: The New Media Consortium.

Kuhlthau, C. C. and Maniotes, L. K. (2010) Building Guided Inquiry Teams for 21st Century Learners, *School Library Monthly*, **26** (5), 4.

Ladbrook, J. and Probert, E. (2011) Information Skills and Critical Literacy: where are our digikids at with online searching and are their teachers helping? *Australian Journal of Educational Technology*, **27** (1), 105-21, www.ascilite.org.au/ajet/ajet27/ladbrook.html.

Lamb, A. and Johnson, L. (2010) Divergent Convergence Part 2: teaching and learning in a transmedia world, *Teacher Librarian*, **38** (1), 64-9.

Lankes, D. R. (2011) *The Atlas of New Librarianship*, Cambridge, MA: MIT Press.

Loertscher, D. V. and Marcoux, E. B. (2010) *Learning Commons Treasury*, Teacher Librarian Press.

Mackey, T. P. and Jacobson, T. E. (2011) Reframing Information Literacy as a Metaliteracy, *College and Research Libraries*, **72** (1), 62-78.

O'Connell, J. (2008) School Library 2.0: new skills, new knowledge, new futures. In Godwin, P. and Parker, J. (eds.), *Information Literacy Meets Library 2.0*, Facet Publishing.

O'Connell, J. and Groom, D. (2010) *Virtual Worlds*, Camberwell, Victoria: ACER Press.

Ohio Media Spectrum (2008) Preparing 21st Century Ohio Learners for Success: the role of information literacy and libraries, *Ohio Media Spectrum*, **60** (1), 38-44.

Ohler, J. (2010) The Power and Peril of Web 3.0: it's more than just semantics, *Learning and Leading with Technology*, **37** (7), 14-17.

Oliver, C. (2010) *Introducing RDA: a guide to the basics*, American Library Association Editions.

Ribble, M. and Bailey, G. D. (2007) *Digital Citizenship in Schools*, 1st edn, Eugene, OR: International Society for Technology in Education.

Subel, S. (2007) Facility Design as an Agent of Learning, *Knowledge Quest*, **35** (3), 38-41.

Thomas, D. and Brown, J. S. (2011) *A New Culture of Learning: cultivating the imagination for a world of constant change*, CreateSpace.

Todd, R. J. (2010) *Curriculum Integration*, Camberwell, Victoria: ACER Press.

Valenza, J. K. (2010) Manifesto for 21st Century School Librarians, www.voya.com/2010/09/15/tag-team-tech-october-2010/.

Williamson, K., Archibald, A. and McGregor, J. (2010) Shared Vision: a key to successful collaboration? *School Libraries Worldwide*, **16** (2), 16–30.

Young, S. (2007) *The Book is Dead: long live the book*, Sydney: University of New South Wales Press.

Chapter 20

Information literacy: a path to the future

Peter Godwin

Introduction

We can no longer think just in terms of 2.0. Its transformation into social media and merger with mobile devices require librarians to look right across the information landscape for the literacies that are required in the future. This has been a journey of discovery for me: for the first time many things have begun to make sense, and I want to share that vision with you. I hope that you last the whole journey and do not lapse into sleep and swerve dangerously into the ditch on the way!

I believe we have to survey the whole information landscape if we are to understand the complex blend of literacies that we, as educators, and our students, as learners and 21st-century citizens, have to experience. Many writers have attempted to do this. As we go through some of these explorations we may see occasional shafts of light through the trees and clearings along the way, before we grasp that what we see keeps subtly changing and will always depend on the context.

A confusion of literacies

In recent years there have been a number of attempts to create maps of literacies, and this has sometimes implied that information literacy (IL) is no longer the central literacy for the 21st century. Twenty-first-century literacy is 'the set of abilities and skills where aural, visual, and digital literacy overlap' (New Media Consortium, 2005). As we have seen already, literacies can be divided into three main types: generic, situated and transforming. From the first type, Bawden (2001) traced a variety of skill-based literacies that fitted the requirements of the more varied information environment with its new technologies. This included the development of computer and, later, ICT literacy, which initially was frequently confused with IL. I will now *briefly* outline some of these literacies.

Digital literacy (DL)

This is 'the ability to understand and use information in multiple formats from a wide variety of sources when it is presented via computers' (Gilster, 1997). Gilster's view of DL went wider than the internet, which he saw as only one major digital source. It was more about literacy in the digital age. Discussions about IL and DL have not impinged much on the library practitioner (Bawden, 2001). Perhaps surprisingly, a framework devised by Markless and Streatfield (2007) was very similar to Gilster's original concept. Recently, Hague and Peyton (2010) have produced an excellent DL handbook for teachers in schools. It talks about the process of 'young people becoming active meaning-makers' (ibid., 8) and provides a visual map of DL skills, such as critical thinking and evaluation, e-safety and the ability to find and select information. Contrastingly, DL has also been described as merely the ability to perform IL tasks within a digital environment (Weetman DaCosta, 2011).

Media literacy

Media literacy is another skill-based literacy and involves critical thinking as a result of getting information from mass media sources like newspapers, television and radio. These skills overlap significantly with IL (Bawden, 2001). Media literacy is most frequently associated with schools (Koltay, 2011), but it is sometimes weakened by teachers who assume that their pupils know more about it than they themselves do (Hobbs and Jensen, 2009). Digital media literacy skills are seen as a key 21st-century skill in the Horizon Report (2010). Again, teachers are limiting their students by their own lack of training and this is not helped by skills, and standards for their measurement, being based too much on tools, and not enough on critical thinking (Horizon Report, 2010). UNESCO's adoption of a combined concept of information and media literacy recognizes the overlap and may have helped to raise the status of the term. (UNESCO, 2011). Rheingold (2010) has gone further, outlining five literacies for social media (attention, participation, collaboration, network awareness and critical consumption). His analysis requires these five social media literacies to be combined:

- Learn to turn on high attention when required.

- Understand the huge potential of participation, following mass access to the internet and via mobile devices.
- Collaborate in powerful new ways.
- Understand how networks operate and decide who we trust to take up our time online.
- And finally, decide what is trustworthy online.

Clearly there are major connections with IL here.

Visual literacy

Visual literacy addresses knowing how to assess the value and credibility of images: a set of skills that has grown in importance in the digital environment. Harris (2010, 526) notes overlap with IL and that 'the borders do exist, will continue to exist, but that they are not discrete or static'. This could apply right across all the literacies. He goes on to show some synergies between the visual literacy standards of Maria Avgerinou (2010) and the ACRL IL standards (Association of College and Research Libraries, 2000). He sees opportunities for librarians to assist in the cross-fertilization of literacy development in the classroom.

Enter Web 2.0

So far we have been looking at literacies that attempted to engage with the Web 1.0 world of static documents, but within a rapidly expanding digital environment. Web 2.0 has changed all this. Wikis, blogs, Facebook, Delicious, YouTube: the point is less about what the new technologies can enable us to do (easy research, photo stories, movies) and more that the kind of behaviour that they foster is different from that outlined in previous literacy models (Lankshear and Knobel, 2007). Behaviour is participatory, collaborative, distributed and less dominated by experts. We have the ability to take content and freely use and adapt it. The book was seen as the major carrier of text, but in the new world text will be less rigidly fixed and controlled.

Here we must return to the question posed in Chapter 2: does this all require a reconceptualization of IL? From an exhaustive (and exhausting) exploration of this question it is clear that many attempts are being made to chart this new ground.

Špiranec and Zorica (2010) have come up with the idea of IL 2.0. They begin by seeing a connection between education as a process that involves creation, reflection and critical awareness (sometimes called constructivism) and the increasing importance of IL. In addition, the information landscape, with its 2.0 aspects of user participation and collaboration, was a fundamental change that cried out for the label 'Information Literacy 2.0' as a subset of IL. Špiranec and Zorica also embrace the view that information is socially produced in a group via social relationships and that literacies should be seen within a particular social context. All this chimes very well with what is presented in this book, except for simply seeing IL 2.0 as a subset. A more thorough understanding of how the literacies interrelate is still required.

Helen Partridge (Queensland University of Technology) is researching how people experience IL in a social media context. Social media are changing the way in which people find and use information, and this means seeing IL in a richer, more dynamic way. She states: 'Previous studies have looked at information seeking and my research will go beyond this to look at people's information practice, which is the ways they find and use information, form a relationship with information and create their own information style' (Campus Daily, 2010).

Practitioners have also begun to alter their practice and document it. Walstrum, Garcia and Morisson (2011) explain how they have moved into what they call 'digital IL' at National-Louis University. As information has moved into new, digital, 2.0 formats, they felt that they should transform their IL teaching in the 21st century to include social bookmarking, Wikipedia and blogs. The module that they offer moves from just a library focus to critically assessing IL and social media in society - for example, business students look at Twitter's validity as a business information tool.

Metaliteracy

This is one solution to the search for ways of charting the literacies necessary in the 21st century. Mackey and Jacobson (2011) feel that social media have required IL to be recast as metaliteracy, to support various types of literacy. They do not feel that the old SCONUL framework is applicable to the new trends in information creation and distribution. They see 'information fluency' as 'a set of intellectual capabilities, conceptual knowledge, and contemporary skills associated with information technology'. IL is wider than and independent of technology. Metaliteracy in practice covers the understanding of format, type and mode of delivery. It would provide a platform foundation for media, digital ICT literacy and visual literacy. They conclude that 'Information itself is constantly variable and to fully gain knowledge about interacting with it, as something dynamic and collaboratively produced, requires the ability to adapt to shifting formats.' This helps us to make sense of the literacies, but I remain unconvinced about the need for the term as a brand for internal staff consumption, and particularly as a selling point to a university or any other organization.

Multimodal

Another solution is proposed by Cordes (2009), whose preferred term is 'multimodal literacy'. It is a synthesis of numerous modes of communication that leads to a transformation of the singular modes, producing new or multiple meanings. The idea of new literacies and multi-literacies emerged in the 1990s (Lloyd and Talja, 2010). It seemed that there could be endless numbers of literacies to deal with the different spheres of life and knowledge. Urena (2010) also refers to a multimodal approach, a constellation of skills that could 'allow us to determine – for each situation or specific problem anywhere in the world, or for any social segment and at any level of complexity – what constellations of literacies are the most essential and effective in order to deal with that situation or problem' (Urena, 2010, 20). I sympathize with this, but it would be difficult to achieve, and the concept of transliteracy (TL) might be a better solution – to which we shall return later. Urena regards digital literacy as the collision between ICT literacy and IL, seeing multiliteracy as revolutionary in a school environment, in terms of the critical questioning of all sources of data and the ability to produce multimodal material. This is not happening in his native Spain, where it is assumed that the skills are being learned. Surely this is often the case elsewhere: the skills are expected to be gained by a form of osmosis.

Transmedia

A further suggestion is the transmedia approach, which recognizes the need to teach communication in all forms (Jenkins, 2009): not just words, but also graphics, music, film. Students no longer rely on expert gatekeepers but need to be able to reflect for themselves on how they know what they know and how to assess the motives and knowledge of other communities. Transmedia is about different media systems and the ability to navigate across social communities. The way it is taught should alter the way all subjects are taught: it should not be a 'bolt on' (Jenkins, 2009).

Transliteracy

Finally, we have the concept of transliteracy. We have already met it in this book (Chapters 5 and 15) and have seen that it can be a useful way to articulate the nature of our contribution to supporting individual learning. The concept was much discussed in the USA in 2010, receiving particularly strong criticism in the blog world in David Rothman's critique in late December 2010 (Rothman, 2010). I still believe that it is the most helpful way of looking at the future information environment.

Transliteracy is 'the ability to read, write and interact across a range of platforms, tools and media' (Thomas, 2010). It is a difficult concept to pin down and is like the old story of the blind men and the elephant, where everyone encounters the animal (in this case communication media) and adds their own meaning, whether by talking face to face, by mobile phone, reading a newspaper, using the web and a host of other methods, yet no one sees the whole animal (Thomas, 2010). Add to this the fact that this animal keeps changing shape. This seems to me a most useful way of thinking about the reality of the situation of literacies: particularly IL. The brief analysis of literacies above has shown that overlap is common and that literacies change and develop. This is where taking a transliteracy approach helps me: 'Seeing the whole elephant is about realizing that ALL of these are interconnected and can be understood in relation to each other through history, culture and context' (Thomas, 2010).

Susie Andretta in Chapter 5 has taken a long-term, evolutionary view of transliteracy and Lane Wilkinson in Chapter 15 has taken an immediate, pragmatic view of it as a cognitive skill to be emphasized in our IL interventions. So what does this amount to? Literacies change and develop in any country according to the technological, economic and cultural requirements they have to address. Therefore literacy will be different in the UK in 2011 from literacy in Somalia. Literacies are progressive, so reading and writing precedes being able to appraise a newspaper article. I am reminded of trying to help a student, some years ago, who was unable to use a web browser but needed to access old newspaper articles from NewsBank. A person has first to be information literate, before becoming transliterate. It is useful to work with students from a position or mental model that they understand or adopt. Ipri (2010) believes that transliteracy stresses the social meaning of literacy, the benefits of knowledge sharing via social media. A transliteracy approach that could assist in building people's mental model of search could be very valuable (Wilkinson, 2011). Holman (2011) did a survey of 21 carefully chosen students at the University of

Baltimore in late 2008, and their search methods showed a preference for simple, natural language queries which contrasted with the kind of print-based search strategy instruction sometimes given in libraries. Examples of a transliteracy approach are to compare the use of hashtags and subject headings, or Amazon reviews and abstracts. Lane Wilkinson in Chapter 15 speaks of his students comparing results from Wikipedia with those from a library database, and of the importance of knowing which type of resource is appropriate for a variety of needs.

Potter (2011) sees transliteracy as an umbrella term for IL literacies (IL, DL, technology literacy, media literacy and any literacies that will be of importance in the future). He likes the idea that it allows literacies to exist together with equal merit. He believes we should be taking a transliteracy approach in our interventions, which should vary according to the context. Transliteracy can be helping a student to transfer files to Dropbox or Google Docs, to put videos on YouTube, or to create interactive video presentations (McDonald, 2010). It can be about the convergence of work and play. It can be a way of helping the disadvantaged to close the digital gap (Newman, 2010). It is about mapping meaning across different media. It is not about the individual literacies (e.g. visual or media), but about their interaction. A vook is an example of transliteracy in action - a book with high-quality video and internet together - see http://vook.com/. How long will it be before anybody will be able to create something like this?

Wheeler (2010) explains transliteracy by saying that it is about being able to vary your style according to the medium used to communicate. A professional style, as in LinkedIn, for example, will be very different from Facebook socializing. We need to know that joining up Twitter and Facebook, for example, may not be helpful. We need to know which is the most effective tool for the task in hand, and be comfortable with how to use it, becoming application magicians (Watt, 2011). This is why transliteracy will be so important.

One of the criticisms of transliteracy is that librarians have often been adopting its approach without being aware of the term. As Meredith Farkas (2010) writes, 'The way librarians and other instructors teach information literacy instruction has grown and changed in response to the changing information ecosystem ... And while there are librarians who don't change the way they teach, that's just being a bad instructor. It has nothing to do with information literacy instruction somehow being insufficient.'. I am sure a transliteracy approach has been applied beneficially already in many places without its being labelled as such. For example, the advantage of fostering media scepticism is advocated by Van de Vord (2010) at Washington State University. An online survey was undertaken (363 respondents, a 15% response rate) relating to work in which students had to reflect on advertisements and YouTube. It showed that a transliterate approach was a direct help in fostering IL.

The implication here is that transliteracy as a label or concept is unnecessary. Wilkinson (2011) examines how far transliteracy is covered within three existing IL standards, including ACRL's. He concludes that it is an open question as to whether or not IL includes transliteracy. Even if it could be proved, and even if only some progressive librarians are familiar with its concepts, I conclude that it is still the most useful approach to help us develop our future practice.

Informed learning

This concept (see Chapters 6 and 13) is another approach to IL that goes beyond the standard frameworks and skills/competencies approaches, and more towards using information in a Web 2.0 world to engage with academic or professional content or practices within a specific study area. This seems to be similar to a transliteracy approach, which builds upon prior knowledge, promoting problem solving within a particular discipline or context, while building up learners' flexibility and confidence to use information within a changing information environment. It can be reflective too, as students look back on their use of information during their learning experiences, because informed learning provides the opportunity to discover and use subject content and reflect on the experience of using it. Web 2.0 is ideal for this sharing and communication, as it can encourage curiosity and creativity in familiar 2.0 environments. Hilary Hughes (Chapter 13) has given us a useful list of Web 2.0 tools that lend themselves to this approach, which would encourage, and likely require, considerable dialogue with relevant academics in order to be successfully embedded into course practice.

Conclusion: a way through the maze

So, there are many literacies, and they shift in importance, according to the level of the activity, social discourse and subject discipline. Web 2.0 has affected this, affording us the technical ability to create, share and connect in so many new ways. We have not seen the end of this: maybe hardly even the start. Literacies are connected, and most of them have some kind of critical thinking and development of scepticism at their core. This is what should form the basis of IL in 2012, and in the immediate future. For convenience, we will continue to call it information literacy: not because we like it, but because it is the best label we have. Not everyone will agree, and any of the other labels will persist in covering similar ground. Informed learning seems to offer a practical and more defined approach to meeting the needs of 21st-century literacy (certainly within higher education) because it can accommodate the learning involved in IL, 2.0 elements, and use of mobile devices or a transliteracy approach.

Does it matter that we don't have clarity here? It is no use waiting to agree on strict definitions and titles. I believe that the literacies shift around and interrelate, and that, to me, is transliteracy – but this does not mean that I want to champion this term to my constituencies or recommend that you do so. It is merely a device for helping us to adapt our thinking about literacies, to be able to operate in a post-Web 2.0 world as it is – exciting, unknown and unpredictable. It also resonates with many of the approaches taken in this book, in a world where we seek to join up our learning across platforms and devices.

References

Association of College and Research Libraries (2000) *Information Literacy Competency Standards for Higher Education*, American Library Association.

Avgerinou, M. D. (2010) What Is Visual Literacy?, International Visual Literacy Association, www.ivla.org/org_what_vis_lit.htm.

Bawden, D. (2001) Information and Digital Literacies: a review of concepts, *Journal of Documentation*, **57** (2), 218-59.

Campus Daily (2010) QUT Academic Appointed Oxford University Fellow, *Campus Daily*, www.campusdaily.com.au/read_university_news. php?title=qut_academic_appointed_oxford_university_fellow_16097.

Cordes, S. (2009) Broad Horizons: the role of multimodal literacy in 21st century library instruction. IFLA Conference, Milan, 2009, www.ifla.org/files/hq/papers/ifla75/94-cordes-en.pdf.

Farkas, M. (2010) Transliteracy from the Perspective of an Information Literacy Advocate, *Information wants to be free* (blog), http://meredith.wolfwater.com/wordpress/2010/12/21/transliteracy-from-the-perspective-of-an-information-literacy-advocate/.

Gilster, P. (1997) *Digital Literacy*, New York: John Wiley.

Hague, C. and Peyton, S. (2010) *Digital Literacy across the Curriculum, a Futurelab* handbook, Futurelab, http://archive.futurelab.org.uk/resources/documents/handbooks/digital_literacy.pdf.

Harris, B. R. (2010) Blurring Borders, Visualizing Connections, *Reference Services Review*, **38** (4), 523–35.

Hobbs, R. and Jensen, A. (2009) The Past, Present, and Future of Media Literacy Education, *Journal of Media Literacy Education*, **1** (1), 1–11.

Holman, L. (2011) Millennial Students' Mental Models of Search: implications for academic librarians and database developers, *Journal of Academic Librarianship*, **37** (1), 19–27.

Horizon Report (2010) *2010 Horizon Report*, Austin, TX: New Media Consortium, http://wp.nmc.org/horizon2010/.

Ipri, T. (2010) Introducing Transliteracy, *College and Research Libraries News*, **71** (10), 532–67.

Jenkins, H. (2009) *Confronting the Challenges of Participatory Culture: media education for the 21st century*, Cambridge, MA: MIT Press.

Koltay, T. (2011) The Media and the Literacies: media literacy, information literacy, digital literacy, *Media, Culture and Society*, **33** (2), 211–21.

Lankshear, C. and Knobel, M. (eds) (2007) *A New Literacies Sampler*, New York: Peter Lang.

Lloyd, A. and Talja, S. (eds) (2010) *Practising Information Literacy: bringing theories of learning, practice and information literacy together*, Wagga Wagga, New South Wales: Centre for Information Studies, Charles Sturt University.

Mackey, T. P. and Jacobson, T. E. (2011) Reframing Information Literacy as a Metaliteracy, *College and Research Libraries*, **72** (1), 62–78.

Markless, S. and Streatfield, D. (2007) Three Decades of Information Literacy: redefining the parameters. In Andretta, S. (ed.), *Change and Challenge: information literacy for the 21st century*, Adelaide: Auslib Press.

McDonald, S. (2010) Making Sense of Transliteracy? *Miss Sophie Mac* (blog), http://misssophiemac.blogspot.com/2010/12/making-sense-of-transliteracy.html.

New Media Consortium (2005) *A Global Imperative: report of the 21st Century Literacies Summit, 2005*, Austin, TX: New Media Consortium.

Newman, B. (2010) Why Transliteracy? Bobbi's two cents (or less), *Libraries and transliteracy* (blog), http://librariesandtransliteracy.wordpress.com/2010/12/22/why-transliteracy-bobbis-two-cents-or-less/.

Potter, N. (2011) The Future of Libraries Is Transliteral – a Guest Post by Ned Potter, *Libraries and Transliteracy* (blog), http://librariesandtransliteracy.wordpress.com/2011/03/15/the-future-of-libraries-is-transliteral/.

Rheingold, H. (2010) Attention, and Other 21st-Century Social Media Literacies, *Educause Review*, **45** (5), 14-24.

Rothman, D. (2010) Commensurable Nonsense (Transliteracy). Davidrothman.net, http://davidrothman.net/2010/12/19/commensurable-nonsense-transliteracy/.

Špiranec, S. and Zorica, M. B. (2010) Information Literacy 2.0: hype or discourse refinement? *Journal of Documentation*, **66** (1), 140-53.

Thomas, S. (2010) The Whole Elephant: librarians arguing about transliteracy, *Transliteracy* (blog), http://nlabnetworks.typepad.com/transliteracy/2010/12/argue.html#.

UNESCO (2011) Media and Information Literacy, http://portal.unesco.org/ci/en/ev.php-URL_ID=15886&URL_DO=DO_TOPIC&URL_SECTION=201.html#topPage.

Urena, C. P. (2010) Multiliteracy and Social Networks in Higher Education, *Revista de Universidad y Sociedad del Conocimiento*, **7** (2), 16-24.

Van de Vord, R. (2010) Distance Students and Online Research: promoting information literacy through media literacy, *The Internet and Higher Education*, **13** (3), 170-5.

Walstrum, M., Garcia, L. and Morisson, R. (2011) From Embedded to Integrated: digital information literacy and new teaching models for academic librarians. ALA Conference, 2010, Philadelphia, http://www.ala.org/acrl/sites/ala.org.acrl/files/content/conferences/confsandpreconfs/national/2011/papers/from_embedded.pdf

Watt, D. (2011) Becoming the Embedded School Librarian Begins with Understanding Our Place in the New Zealand Curriculum, *Half Pint of Wisdom* (blog), www.scoop.it/t/personal-learning-networks-for-librarians/p/361639738/becoming-the-embedded-school-librarian-begins-with-understanding-our-place-in-the-new-zealand-curriculum-half-pint-of-wisdom.

Weetman DaCosta, J. (2011) Information Literacy in the Digital Environment. In Dale, P., Beard, J. and Holland, M. (eds), *University Libraries and Digital Learning Environments*, Ashgate.

Wheeler, S. (2010) Digital Literacy: crossing the divide, *Learning with 'e's* (blog), http://steve-wheeler.blogspot.com/2010/11/crossing-divide.html.

Wilkinson, L. (2011) Transliteracy and Millennial Students' Mental Models of Search, *Libraries and transliteracy* (blog), http://librariesandtransliteracy.wordpress.com/?s=mental+models+of+search.

Chapter 21

Thoughts about the future

Peter Godwin

Introduction

The speed of change fascinates me. With the coming of the internet everything changed, and with Web 2.0 it has changed yet again. YouTube took up more bandwidth in 2007 than the entire internet in 2000. Many mobile phones now have more computing power and internet capability than the average home computer of 2000 (Thomas and Brown, 2011). However, education changes slowly. Institutions are changing far more slowly than are modes of learning, which are becoming more participatory and collaborative (Davidson and Goldberg, 2009). Think of your own workplace and your own colleagues and friends. Real change is slow. In this chapter I will cover some important likely trends and what they may mean to us, as IL practitioners, in the future.

Streams of information and coping with the flow

Information overload is going to increase. This is not just the amount of information being added to the web every day, and its being searchable via Google. It is about coping with the flow of information: the flood of RSS feeds, blog posts or tweets. We need to be able to 'sample' the flow (Rheingold, 2010). The tools we use to do this will change, evolve and interrelate. The challenge will still be to channel the right stuff and to control it. Web 3.0 could bring search engines that bring together results into a synthesized report - but many of the promised improvements in search have not yet occurred (Herring, 2011). So we can still say 'Information overload is not the problem. It's filter failure' (Shirky, 2008). Boyd (2010) places us all in a stream of networked content that we grab as it goes by, as opposed to broadcast models of information and entertainment. In Chapter 4, Phil Bradley and Karen Blakeman have shown how search engines now take our location, occupation, interests and social media activity into consideration when presenting results to us. How many of our users (or our librarian colleagues, for that matter) realize that different results appear for the same search in different locations? In a world where Google is so trusted, it is important that someone should inform people that the results they get will vary: from person to person, from place to place, at the same time and at different times. It is so easy to accept what Google tells us: like oven-ready fast food (Brabazon, 2009). Librarians should be including this caveat in their IL interventions.

Lankes (2011) pushes the view that we do not talk about a 'good' or a 'bad' site. In the contextual view of knowledge and conversation, in order to gain trust we offer a variety of approaches, so that the user can make choices – a source may be great for one user, but not for another. We have conversations, building credibility, and creating a picture of what IL means in the context of each user. Credibility is the greatest asset that we can have, and is established by conversation rather than by policies and decrees. Lankes continues: 'Life is complex and messy. As a librarian, your focus must be on context and the needs of the user, not the artefact or object. The artefact only takes on value and only has meaning in its use' (Lankes, 2011, 123).

With the growth of the public perception that 'everything' is on the web, and with search engines returning masses of indiscriminate content, I believe we are seeing the breaking down of the old differentiation of content into book, journal, report and so on. Tuominen (2007) sees this as an 'erosion of information contexts'. She describes how she reads hundreds of items daily via RSS feeds derived from Netvibes, and how they so easily become anonymous and deprived of context. Books had a permanence that web documents do not have. Tuominen speaks of a digital information 'flatness', and it is a real challenge for us to provide innovative ways of overcoming it. Karen Blakeman and Phil Bradley in Chapter 4 also drew attention to the disjointed nature of much of what we retrieve via search engines and how, online, the nature of a business report may change over time. The increasing decontextualization of information raises the importance of critical evaluation. Mobile devices will accentuate this trend, because news will feature on mobiles next to status updates (Boyd, 2010, 36). As Tuominen (2007) wrote, 'the most important goal of IL education should be to increase users' conceptual understandings of their information environment. In this sense, the tricks of information retrieval like truncation or Boolean logics are not so significant. Who even uses Boolean searches anymore?'

New IL frameworks

It is therefore good to see that change is occurring in some IL frameworks. The new SCONUL framework came out in April 2011 (SCONUL Working Group on Information Literacy, 2011). This generic core version for higher education is intended to be followed by versions for other sectors. This is very encouraging, and responds to much of the criticism that one scheme does not fit all, recognizing the need to cater for different user communities. Furthermore, the model is circular rather than linear. The pillars of SCONUL's Seven Pillars model do not have to be regarded or taught sequentially, and users can develop within pillars at differing rates, according to their needs. The intention is that different versions (for different user communities) will articulate different information attributes and use language that makes sense to that particular group. It remains to be seen how quickly this will take root, and change may be slow.

The Welsh Information Literacy framework was launched in July 2011 and is an ambitious attempt to chart all sectors, from school (14-year-olds) to PhD level, in Wales (Welsh Information Literacy Project, 2011). It uses elements from the new SCONUL and other UK IL models. It also draws attention to the importance of IL for lifelong learning and to the (underrated) support given in schools by school librarians.

IL remains the chosen title for these initiatives, and both the SCONUL and the Welsh frameworks will be important reference points for advancing the cause of IL in the education sector. However, just as the different versions of the SCONUL framework will use different vocabulary to address the different sectors, so we can expect library practitioners to use labels other than IL in order to relate to the communities they serve.

It's mobile and social

Social media are everywhere. Over 110 million tweets per day are sent on Twitter (Swallow, 2011). We know how social media is empowering – see the demonstrations in Iran in 2009, for example. Mobile phones are ubiquitous. Harris Interactive (2008) reports that 57% of teens say that mobile technology 'has improved the quality of my life'. Of those with smartphones, 59% said that it was an indicator of their personal style (Bridges, Rempel and Griggs, 2010). Our users will have increasingly high expectations of our mobile services as time goes on.

Kristen Yarmey has been concerned with meeting this challenge in Chapter 9. She also demonstrated the desirability of starting where the students are by discussing with them the use of Google and other mobile device apps and encouraging them to be critical in their choices. The tendency not to look beyond the first five results of a search, and uncritical acceptance of material, can be even more dangerous in the mobile environment. Students' use of applications of questionable scope and authority on mobile devices adds another serious dimension to our IL challenge. Andrew Walsh in Chapter 10 shows us that mobiles have scope for use in our IL interventions. Poll Everywhere is a good example, allowing up to 30 users to participate in an activity via mobile phone using Twitter, text message or the web.

Virtual reference services will become more important and will improve the student experience and help us to meet students where they are, especially in the mobile environment. We will be challenged to provide the quick, minimum-clicks kind of interface that they are likely to prefer. Information presented to them will not have to be as structured as a conventional website and will appear 'disaggregated into bite-sized chunks' (Geeson, 2011, 101).

We have yet to discover the range of services our users will accept via mobile devices. Seeholzer and Salem (2011) held a focus group at Kent State University about interest in use of facilities on the mobile web and found that the students ranked researching possibilities higher than information about our services and 'About Us'. They would look for what was available on a topic and, as one participant said, 'I would not read the whole articles in the mobile device, but search'. Another said, 'Especially if I were standing in line somewhere and waiting, I would absolutely start doing research for something and then save citations.'

GPS and augmented reality

We have seen how GPS (the Global Positioning System) is being incorporated into web and mobile applications, and its potential for use in IL on mobile devices (see Chapter 10). Car navigation systems use GPS. They operate in a very focused way, much like an expert information searcher. In an excellent tutorial on the 21st Century Information Fluency site, Balzer (2010) demonstrates how GPS and internet navigation intersect.

GPS Foursquare and Gowalla are examples of GPS which provide free services to enable individuals to indicate where they are at the time. Libraries can take advantage of this to deliver news and advice (Walsh, 2010). The arrival of mobile devices is encouraging game-based learning. For example, the State Library of Queensland used a 'scavenger hunt application' to set up self-guided library tours using GPS (Barron, 2011). The University of Technology Sydney (UTS) and Charles Darwin University have used QR codes to create a treasure hunt (ALIA Sydney, 2011).

Augmented Reality (AR) operates on smartphones that usually contain a camera, accelerometer, compass and GPS. An object that is recognized by the camera, compass and GPS will trigger the retrieval and display of data. Lankes (2011) shows that AR is already in operation (in traffic control systems). So it is really like a merger of the real with the virtual world. However, developing AR can be expensive. For a pioneering example of AR, see Wolfwalk, the mobile library project at North Carolina State University, which uses location-aware software. The first version was put out in March 2010, working across several newer mobile devices, such as iPhone, iPod and Android-based smartphones (NCSU Library, 2011).

AR takes QR codes one step further, and could be used by the library to link to information and guidance at point of need. As the user views a building or an object via a mobile, information about that object, which has been written by the library, will appear. The iPad 2, with its twin cameras, could be poised to take this technology further. Aurasma is recommended by Tay (2011) in a fun experiment recording a talking-head book review, which could be accessed by scanning the book's jacket. He acknowledges that there will be a question as to which device will be able to take advantage of this technology. However, his experiment demonstrates that creating an AR application can be easy. I would hazard that, at present, AR is only something to be aware of, featuring as it does in the two-to-three-year adoption frame in the *2010 Horizon Report* (Horizon Report, 2010).

Active learning and gaming

The power of active learning techniques, where the emphasis moves from teacher-centred to learner-centred learning, is well established in IL. Walsh and Inala (2010) have produced a great resource for implementing it and have shown that Web 2.0 has opened up even more possibilities. The power of gaming in learning is well demonstrated in the case studies by Susan Boyle in Chapter 8 and Sophie McDonald and Jemima McDonald in Chapter 7. Play, questioning and imagination should be at the centre of learning (Thomas and Brown, 2011). Vecchione and Mellinger (2011) tell of interesting uses of the application SCVNGR for new international student orientation at Oregon State University and for delivering bibliographic instruction at Boise State University. Linda

Barron told of the use of SCVNGR for tours of the State Library of Queensland at the 2011 M-Libraries conference (Barron, 2011). We should not be using such technology purely as a means of getting our users interested, but as a way to empower them and to start them on their way to creating their own knowledge. In Chapter 10 Andrew Walsh gives an example of this approach when he describes a new project called Lemon Tree, which links virtual rewards to normal library interactions such as borrowing books, or writing comments about books.

... and it's about cross-device working

We will have to get used to our users employing multiple devices (mobiles, tablets, laptops and PCs) to access, mash and store all kinds of material. The challenge will be for them to be able to access, move around and use this stuff efficiently, on whatever device is to hand. IL will include ways of managing it, from social bookmarking, e.g. Delicious, Diigo, to storing and exchanging documents kept in the cloud, e.g. Dropbox, and referencing, e.g. EasyBib (see Stacey Taylor's Chapter 11). Whereas an individual might once have expected to manage material on a home computer and an institutional PC, now they will want to access it wherever and whenever needed. One student may be accessing a library database on a mobile, marking or e-mailing the results and reviewing them later. Another may be reading an online book, making notes and wanting to incorporate them into an assignment. Yet another student may want to use images found while searching Flickr on an iPad, plus some photos taken with an Android phone, and incorporate them into a PowerPoint presentation using an institutional PC. The learning commons concept, popular in recent years, at least in the USA (Lippincott and Greenwell, 2011), is intended to provide students with a place where they can undertake work and receive support and advice at different stages in their research, including access to e-resources, multimedia and social media. This is very much an image of the library of the future.

New ways of communicating with users

At the time of writing, Google+ has a 'hang-out' feature that could be the 'killer app'. It is like a group video chat. A librarian could contact a group of students and get a conversation going. If no one answered, the librarian could wait until someone came along. Instant uploads allow you to take a photo on a mobile, upload it to Picasa or YouTube, and then share it via Google+ with a particular circle of users. I look forward to trying this out with a focus group or with discrete groups of students.

The use of short movies or screencasts is here to stay. In my experience, this medium has two types. The first, more professional type, aimed at large audiences, which may also be promotional; and the second, quick-fire type, aimed at dealing with a single issue. The latter might be uploaded to a course's virtual learning environment or sent as a reply to an enquiry via remote messaging service. The first may need scripting and a more advanced platform, while the second is likely to be very short and might be produced on something like Screenr in about half an hour.

Impact of search discovery

Recently the major library system companies have been developing and selling us discovery systems, as a response to Google-type search. This could be regarded as an answer to our prayers. Holman (2011) looked at the way that modern students might search and whether they think in a different way from their predecessors. She questioned whether modern technology should be able to cope with simpler searching in natural language, or whether we should concentrate on helping users to undertake the perfect search. She saw that students did not operate in a linear fashion, nor work in a discovery fashion. Thus, we should be working to help them to refine, rather than to hit on an initial perfect search. Furthermore, we should concentrate on developing students' evaluation and critical thinking skills, rather than trying to make students into great 'advanced' searchers! Synonym tools and spelling variants on the discovery platform, rather than advanced Boolean search tuition, should be our focus, or we may lose our younger student users. I suspect that in the past the librarians have wanted to push users towards advanced searching. Very few of them ever wanted it, and now it is clear that nor do researchers use the fancier facilities (Research Information Network, 2011). Discovery systems can be great for getting quick results, and also for enhancing the reliability of results through the use of peer-reviewed filters. However, so long as not all databases are included in these systems (will the law database monopoly ever join the 21st century?) the picture can only be partial. Also, the most relevant individual databases are still likely to provide the best results for serious higher-level research. Just as Google results can be dangerous and misleading, so can discovery system results, but for different reasons.

E-books

By the time you read this, the e-book will be firmly established in the public consciousness. There will be platform divergences for some time to come, but the breakaway success of the Kindle at the time of writing indicates the direction of travel. Amazon e-book sales for Kindle e-versions in the USA overtook hardcover book sales for the first time in July 2010, and paperbacks in January 2011 (Price, 2011). But what is going to be the best fit for education? Lloyd Sealy Library surveyed the alternatives but was not ready to recommend a device in these tough times (Kiriakova et al., 2010). Princeton University's Kindle pilot with Kindle DX identified a range of issues concerning annotations, highlighting, navigation between documents and applicability to HE. Will it be the mobile or the iPad? Will students use them as textbooks? Are there equal measures of preference for print, e-solution and hybrid? The Pearson Foundation survey (Rachlin, 2011) found that 55% of students surveyed preferred print over digital textbooks, but of the 7% who had a tablet, 73% preferred digital textbooks. We could pre-load e-book devices with the content desired for a course. This could include subject-related content, guides on referencing, podcasts and other IL material (Drinkwater, 2010).

The e-book is only in its infancy and the full potential of the medium is yet to be realized. No single device will meet the requirements of all activities, disciplines and users. The e-book of the future could be more than the Kindle, more than book simulations and more of a multimedia experience. How will this affect IL? How this type of content can be accessed and read, and issues of copyright, especially with sound and video, will be problematic.

Areas of biggest challenge
Public libraries

I am convinced that the two areas where IL presents both the greatest challenge and the greatest opportunity is in public libraries and in schools. Nielsen and Borlund (2011) demonstrate the importance of IL support in public libraries. The public librarian can be 'a person who assists, guides, enables and otherwise intervenes in another person's information search process' (Kuhlthau in Nielsen and Borlund, 2011). Nielsen and Borlund (2011) carried out a phenomenological study of the perceptions of 12 high school students with regard to the place of the public library in learning, user education and IL. Their key finding was that there was a perception that IL was about 'finding information' and that public libraries should develop their learning support, using either Kuhlthau's Information Search Process model (Kuhlthau in Nielsen and Borlund, 2011) or McNicol and Dalton's Cycle of Learning in Public Libraries as a starting-point (McNicol and Dalton in Nielsen and Borlund, 2011). Lloyd (2010) is concerned about the critical role that public libraries would have to play in order to meet the aspirations for active citizens throughout the world, as expressed by meetings such as that which produced the Prague Declaration (UNESCO, 2003). Koltay (2011) sees public libraries as dealing primarily with amateurs or recreational users, where use of Web 2.0 tools would often be a good fit for the kind of information support required and provide opportunities for public participation in the creation of local content. I can only conclude that IL can be much more difficult in the public library than in HE. In the latter setting there are known user groups, as compared to the multiplicity of demands in the public library, ranging from primary school readers through to secondary school children, HE students, lifelong learners and 'third agers'. Tackling this will be complex without a national strategy. Helen Leech in Chapter 18 has shown how public libraries are developing services via initiatives such as MyGuide and using the BBC's WebWise site. In the past, public libraries have often been held back by local authority bans on the use of 2.0. Recently, we have seen the UK version of 23 Things spearheaded by four UK county library authorities. Chat reference using the OCLC Questionpoint software has also begun. Public libraries should be experimenting with these exciting new technologies as ways to bring them closer to their communities.

Schools and transfer literacy

Judy O'Connell in Chapter 19 has enthused about the school library as a learning commons or flexible learning space that offers possibilities for the promotion of literacy in multiple ways by librarians who are informed learners. Informed learning could be instituted as early as secondary school (11-15) level, in order to make students aware of their learning experiences. Avoidance of plagiarism should most definitely be highlighted at this stage. Stacey Taylor has shown in Chapter 11 that referencing can be inculcated in school pupils well before they go on to HE.

Just as IL cannot be a one-shot injection in HE, so it cannot be restricted to a single stage of an individual's life. The Jesuit would say, 'Get them young'; and we could say that IL development should begin from early childhood. Then, by the time that students transfer from secondary school to university or college they will have obtained a good grounding. Schools often assume that when students are shown a particular skill they will automatically be able to transfer it. In universities we like to think that the skills learned in school can be transferred to HE. However, it is far from clear whether or not information transfer does or can occur. Markless (2009) quotes research suggesting that only what can be deemed low-level transfer (reflexive, automatic triggering) is easily carried across from one situation to another. This means that lessons learned at school (e.g. in media studies) may not be carried forward by students into their core subject area at university. Research by Herring (2011) on skills such as concept mapping and question formulation shows that this connection is unlikely to be made, except in the case of a few high-achievers. The study of three secondary or high schools in Australia showed that there were three types of student: a minority who were actually able to transfer skills and abilities; a few who did not understand the idea of transfer; and the majority who appreciated the idea but did not carry it through. The reality of transfer literacy is that it is for the whole school to embrace, including the students. Ellis and Salisbury (2004) surveyed six first-year arts groups at the University of Melbourne in 2003. Of the students surveyed, 24% had had no previous IL instruction at school; 65% identified the internet as their preferred way of searching, although most rated it 3 out of 4 in a ranking of reliability. The authors stressed the importance of building on what the students already know: that is to say, their previous internet searching ideas.

From this brief exploration, we can see that the approach to the problem of IL transition is based largely on skills transfer. IL is not going to be the same in schools as in HE because the context is different, HE having a higher level of discourse and variations according to subject discipline. The transfer is thus hard to achieve. In addition, schools may be doing less to help their students, because in the digital world the problems seem fewer and teachers think that students can do their own searching using search engines (Fieldhouse and Nicholas, 2008). Many people will think that because information is everywhere, it can be easily sourced and understood (Herring, 2011). This conception is amplified by the ease of access via mobiles. Users themselves mistake easy access for effective search and don't feel that they need guidance. They have to become convinced of the need. Demonstrating this from data is hard, and this could be an area for more research.

A future for librarians, with bright sparks for the future

As information professionals, our great strength is our personal service: being a better friend than Google. This should be our goal, but it is often hard to practise in organizations, especially large ones. Enter Web 2.0. We now have so many ways of promoting ourselves and our services, and of networking. We need to know our users. This is 2.0, and what is important is to know your client group: don't assume they are all the same, because one size does not fit all.

However, we must not assume that users will easily change their perceptions of what librarians offer. Here the new learning commons at the University of Sheffield provides an illuminating cautionary tale. Bickley and Corrall (2011) carried out a survey to uncover the Sheffield student experience. The majority of those surveyed had asked for help at some point and held positive views of librarian assistance. However, the continuing failure of respondents to grasp the academic function of librarians was alarming. Despite inductions and the provision of web pages and blogs, the correct messages were not getting across. The survey reported that some academic librarians were also going out on the floors to provide roving support. I conclude that this shows the continuing need to try all the possible 2.0 weapons at our disposal and keep experimenting: change will not come overnight.

The potential for use of Web 2.0 in instruction is still great. Project Information Literacy (Head and Eisenberg, 2010), on how undergraduates use information sources in their research, and the Ethnographic Research in Illinois Academic Libraries study (Asher, Duke and Green, 2010) both indicate that students don't know how to go about starting their research (Hill, 2010). New technologies such as Web 2.0 'hold the promise of bringing the library into the classroom and the classroom into the library in ways that we are only just beginning to imagine and realize' (Hill, 2010).

The sharing of ideas and resources will be fundamental to our future success. In Chapter 17 Niamh Tumelty, Isla Kuhn and Katie Birkwood show how the 23 Things initiative in Cambridge led to a desire to share via a new mechanism: the TeachMeet. This open and flexible model seems ideal at a time of national recession, generating new ideas and enthusiasm in a non-threatening environment, and is one of the great success stories of recent years.

The importance of sharing is obvious, and Carmen Kazakoff-Lane (Chapter 12) has shown us one of the best examples of sharing through the tutorials in the Animated Tutorial Sharing Project (ANTS).

Susan Boyle in Chapter 8 has suggested the idea of establishing an international creative commons for IL game design, to serve as a collaborative space for sharing treatment game ideas, as well as experiences of both using games in IL and overcoming difficulties in using them.

Social media should be part of the new professional librarians' curriculum, if we are to understand the information landscape and best connect with our student body. We have seen examples of this: Dean Giustini has shown us in Chapter 14 how it has been done at University of British Columbia, making students engage with new digital formats and critiquing the use of SNS tools for information services. Also, Hilary Hughes (Chapter 13) has used 2.0 tools for informed learning in the Queensland University of Technology cyberlearning unit of the Master of Education degree (Teacher-Librarianship).

Jane Secker and Emma Coonan have provided a thoughtful curriculum for HE students (Chapter 16) that claims to be transitional, transferable and transformational. This wide interpretation of IL fits very well with views expressed in this book. The mapping against some of the standard IL frameworks shows the curriculum's breadth in extending into other areas, e.g. transition into HE. The emphasis on students developing knowledge of their specific discipline underlines the importance of context, which has been identified in this book as being so crucial. Perhaps only Strand 6, on managing information, will need to be developed in order to cope with the cross-device and information-handling challenges that students will face. Secker and Coonan's curriculum for information literacy is a formidable document that will be of great use to HE practitioners. Although delivery by a variety of staff is expected, its implementation does imply a greater amount of liaison and planning than is usually possible, so we must hope for some pilot schemes in the near future to test the structure.

So what of the future for our users? As Susie Andretta said in Chapter 5, we need to foster a literacy in our users that is learner centred, building interpersonal and communication skills, critical thinking and synthesis as a preparation for career change and uncertainty. Or as Judy O'Connell said in Chapter 19, 'adaptability' is the key attribute, stemming from our support of users' use of information to learn (informed learning) and their growing awareness of the way in which they use information as they learn. Finally, if we have taken a transliterate approach that acknowledges shifting literacies, we will have found a winning formula for really helping people to cope in the 21st century.

References

ALIA Sydney (2011) Game Based Learning: or how to make learning fun! *ALIA Sydney* (blog), http://aliasydney.blogspot.com/2011/06/game-based-learning-or-how-to-make.html.

Asher, A., Duke, L. and Green, D. (2010) *The ERIAL Project: ethnographic research in Illinois Academic Libraries*, www.academiccommons.org/commons/essay/erial-project.

Balzer, D. (2010) Finding My Way: how GPS and internet navigation intersect. 21st Century Information Fluency, http://21cif.com/rkitp/features/personalside_internetgps_vol1n2.html.

Barron, L. (2011) Location-based Gaming: meeting the overwhelming demand for school visits. M-Libraries 3 Conference, May.

Bickley, R. and Corrall, S. (2011) Student Perceptions of Staff in the Information Commons: a survey at the University of Sheffield, *Reference Services Review*, **39** (2), 223-43.

Boyd, D. (2010) Streams of Content: limited attention: the flow of information through social media, *Educause Review*, **45** (5), 26-36.

Brabazon, T. (2009) Ready Meals for the Mind, *Times Higher Education*, (16 December), www.timeshighereducation.co.uk/story.asp?storycode=409627.

Bridges, L., Rempel, H. G. and Griggs, K. (2010) Making the Case for a Fully Mobile Library Web Site: from floor maps to the catalog, *Reference Services Review*, **38** (2), 309-20.

Davidson, C. N. and Goldberg, D. T. (2009) *The Future of Learning Institutions in a Digital Age*, Cambridge, MA: MIT Press.

Drinkwater, K. (2010) E-book Readers: what are librarians to make of them? *SCONUL Focus*, **50**, 15-21.

Ellis, J. and Salisbury, F. (2004) Information Literacy Milestones: building upon prior knowledge of first-year students, *Australian Library Journal*, **53** (4), 383-96.

Fieldhouse, M. and Nicholas, D. (2008) Digital Literacy as Information Savvy: the road to information literacy. In Lankshear, C. K. M. (ed.), *Digital Literacies: concepts, policies and practices*, International Academic Publishers.

Geeson, R. (2011) Virtual Advice Services. In Dale, P., Beard, J. and Holland, M. (eds), *University Libraries and Digital Learning Environments*, Ashgate.

Harris Interactive (2008) *A Generation Unplugged: a national survey by CTIA and Harris Interactive*www.ctia.org/advocacy/research/index.cfm/aid/11483.

Head, A. J. and Eisenberg, M. B. (2010) *Truth be Told: how college students evaluate and use information in the digital age. Project Information Literacy Progress Report*, http://projectinfolit.org/pdfs/PIL_Fall2010_Survey_FullReport1.pdf.

Herring, J. E. (2011) *Improving Students' Web Use and Information Literacy*, Facet Publishing.

Hill, T. (2010) Learning to Navigate the Library an Invaluable Skill, *The Miscellany News*, www.miscellanynews.com/2.1577/learning-to-navigate-the-library-an-invaluable-skill-1.2409609#.TnywZdTEm7B.

Holman, L. (2011) Millennial Students' Mental Models of Search: implications for academic librarians and database developers, *Journal of Academic Librarianship*, **37** (1), 19-27.

Horizon Report (2010) *2010 Horizon Report*, Austin, TX: New Media Consortium, http://wp.nmc.org/horizon2010/.

Kiriakova, M. et al. (2010) Aiming at a Moving Target: pilot testing e-book readers in an urban academic library, *Computers in Libraries*, **30** (2), 20-4.

Koltay, T. (2011) Information Literacy for Amateurs and Professionals: the potential of academic, special and public libraries, *Library Review*, **60** (3), 246-57.

Lankes, R. D. (2011) *The Atlas of New Librarianship*, Cambridge, MA: MIT Press.

Lippincott, J. K. and Greenwell, S. (2011) Seven Things You Should Know about the Modern Learning Commons, Educause, www.educause.edu/Resources/7ThingsYouShouldKnowAbouttheMO/227141.

Lloyd, A. (2010) *Information Literacy Landscapes: information literacy in education, workplace and everyday contexts*, Chandos Publishing.

Markless, S. (2009) A New Conception of Information Literacy for the Digital Learning Environment in Higher Education, *Nordic Journal of Information Literacy in Higher Education*, **1** (1), 25-40.

NCSU Library (2011) Wolfwalk, www.lib.ncsu.edu/dli/projects/wolfwalk/.

Nielsen, B. and Borlund, P. (2011) Information Literacy, Learning, and the Public Library: a study of Danish high school students, *Journal of Librarianship and Information Science*, **43** (2), 106-19.

Price, G. D. (2011) Publishing Milestone; 'Amazon Kindle E-Book sales top print', http://infodocket.com/2011/05/19/milestones-publishing-amazon-kindle-e-book-sales-top-print/.

Rachlin, N. (2011) Digital Textbooks Slow to Catch On, *New York Times*, 8 June.

Research Information Network (2011) *E-journals: their use, value and impact*, Final report.

Rheingold, H. (2010) Attention, and Other 21st-Century Social Media Literacies, *Educause Review*, **45** (5), 14-24.

SCONUL Working Group on Information Literacy (2011) The SCONUL Seven Pillars of Information Literacy Core Model for Higher Education, SCONUL, www.sconul.ac.uk/groups/information_literacy/publications/coremodel.pdf.

Seeholzer, J. and Salem, J. A. Jr (2011) Library on the Go: a focus group survey of the mobile web and the academic library, *College and Research Libraries*, **72** (1), 9–20.

Shirky, C. (2008) Information Load is Not the Problem. It's filter failure, *Web 2.0 Expo*, New York, http://blip.tv/web2expo/web-2-0-expo-ny-clay-shirky-shirky-com-it-s-not-information-overload-it-s-filter-failure-1283699.

Swallow, E. (2011) How Semantic Search Is Redefining Traditional and Social Media, *Mashable* (blog), http://mashable.com/2011/03/04/semantic-search-media/.

Tay, A. (2011) Libraries and Augmented Reality, Adding Video Reviews to Books – Aurasma, *Musings about Librarianship* (blog), http://musingsaboutlibrarianship.blogspot.com/2011/05/libraries-augmented-reality-adding.html.

Thomas, T. and Brown, J. S. (2011) *A New Culture of Learning: cultivating the imagination for a world of constant change*, CreateSpace.

Tuominen, K. (2007) Information Literacy 2.0, *Signum*, **40** (5), 6–12.

UNESCO (2003) Prague Declaration: Towards an Information Literate Society, UNESCO, www.unesco.org/new/fileadmin/MULTIMEDIA/HQ/CI/CI/pdf/PragueDeclaration.pdf.

Vecchione, A. E. and Mellinger, M. (2011) Beyond Foursquare: library treks with SCVNGR. Handheld Librarian IV Conference, February 2011, http://works.bepress.com/amy_vecchione/23/.

Walsh, A. (2010) Mobile Technologies in Libraries, Fumsi, http://fumsi.com/go/articale/use/60968.

Walsh, A. and Inala, P. (2010) *Active Learning Techniques for Librarians*, Chandos.

Welsh Information Literacy Project (2011) *Information Literacy Framework for Wales: finding and using information in 21st century Wales*, http://library.wales.org/uploads/media/Information_Literacy_Framework_Wales.pdf.

Chapter 22

Last word: information literacy beyond Library 2.0

Peter Godwin

Web 2.0 has become social media and is here to stay. The opening up of the web to everyone, and the authoring and sharing capabilities inherent in this, have been embraced by libraries. We may not be speaking about Library 2.0 any more, but the possibilities opened up for libraries have by no means been exhausted. Take-up has been variable and the opportunities for marketing have sometimes obscured the educational possibilities exemplified by IL.

In the past, IL has too often been seen as a higher education (HE) concern. We should see it as a process, from childhood, through school, college, university and into lifelong learning. This only begins to make sense if we always view IL as conditioned by its context: the social conditions, the discipline and the language used within its discourse. IL is a social construct, and what it means to be information literate will vary according to the context. It will even vary according to the individuals within a group, because the participants will be creating their own meaning. The concept of informed learning (see Chapter 6) is helpful here because it explains how students can use information to learn, and then reflect upon their own learning. The curriculum can allow us to use information to develop individual and collective exploration of information, to enable learners to develop their own experience. It is no longer about rote learning, or being directive in terms of the 'best' way to do things: we do not write prescriptions, we encourage and guide.

IL is not just for librarians: yet amongst librarians is mostly where it is discussed, and it is rarely discussed outside the library silo. Other players have actually been interested in IL for years, but they call it different things – critical thinking, workplace skills, learning to learn and so on. IL is far more than bibliographic instruction, user education or how to use a library. In our policy documents we may speak about IL, but in our marketing and delivery we adapt our language to suit the consumer. We need to take a broad view, work with colleagues from other departments and be as unafraid of veering into their territory as they often are when they venture into ours. IL is far bigger than librarians, but we are extremely well placed to help with the multifaceted challenge that is 21st-century IL.

We have highlighted that schools and public libraries are areas of particular importance (see Chapters 18 and 19). The seeds sown in the school environment, particularly developing critical thinking and awareness of plagiarism, may be transferable into HE. Too much should not be expected, because the HE context is quite different. Unlike HE and schools, public libraries have to accommodate anyone who crosses their threshold. The huge variety of individuals and demands makes their IL role more difficult, yet no less crucial, because they can assist people of all ages and from all walks of life. In both the education and the public library sectors, IL work goes on, under other names, but the 2.0 world gives it both new urgency and new tools to exploit.

The shape of information is changing fundamentally and has become more complex as a result of the 2.0 phenomenon. As we have seen, it is chaotic and becoming more social and mobile. The seeming simplicity of Google disguises the greatest challenge of all, around which most literacy concepts revolve: critical awareness and critical thinking. The danger of using mobile apps of dubious credibility, and the temptation to accept Google results uncritically, is our major problem.

We need to go back to basics and grasp how literacies change and evolve. In this book we have looked briefly at some of the literacies and whether other labels or all-embracing concepts would now be better than 'IL'. Overlaps between literacies have often been obvious, but, despite the difficulties involved with IL as a term, this is still the best one that we have. It is in understanding the movement of the tectonic plates of the literacies and through the insights that the concept of transliteracy (TL) can provide that we can be better equipped to deal with a post-2.0 world. TL is an open concept that lets us see the significance of being able to express ourselves in different ways. It recognizes that literacies move around, cannot be tied down and are essentially messy. Taking a TL approach in our IL interventions can help us to demonstrate and compare how meaning is communicated and shared across different channels; for example, the use of SlideShare and YouTube as information sources; how to write on

Twitter or Facebook, including the use of photos or video; composing an essay and storing materials for it on a mobile device, iPad or laptop.

We must encourage the students of the future to construct their own meaning. It will not be a one-off experience, but a developing, living thing that accompanies them as they learn throughout their lives, in their study, in their work and in their practice. At the centre of this must be a capacity to adapt, to cope with uncertainty, and to have confidence in their interpersonal and communication skills and, above all, critical thinking. But wasn't this true in 1900, 1700, 1500 too? Yes, but the pace of life and the speed of communication make it quite different.

The librarian of the future keeps abreast of social media so that he/she can experiment and critique their use in his/her own information behaviours, and to facilitate the learning of others. The creation of nuggets of learning, as screenshots, podcasts or screencasts, for classes or to answer individual queries (and then perhaps to use as FAQs) will take up an increasing amount of time. The ease of creating them can be expected to grow. Together with the ways of distributing them via RSS feeds, blogs, YouTube, virtual learning environments, this marks the great step forward that 2.0 represents. Their use via mobile devices will add considerably to our fire-power in reaching our users wherever they are, and whenever they want.

Index